**THE SUCCESSFUL
COMPUTER SYSTEM**

The Successful Computer System

Its Planning,
Development, and Management
in a Business Enterprise

JOSEPH ORLICKY

McGraw-Hill Book Company
New York　　*San Francisco*　　*Toronto*　　*London*　　*Sydney*

THE SUCCESSFUL COMPUTER
SYSTEM

to
JOHN HINCHCLIFFE
for his role in making this book a reality

Preface

Every book traces its origin to some point in time, to some event. The seed of this one was planted on the occasion of the 1966 national convention of the American Production and Inventory Control Society (APICS) in Philadelphia. Having been invited to speak on the subject of computer-based system planning and implementation, I found myself addressing some 750 people who jam-packed a room that held only 600 chairs. The fact that so many were willing to stand through a two-hour presentation made an especially strong impression on me. I had been aware of the general popularity of the subject of my talk, but what was the reason for a show of such an intense interest?

There certainly had been no dearth of literature, seminars, and lectures by competent specialists on every facet of computer technology and methodology. Why, then, were all these men bent on attending this particular session? I suddenly understood. I was *not* a computer specialist but a business manager like themselves—they expected me to deal with the subject on the basis of experience in the practical use of computers in industry—and to discuss it in their own terms and from their point of view.

I had been only too well aware of difficulties that many managers were experiencing in their endeavor to extend the utilization of computers beyond payroll and accounting applications into areas of business operation. I saw in the overflow crowd a manifestation of the business management community's pent-up hunger for systematically organized, practical, management-level information about principles of successful computer use and advice on the application of these principles.

I have had the opportunity to participate in, or to direct, several data-processing systems projects in what is considered a rather tough area—production control and materials logistics. I had learned quite a few lessons, and had the scars to prove it. Following the speech in Philadelphia, I began to feel that I had a larger contribution to make—beyond an occasional speech or article—toward satisfying the business manager's need for sound usable advice on computer system implementation. That is when the thought of writing a book on the subject first entered my mind.

The idea was seized upon by several of my friends and associates, who declared it to be my professional duty and who urged, cajoled, and prodded me into eventually undertaking the project in earnest. This book is the result.

It represents an attempt at comprehensive coverage of the whole spectrum of management considerations that bear on the subject of successful computer use in business. It is meant to serve as a guidebook or a blueprint that can be followed through the various stages of computer system development, from the initial study and computer selection to installation and system operation. But this book attempts to be more than a manual of practical advice. It also contains selected general information about computers and methods of their use; i.e., it offers the education needed to appreciate and use the advice.

A book, and its purpose, can also be described by pointing out what it is not. This book does not deal with individual specific applications but with principles and considerations pertaining to *all* applications in the commercial sphere. It does not draw on sources in literature but on lessons learned in practice. It does not pretend to scientific objectivity or detachment but freely offers opinions and recommendations. I have not consciously avoided any controversial area, nor have I side-stepped an issue. This much I can promise the reader—he will always know where *I* stand.

This brings up a final point that I particularly wish to stress. I am solely responsible for any of the recommendations and opinions expressed in the text. They are my own professional opinions, and they are not necessarily shared or endorsed by any other individual or organization.

ACKNOWLEDGMENTS

I owe thanks to many people who helped me, in different ways, to create this book. My wife, Olga, acted as an on-the-spot editor and conscientiously read every portion of the manuscript as it was being generated. In her, the lay reader had a staunch champion—she kept me from lapsing into "systemese" and made me rewrite many a paragraph that to her was unintelligible or that she had to read more than *twice* to get its meaning. She also objected to my use of "big words," most of which, with some regret, I eventually eliminated. I did keep *simulacrum, ad hoc,* and *postulate,* though, so as not to give in entirely.

Many friends and associates contributed to the book either by reading and critiquing the manuscript or by submitting to interviews on subjects of their particular competence. Among these, major substantive contributions were made by Messrs. Charles E. Hawkins (data processing methods and programming languages, Chapters 2 and 3), Paul M. Howe (organizational considerations, Chapters 6 and 9), Irwin J. Reps (project controls, Chapter 6), Edward E. Souders (corporate systems planning, Chapter 9), and Joseph L. Wise (system growth, compatibility, and modularity, Chapter 4). A special expression of my gratitude is due my friend Oliver W. Wight, who simply decided that I must write this book and then unmercifully kept after me until I did. His reviews of the manuscript and the many suggestions he offered were extremely valuable to me.

In the text, I am quoting from, paraphrasing, and otherwise making free use of my own past writings which previously appeared in the following copyrighted publications: The *1961, 1966,* and *1967 Proceedings* of the national conference of the American Production and Inventory Control Society. The July, 1963, and the October, 1964, issues of the APICS *Quarterly Bulletin,* published by the mentioned society. *Technical Paper MM67-677,* published by the American Society of Tool and Manufacturing Engineers (ASTME). The May, 1965, issue of *Modern Machine Shop* magazine, published by Gardner Publications, Inc. The February, 1967, issue of *Automation* magazine, published by the Penton Publishing Company.

In Chapter 1, some of the arguments concerning the choice between the business manager and a systems specialist to lead the system development effort, discussed on pages 3 and 4, have been adapted from an article entitled *Who Should Control Information Systems?* by Philip H. Thurston, published in the November-December, 1962, issue of the *Harvard Business Review.*

In Chapter 4, section on The Study, some of the discussion on pages 64 and 65 is based on the article by R. George Glaser, *Are You Working on the Right Problem?* in the June, 1967, issue of *Datamation* magazine, published and copyrighted by F. D. Thompson Publications, Inc., Greenwich, Connecticut.

As the text contains neither footnotes nor bibliographical references, I also wish to acknowledge, in this place, a number of individual observations or thoughts expressed by writers in a variety of periodicals, that I have incorporated into this book.

Joseph Orlicky

Contents

xi

**THE SUCCESSFUL
COMPUTER SYSTEM**

Chapter One
The Problem

We are in the business of making motors, not programming and installing computers.

This statement was recently made by one of the top executives of a European manufacturing company with their first computer on order, who came here to learn from American experience and who, in a discussion with the author, thus countered a recommendation of maximum participation by business management in the system development effort. The quotation represents a variation on a frequently heard theme —the business manager is too busy making freight cars, or pipe, or whatever, to be bothered with the development of a computer-based system in his company.

The executive who feels this way has started off on the wrong foot—his attitude stems from ignorance of *what it takes* to put a computer system in, successfully. Like the visitor from Europe who engaged an outside firm of specialists in systems work and programming (his company had never used any data processing equipment before, hence no one knew much about this subject), he considers the problem to be a purely technical one and therefore susceptible of a strictly technical solution. It is, perhaps, unfortunate that this is simply not so.

The argument that the company is in the business of making widgets and not in the business of designing systems and programming computers is a pernicious one, because it seems so logical on its face. It is also false. First, let us observe that whoever advances this type of argument fails to distinguish between system design and development on one hand and programming on the other. Programming can be bought. But buying the right program specs for a system that is to support a business operation is quite another matter.

Is the making of widgets the company's sole business? Certainly not. They are in the business of making money, earning a fair return on their stockholders' investment, providing jobs for their employees, and surviving as a business. The making of widgets is incidental to their purpose, a means to an end. Making the best of products will mean little if this product cannot be produced economically or in time to meet the customer's demand. A company may be in the business of making widgets, but it is also in the business of keeping up its capability (*and this includes a continuous effort to improve the system which supports and controls operations*) to do so profitably.

The management of a company that is introducing a computer into business operations should expect to become involved in system planning and development. They should plan on becoming involved. They should make time, by drastic means if necessary, for becoming thus involved.

This goes doubly for the primary *user* of the new system, the operating manager or department head directly responsible for the function that the computer is intended to support. Ideally, this manager should be reassigned to the system development project on a full-time basis. Where this is not feasible, he should free up the ablest of his lieutenants to represent him on the project team. In addition, he himself should plan to be available for frequent consultation. *It is simply not practical for a functional manager to devote his full time to operations while the system that is to control these operations in the future is being designed and implemented.* Where this principle has been violated—as it in many instances has been—the computer system in question eventually always proved disappointing.

In planning and designing a system for the support of business operations, the user's role is paramount. He is, or should be, the one most important contributor to the system development effort. The reason why he and not the system and computer specialists should control system design is twofold:

1. The user has a better understanding of the function that the computer is to support or control.

2. It is he who will have to use the new system and operate through it.

These two points represent the *aspect of business knowledge* and the *aspect of human psychology*, respectively.

The requirement that people who are automating a business function possess a good understanding of this function is self-evident. The system's user knows the most (or so it must be assumed) not only about his function as such but also about the *needs* of the company, as they relate to this function. In designing computer-based systems for the control of operations, operating people have the distinct advantage of an in-depth understanding of the job they perform, which helps them in determining the information requirements of the function, as well as in assembling information necessary for system design decisions. Without the user's active participation, there can be no real assurance that the logic of the system and the forms of its output will be fully suited to the needs of the people who eventually will have to work with the system's outputs, evaluate them, and act on them.

Computer-based system design and development also have a psychological aspect. Operating people resist planning in which they have no part. They know they will have to live with whatever is developed, but if they are not invited in on the design and planning of the system (or sometimes if the invitation is not forced on them), they tend to resist the efforts of the specialists seeking information or attempting innovation. They also delay accepting responsibility for the way a computer-based system installed by specialists functions. NIH (Not Invented Here) is a well-known factor that prevents people in laboratories, research institutes, universities, and business offices from wholeheartedly embracing something they had no part in creating. At the bottom of this resistance probably lies mistrust, which, in turn, stems from a lack of full understanding. A person often gains a thorough understanding only through participation, by *doing*. At any rate, there is no better way to educate a user in the system's makeup than by having him help design it.

The manager of the function for which the new system is intended should assume a role of leadership in the design and development of the system. If it turns out that organizational and procedural changes within his area of responsibility are needed before the new system can successfully be installed, he is the one who should take initiative in making them. If it develops that certain management policies should be reappraised in light of the proposed system, he is the one who should convince his superiors of the desirability of such a reappraisal. He should play an *active* role in the whole effort and should never allow the specialists or outsiders to make the important system design decisions for him.

Failure on the part of operating management to act this way, and letting all system responsibility rest with technical personnel, is not only dangerous but a disservice to the company. A system entirely developed by experts is likely to reflect pet theories of the computer specialist—*his* notion of how the business should be run—and is equally likely to fail in practice, because his technical expertise is not necessarily coupled with business experience and judgment.

The system specialist probably has a limited, inadequate understanding of the business function being automated—a fact he may not be aware of. Letting the systems man carry the whole burden of system design is both risky for the business and unfair to him. The business manager will be wiser to learn something about systems and computers rather than depend on the technical experts to learn the business.

There are five principal requirements for a system development effort to turn out successfully:

1. A good understanding of the business function that is to be automated, and of its objectives.

2. Motivation to innovate.

3. Competence in the design of computer-based systems and the ability to relate the system's functions to operating needs.

4. Authority and prestige of a position that can work with operating people and also otherwise can make things happen.

5. Insight into how human factors affect the success of a computer-based system.

When a top executive is deciding where to assign responsibility for a systems project, and when he matches the attributes of the systems specialist and those of the operating manager against the above five requirements, the result is usually that the systems man scores higher on points 2 and 3, the business manager on points 1, 4, and 5. It is true that the operating man, conditioned to concentrate on his particular sphere of operation, its day-to-day problems, and current period expense performance, tends to take a narrower point of view than the systems man on questions of new operating patterns and systems. As to the business manager's skills in computer-based system design, he may have none. But although he may lack the technical skills, he possesses all the attributes necessary to "make the system work." The spirit of innovation and the technical skills can be contributed by the specialist *teamed up with him.* The specialists are definitely needed, and their contribution is important, but responsibility and control should be vested in the business manager.

This is not to suggest that the business manager need not know anything—or should not try to learn something—about systems and data processing by computer. The idea of a computer-based system supporting business operations obviously implies the bringing together of two separate disciplines, that of the business function and that of data processing. The successful synthesis of the two will depend to a large extent on whether the key individuals in position to influence the outcome of the system development effort possess the combined knowledge of the two fields that are involved, in the required degree.

Considering the size of the investment in computers, systems, and programming that so many businesses now have, it is desirable that business management become more systems-oriented and better systems-educated. Because computer-based systems are becoming a way of life in business operations, it is the modern business manager's responsibility to educate himself in the use of these new tools he will have to work with.

The principal difference between a butcher knife and a scalpel lies not in their physical characteristics but in their purpose and in the *degree of skill* required for their proper use. The computer, like the scalpel, calls for new and finer skills on the part of its user. In the industrial environment, this user is not the programmer or computer system specialist, but the business manager. The skill required on his part consists primarily in a better, deeper understanding of the operation into which the computer is to be introduced. To acquire the desired degree of understanding, the manager must be trained, or must train himself, to abstract certain aspects of his operation from other, traditionally better understood characteristics such as the physical or human side of the business.

He must learn to synthesize the business functions and data processing, i.e., be able to think about operating problems in terms of their data-processing solution potential. He should view, redefine, and analyze his operation in terms of data sources, information flow, procedure, and decision logic. This will then enable him to see the function of managing as the process of converting information into action—and will provide the insights necessary for the proper use of computers.

Managers who desire a truly successful computer installation for their company must also be prepared to educate themselves about the computer and the principal methods of its use. In addition, they need to become familiar with considerations of system design and development, as well as with psychological factors that bear on the success of computer-based system operation. And, at any rate, they need to know enough about computers and systems work so as to be able to communicate with the specialists without the possibility of becoming overwhelmed, intimidated, or misled.

These new demands on the business executive are often resisted. He wants to know why, since the computer is a tool, he should have to know more about it than about any of the other tools and machines used in his business. The executive need know little about individual machine tools on the floor of his factory, or about materials handling equipment, or about the design and maintenance of production tooling. He safely delegates responsibility for all these to subordinate specialists and technicians. Why should he not treat the computer the same way?

The reason why he should not lies in the computer's all-pervasiveness. All other tools, machines, and technical functions are of limited scope and specialized purpose. Individually, they can have only a limited effect on the overall operation. A computer system, on the other hand, tends to get into the very bloodstream of the enterprise. As it is being developed and as it grows, it tends to take over the function of the company's nervous system—the sensing, operating decision making and responding—and it directly affects more and more functions of the business.

A decision about, say, the selection and use of materials handling equipment can be made by a specialist competent in this area of the operation. If he makes a poor decision, it merely means that materials will not be handled as efficiently as they should. If responsibility for decisions about computer systems, and their use, is completely delegated to technical specialists, errors of judgment on their part may have far-reaching consequences that can jeopardize the performance of the whole enterprise. As computers, and their effective use, become essential to competitive survival, business management will be well advised to reclaim control over computer-related activities from the specialist to whom it has fallen by default.

To exercise such control effectively, the business manager needs to acquire new knowledge. But he does not find it easy to determine precisely what it is he has to learn and where to learn it. Much of the information he needs is available, but it is contained in such a mass of technical literature, written in a jargon and from a viewpoint so foreign to him, that he is not able to take advantage of it. In addition to the more technical, machine-related information, he also has a need of systematically organized advice on how to *use* computer systems and *manage* their development.

This book attempts to meet the business manager's needs. Its purpose is to aid him in the difficult task of evaluating, directing, and managing computer-systems development activities taking place in his company. The scope of the book encompasses a digest of technical data-processing information related to the computer and methods of its use, as well as an extended review of practical considerations pertaining to system design, system development, and system operation. This is a book written for the computer user in the broad sense of the word, whether he is a top executive, a data processing manager, or a systems analyst. It is primarily, however, a book for business managers, by a business manager.

There are few examples or references to actual situations, and the points made in the text are intentionally kept general. This may place more demands on the reader with exclusively practical orientation. No doubt some business managers would prefer a guide in terms of specific dos and don'ts without extensive reasoning and elaboration. Such a book, however, would not do the job, particularly where it is based on the author's opinions, experiences, and conclusions, which should be *adapted* to the reader's own situation. To the extent that the book encourages the reader to examine critically, and to adapt, opinions and recommendations contained in the text, it will have equipped him to deal with future challenges in the computer systems area with more confidence as well as more effectiveness—and it will have succeeded in its purpose.

The book is organized into ten chapters and an appendix, and the material they contain is essentially the following:

1. **Introductory.**

2. **Conceptual and historical perspective,** and considerations of **transferring work from man to computer.** The discussion covers three concepts that are directly pertinent to the subject of the book: automation, systems, and the computer. The second part of this chapter is devoted to the question of how, in effect, procedures must be stated for the computer to follow. This includes a review of the subject of computer programming and of so-called programming aids.

3. **Approaches to the processing of information.** This chapter deals with the various categories of computer use and with the main philosophies, or methods, of information processing. Topics covered include data communications, multiprogramming, time sharing, and management information systems.

4. **Initial computer system development activities and functions.** The discussion is aimed at answering questions of how to conduct a feasibility study, how to prepare a management proposal, how to justify and how to select a computer.

5. **How to design a computer-based system.** A review of the most important considerations, principles, and methods of system design. Included are twelve system design pointers that can serve the system designer as a practical guide and checklist.

6. **Organizational considerations.** Departmental organization of the

functions of data processing, programming, and systems, as well as the organization of a system development project.

7. System development phases. A review of the different activities, from system design detailing to system conversion, that have to take place before a computer system can go "on the air."

8. Problems of system operation. The discussion in this chapter centers on difficulties that plague most business computer installations, with particular emphasis on file maintenance, faulty input data, and injurious action by system users.

9. Special considerations in large corporations. This chapter should be of particular interest to the executive of a multidivision or multilocation company, who faces issues discussed here: centralization, long-range system planning, corporate systems management, system standardization, and the conduct of corporate system projects.

10. Conclusion. A summary of management considerations, economic factors, and the impact of computers on the conduct of business. A final argument for an increased management involvement in computer system planning.

Appendix. A review, in condensed form, of **computer characteristics and technology.** This material has been placed at the end of the book so as not to break the flow of discussion. The reader who is familiar with computers will not need to read it. The reader who has scant computer knowledge, however, is advised either to read it ahead of the section on programming in Chapter 2, or else to consult it as he may require later on. Beyond the introductory topics, the reader is assumed to have an understanding of basic computer-related terms and functions, throughout the discussion of the various subjects that comprise this book.

There can be no knowledge unless there is structure. The subject of computer system planning and management is of acute importance but so new that its elements have not yet been systematically organized and classified. Most of the subjects covered in the discussions that follow do not, at present, yield to precise measurement and scientific evaluation. Nevertheless, this book represents an attempt at structure in the sense of arranging empirical observations, and conclusions derived from these observations, into meaningful relationships.

Although the text may not amount to knowledge, its author hopes that it will be judged a contribution to knowledge in the making.

Chapter Two
A Machine That Amplifies Man's Intellect

At first the function of brawn *and finally the function of the* brain *behind the brawn, are automated.*

PERSPECTIVE

Before taking up questions of practical computer use, let us establish historical perspective for our current endeavors in this area. What we are really attempting to do is to carry a step further the idea of automatic performance of human tasks. In a business environment, this effort is directed at procedural systems, and the tool that promises to make these systems function automatically is the modern computer. The following review of

1. Automation concepts
2. Systems concepts
3. Computer concepts

will serve to provide the reader with a conceptual grounding for examining many of the issues raised in subsequent chapters in a broader context.

AUTOMATION CONCEPTS

The term "automation" denotes the activity, or the result, of making something automatic, i.e., *self-acting.* Currently, this term is popularly applied primarily to the process of manufacturing and to the movement of material undergoing this process. But we can legitimately speak of automation when referring to any undertaking that aims at creating some apparatus, process, or system that is to contain *within itself* the principle of its actions and that will thus function automatically.

Attempts at automation represent an outgrowth of a centuries-long development of substituting tools for human power, so as to enable man to make fuller use of his brain capacity for social and economic co-operation. In essence, automating means transferring skills from man to machine, in order that the latter may perform certain tasks on behalf, and *instead of,* man. The idea of automating is not at all new. In thirteenth-century Europe, the German Dominican monk Albertus Magnus spent thirty years building a robot that would open doors and greet his visitors. His example typifies early attempts at automating, which took the form of constructing an automaton, i.e., a working simulacrum of a living organism.

Automata are nonbiological devices that exhibit behavior patterns found in man or animal, including what would commonly be classified as intelligent response. An automaton not only duplicates the function of a living organism but performs it in the same manner. Automata of nonindustrial purpose are generally characterized by their emulating not only the behavior but also the appearance of their living models. According to legend, in the sixteenth century Rabbi Loew of Prague created Golem, a mechanical servant-monster made of clay, in the human image. In 1920 Karel Capek, the Czech author and dramatist, produced a play called R.U.R. which eventually reached Broadway and in which the robots (a term invented by Capek) are indistinguishable from their human counterparts. Disneyland animal automata look, of course, more or less like the real thing.

Industrial automata, on the other hand, are process-oriented, and their physical appearance is entirely subordinated to the performance of the functions—often single tasks—that they take over from men. One of the earliest devices capable of controlling a process, the pressure boiler with safety valve, was invented by Denis Papin in the seventeenth century. It is the classic example of an *open-loop* control mechanism, because it has no capability of self-correction and depends on human action to close the loop (regulate the source of the heat causing the pressure). The first device that embodied a capacity for self-correction and could *close the loop* of control was James Watt's flyball, centrifugal governor developed in 1788 to regulate steam pressure.

In post-Colonial Pennsylvania (1784), Oliver Evans built an automated grist mill outside Philadelphia, using a bucketed conveyor belt and an Archimedean screw to grind the grain. The real growth of the factory system started when Watt's steam engine added the turning of line shafting to its original talent for pumping water from mines. In 1793, Eli Whitney's cotton gin automated the heretofore human task of separating cotton fiber from the seed, and in 1801 Joseph Marie Jacquard of Paris perfected a loom that was not just automatic but also versatile, as it was capable of obeying a variety of instructions punched into cards. In the history of automation, Jacquard's loom represents a breakthrough onto new grounds, because it automated not only the execution of a command but the function of command itself.

Thus the development of automation concepts and technological achievements is characterized by progress from open-loop control of automated processes, to closed-loop devices controlling these processes, and finally to command automata (computers) controlling the devices that control the processes. At first the function of *brawn* and finally the function of the *brain* behind the brawn are automated.

It is interesting to note that this new capability tends to solve a serious problem that has gradually developed over the past few decades as attempts were made to automate industrial processes on a more comprehensive scale. This problem is the *loss of flexibility* in production. As individual automated machines, equipment, and work stations were linked together to form larger, integrated productive entities encompassing whole shops and, perhaps, factories, the process got hardened, locked in. Even slight deviations in the materials, manufacturing processes, or production plans could not be accommodated without costly and time-consuming resetups, line rearrangements, and retooling. The more automated the facility, the harder it became to make changes and disruption of production tended to be factory-wide. Modern tooling, including elaborate fixtures and huge dies, defied change; engineering needed to be complete and correct before tooling up, and as tooling took longer to get, marketing and other management decisions had to be made earlier. Thus, because of the automation of the factory, the whole enterprise tended to suffer from a loss of ability to respond to change.

The problem was made more acute by the fact that while such hardening of the productive arteries was setting in, the requirements of the marketplace actually called for the very opposite, namely, improved responsiveness to the vagaries of customer demand and an enhancement of the capability to accommodate changes generally. This development tended to act as a brake on further progress in comprehensive automation, and in fact some of the pioneering companies were forced to retreat, to de-automate.

The fate of the famous A. O. Smith automotive frame production line is a case in point. In 1915 Mr. Smith built a plant in Milwaukee to produce automobile frames automatically. All of the productive machinery and materials handling equipment had been mechanically linked together and, driven by a common, single source of power, acted as one huge frame-producing machine. The frames were being produced, in mass volume, from start to finish untouched by human hand, and the A. O. Smith line was for many years regarded as a marvel of manufacturing engineering. But the weakness that was eventually to prove fatal lay in the fact that it had been designed for large runs of the same frame. All Model-T's used, of course, an identical frame of stable design.

But as an ever-wider variety in automobile body (and frame) specifications was introduced over the years, and as custom assembly to automobile-buyer option, as well as frequent reengineering became the way of life, the A. O. Smith line had to be successively disjointed and generally shrunk back, as more and more individual process steps were separated from it for reasons of flexibility. Finally, just a few years ago, the last vestiges of the erstwhile marvel of automation disappeared entirely.

In light of the above, it might seem that industrial automation, at least in its more comprehensive stages, contains the seeds of its own destruction. Actually, however, the limitations are inherent merely in the "hard tooling" *method* of automation. If we contemplate the essential purpose and function of tooling, we realize that it is to deskill the work. To do away with, or at least to reduce, the requirement of knowledge, deftness, and meticulous attention that may be collectively described as intelligence on the part of the production worker. This intelligence is, in effect, captured and transformed into the tooling, which then positions the workpiece, guides the cutting or forming tool, and generally controls the critical elements of the process.

If the intelligence, instead of being frozen into the tooling, can be supplied from a different source (without loss of effectiveness or economy), tooling can become "soft" or may even be eliminated completely. The proof of this is manifest in the case of modern numerically controlled machine tools which require a minimum of workpiece-related tooling and hence a minimum setup. Thanks to the commands embodied in the control tape, the cutting tool is unerringly guided without benefit of fixture or jig plate and a change of setup essentially consists of the changing of tape reels.

But even the present, tape-oriented numerical-control technology will soon yield to "direct" numerical control (DNC), where the functions of the tape, tape reader, and most of the controller (the command assimilation circuitry) will be taken over by computers, with resultant large economies in the modification of part programs caused by engineering changes (now requiring the creation of an entire new tape), as well as in the maintenance of the control hardware. Computers, often remotely located, will be able to drive multiple machine tools simultaneously, with total flexibility as to the particular mix of different parts being produced by these machine tools at any particular time.

The computer will enable us to move toward the twin goals of *maximum automation with maximum flexibility*. Thus the technology of command automata can be expected to overcome the problems heretofore encountered in automating the factory and should revive the temporarily stalled progress in the automation of the industrial processes themselves.

Because of the recent (since the advent of the computer) forays of automation into higher-level, or mental, functions, there has been a definite change away from the notion that industrial automata should emulate human *method* if not appearance. Human method of work, at any level, is dictated by the limitations of the human body and mind. To the extent that modern automata, exploiting in their makeup the latest technological advances, represent a different mix of capabilities and limitations than is found in men, methods of work different from those that would have to be employed by men can be, and will be, adopted for them. As an industrial process, or plant, is designed "around the instruments" so as to take maximum advantage of available automatic control mechanisms, so will procedures of automated higher-level (i.e., management and administration) functions tend to be designed "around the computer."

Automation is an evolutionary phenomenon the origins of which can be traced back for several centuries. Current developments represent an acceleration of this evolution rather than a revolution, except perhaps in one sense. The historic thrust of automation has been confined to the realm of technology until recent years, when the development of the computer caused a shift in interest, and emphasis, from the automation of movement (physical force) to the automation of communication and control (signals). Computers embody the new technology of control in its highest form, and they fairly beg to be utilized not only for the control of devices but also for the execution of complex administrative procedures and, through them, for the control of business operations.

Automation thus has intruded on the previously exclusive domain of the manager through its extension to the very machinery of managing, i.e., the system of administrative and management controls. The principle of automation is today being applied in management's own bailiwick, and it affects the process of business management itself. Its primary impact on the manager lies in the requirement that he master, on top of the purely managerial skills in the traditional sense, also the new skills he needs, at his own level, to successfully manage the automating of as many of the functions for which he is responsible as possible.

SYSTEMS CONCEPTS

The system of administrative and management controls—the current object of automation—has evolved to facilitate control over operations and the conduct of business in general. It is superimposed on the physical plant and productive process so as to provide a mechanism through which the business can be driven. This system consists, in the main, of a complex or network of related procedures developed according to a central scheme for performing the major functions of the business.

This concept can, however, be expanded, and the system can be regarded as encompassing

1. Policies, procedures, and decision rules
2. People and information processing machines

The term "system" is defined as describing an assemblage of diverse elements or units that are mutually interrelated and interdependent; a system is a *composite* that functions as an entity, and its main attribute is that its utility, or power, is greater than that of its components summed individually. The business system under discussion acts as one large information gathering, information processing, and information generating mechanism. Its basic component is the human beings who activate and animate this mechanism and who use the rules and procedures as their tools. This is the system through which the complex business organization acts, controls, and coordinates its actions. The system combines the roles of both energizing machinery and steering apparatus of the modern enterprise.

In concept, the system of business controls is regarded as an entity, but in reality, it is usually made up of more or less uncoupled *subsystems,* i.e., systems individually developed to serve the various functional and organizational subdivisions of a company. It is only in recent years that such subsystems began to be viewed within an overall or total system framework, as the information technology-induced automation of this area brought into sharper focus the interrelationships and interdependencies between functions that have traditionally been segregated organizationally. The new technology now permits us to organize many different kinds of operations and functions into systems and to control such systems. The linking together of (perhaps already automated) individual functions has as its object the integration of subsystems and represents an effort at a higher degree, or level, of automation. At the highest level, automation ultimately culminates in the establishment of a single, comprehensive system in fact (this has not yet been achieved in any business enterprise) as well as in theory.

It is interesting to note that, from top management's point of view, any system of business controls, even though not automated (i.e., consisting entirely of individuals executing "manual" procedures), may nevertheless be considered automatic in the sense that it contains the mainspring of its action—and the rules for the mode of such action—within itself. In comparison with a fully automated system, however, its "manual" counterpart is characterized by a considerably lower degree of reliability and predictability of its performance, not to mention its relative sluggishness. This is so because its (formal, documented) procedures are quite typically incomplete, of low resolution level, inconsistent, faulty, and in some instances, lacking entirely. It is the judgment and experience of the human beings functioning as part of such a system which compensate and make up for the low quality of procedure. Man's intelligence enables him to function satisfactorily (up to a point) in what is technically known as an *unstructured problem* environment, as he is able to work with incomplete or imperfect instructions.

On the other hand, man is relatively unreliable in his role of procedure implementor and decision maker, as he will not consistently act the same way under the same circumstances; his capacity for processing information in high volume is quite limited, and he is a poor calculator of the dynamic behavior (i.e., the changing relationships) of complex systems. Automation of "manual," or entirely people-based, administrative and management control systems is the result of management's desire to make such systems more reliable, more responsive, and more economical.

In a system consisting of procedures and activators/executors, automation essentially means *transferring* the responsibility for the execution of procedures and the application of decision rules from man to (information processing) machine.

It should be evident, however, that it also means that in the process, procedures will have to be tightened up, i.e., made comprehensive, explicit, and valid.

The automation of a business control system does not mean that all the former human system operators and procedure executors are being replaced by machines, but rather that the role of individuals in an automated activity changes to

1. Designing the system
2. Maintaining the system
3. Activating the system

It follows that, as the process of automating business control systems progresses, the traditional roles of lower- and middle-level management, as well as those of skilled clerical/technical personnel in the *line* organization, will change, and are now changing, in the direction toward *staff* system-related functions. The individuals in question are no longer expected to "run" the operation but to devote their efforts to the maintenance and improvement of the automated system that controls the operation.

⇒ Computer technology employed in the environment of business management permits the automating of much of the *helmsman* function. A computer-based system will now enable the decision maker on an upper management level to do almost nothing but decision making instead of spending most of his time, as in the past, on processing and evaluating information to get into position to make the decision.

THE COMPUTER AS A CONCEPT

This will have been made possible by the computer, the machine that represents the culmination of progress in automation technology. The modern electronic, general-purpose, digital computer itself is an outgrowth of thought and effort spanning three centuries, directed at reducing the time and tedium of human calculation. Blaise Pascal, the French mathematician and philosopher, developed in 1642 the first mechanical calculating machine. Proposals for new, and more powerful, computing devices appear in nineteenth-century literature. In 1812 the Englishman Charles Babbage constructed in mechanical form the recognized prototype of the computer. His "analytical engine" had a "store" (the equivalent of internal memory) and a "mill" (the equivalent of an arithmetic unit), and it was designed to accept input data in the form of cards with holes in them, an idea that Babbage borrowed from Jacquard's loom. In 1889 Herman Hollerith, a statistician employed by the United States government, developed and patented the first line of primitive punched-card equipment consisting of a punch, a sorter, and a tabulator, to aid in the compilation of the 1890 census data.

The era of the modern computer dates from the late 1930s. The years 1939 to 1944 mark the successful development, at Harvard University, of the first automatic, *general-purpose* digital computer (electromechanical).

The Automatic Sequence Controlled Calculator, as the machine was called, was developed by Prof. Howard Aiken with financial and technical assistance from the IBM Corporation. At about the same time, pioneering work in this area was also being done by George Stibitz of Bell

Laboratories, who developed an electromechanical automatic digital computer. Concepts of modern digital computers were defined in detail between 1943 and 1946 by John von Neumann, a Hungarian mathematician working at Princeton University, and by the team of J. P. Eckert and J. W. Mauchly of the University of Pennsylvania, who perfected and built ENIAC (Electronic Numerical Integrator And Computer), the first *electronic* digital computer, in 1946.

Since then, the development of computer technology has accelerated in an explosive fashion. This can perhaps best be appreciated if we realize that not only the original machines themselves, and their programming, but their very *output* is now obsolete. This is because the first computers were primarily used for the calculation of extensive mathematical tables intended as computing-laborsaving tools, which by now have been made superfluous by the capability and speed of successor machines. This is truly a remarkable development. Professor Jay Forrester of MIT has estimated that during the 1950s computer performance increased, on the average, each year tenfold over the year before, as measured in terms of a combination of speed, memory capacity, and reliability. Such technological advancement surpasses that which had been achieved in the transition from conventional to nuclear weapons. Never before has a technological product been developed and improved to such an extent over such a brief period.

The modern computer is a far cry from its calculating precursors indeed. It must be pointed out that the connotation of the term "computer" is now, unfortunately, somewhat misleading as it evokes the image of "computing," i.e., some arithmetic operation with its manipulation of numerical data. The notion that the computer is a strictly numerical device is quite incorrect. It is merely an historical accident that the first computers were designed to carry out exclusively arithmetic, repetitive tasks. A computer is basically a symbol-manipulating device (no distinction is being made here between the attributes of the machine and those of the program that controls it), and numerical symbols are merely one of the symbol classes that the computer can manipulate. As the nonnumerical part of digital information processing continues to grow in importance, the meaning of the terms "computer" and "computing" will change, just as the original meaning of the term "shipping," for instance, has changed with usage.

But if the computer is not merely a computing device, then just what is it? In order to acquire the key to knowledge about computers, to isolate the one root idea to which all such knowledge can relate and be transformed through it to insight, it is important to grasp the computer's essential function and purpose. The computer is *a machine that dupli-*

cates and amplifies certain powers of the human mind. It provides an extension to man's intellect. It has been called the universal machine and man's ultimate machine. In the latter sense, it is seen as the supreme technological achievement, because the computer deals not in raw power but in the sublime, abstract processes of mental work.

In this connection, we should realize that before the advent of computers, practically every other tool or machine ever invented and built served as an extension of man's legs (locomotion), back muscles (materials displacement), or arms and hands (manufacturing). Today's most advanced machines such as the bulldozer, the combine, the automatic machine tool, the jet plane, and the rocket-powered space vehicle all belong to this category. The computer, on the other hand, is in a category all by itself. It does not, alone, achieve any physical feats whatever. It can help plan and control physical action by other machines (and men), but its own output is always symbolic and therefore abstract.

The symbols that a computer has the ability to manipulate are numerical digits, letters of the alphabet, special characters, and subcharacters or bits (see section on computer technology in the Appendix), which represent information in the form of data. A computer processes information by means of receiving, storing (remembering), operating on, and producing (output) data. These information-handling operations are directed by a program of instructions which itself is stored in the computer's memory. This principle of utilizing internally stored, *alterable* instructions to control the action of the machine is what provides the computer with a versatility, a logical flexibility, and an open-endedness that are not matched by anything short of a living organism.

In addition to duplicating certain intellectual processes, a computer is also capable of performing clerical tasks that can be viewed as routines performed by rote, such as the retrieval of records, posting and filing, i.e., recordkeeping, as well as transmitting, regenerating, and display of information over distance. Although the computer is relatively limited, as compared to the human mind, in its range of capability and although it uses rather crude methods of internal processing, it has the advantages of *speed, total recall, and complete accuracy.* Speed is the dominant characteristic, as electronic computer circuitry typically handles signals at rates of millions per second. The computer is also called an *electronic data-processing system* (this use of the term "system" tends to confuse, but is prevalent) because it is actually composed of several connected, interacting, and mutually dependent machines and devices operating in harmony under central control.

Another dimension of the computer concept is the relationship between machinery and stored program (*hardware* and *software*). They are inseparable in that both, in combination, determine the total power of the computer, which has some of its capabilities designed into its physical mechanism (wired-in capabilities) and others supplied through stored instructions (programmed capabilities).

In designing a computer, there are opportunities for tradeoff between these two types of capability. As a general rule, anything that can be programmed may instead be wired in, at an increase in hardware cost. This cost increment is then repetitively incurred with every unit being manufactured. Programmed capability, on the other hand, is more expensive to develop but once provided can be infinitely reproduced at nominal cost. Square root extraction, for instance, could be provided through special circuitry (extra cost, fast execution) or through a string of stored instructions that will produce the same result (no extra hardware cost but slower execution) utilizing the regular arithmetic devices.

Thus hardware and software are but two different aspects of the same thing, the machine called the computer. In discussing it on a conceptual level, one more point remains to be made, i.e., that the computer, in addition to all the attributes mentioned above, is characterized by a universality of its use. Unlike other machines, all of which have a relatively limited, special purpose, the computer is truly a *general-purpose* machine in its sphere of duplicating mental processes. Its *application potential is universal,* in the sense that it can potentially be employed wherever the human mind is at work.

Computers are likely to have an impact on their environment similar, in a way, to that of automobiles. The latter have given us a mobility that exceeds by far what evolution intended to provide us with. Computers may constitute a similar extraevolutionary step with respect to man's intellect. This is of grave concern to the biologist and to the social scientist; to explore the full meaning, and the ultimate consequences, of the effect of computers on the human race is not within the scope of this discussion. Of more immediate concern to us is the fact that, because computer technology has progressed so extraordinarily far with such rapidity, a whole new set of problems has been created for the computer's human users. The tremendous potential of the computer developed with such abrupt speed that its prospective users do not find it easy (or even possible) to learn, with similar speed, how properly to utilize it. At present, we are much better at designing and manufacturing computers than we are at *using* them anywhere near their potential.

It has been estimated that, if further development of computer technology stopped right now, several generations of the computer's users would be kept busy discovering its many unexploited capabilities and generally learning how to use computers more fully, and therefore more successfully. To help close this gap between technology and utilization ever so little, at least in business computer applications, by providing system implementation guidelines for management and other concerned personnel is the purpose of this book.

Figuratively speaking, a computer is a Golem of electronic clay and the program that resides in it is its soul.

CAPTURING THE LOGIC OF THE HUMAN MIND AT WORK

Let us return to a statement made in the preceding section, where we did not dwell on it long enough perhaps for the reader to ponder its significance. It is the concept of the *universality* of the computer's application potential. The grasp of the fact that a computer can potentially be employed wherever the human mind is at work represents an all-important insight, which should prove useful to the business manager in guiding his computer system-related thought and action. In the text that follows, we shall explore the computer's strengths and limitations as far as its procedure-executing, or problem-solving, role is concerned. Specific areas that will be reviewed are

1. The analogy between the computer and the human brain.
2. Who must understand the job, the man or the machine?
3. Considerations of policy and procedure.
4. The art and science of programming.
5. Programming languages.

THE COMPUTER AS AN ANALOGUE OF THE BRAIN

Thinking is defined as the sum of mental processes that occur when information is received, organized, and integrated so that an appropriate response can be made. Because a computer is used to duplicate certain mental processes, the blend of imagination and ignorance on the part of the lay public, press reporters, and popular writers created a myth of the giant or electronic brain endowed with occult innate capabilities. This notion still occasionally prevails, as evidenced by cartoon captions and TV-show episodes in which human beings turn to a computer-monster for an answer to some imponderable question.

The tendency to think of the computer in human terms has been persistent and apparently unshakable. If the computer has not been viewed as a giant brain, it was labeled a moron, because programmers had to feed it very detailed instructions before it would do anything. It is, obviously, this anthropomorphism which fosters the confusion and misunderstanding. It is true that the computer can perform many of the tasks that can be done by the human brain, some much faster and with greater accuracy (like arithmetic) and some with much less space efficiency (like remembering). But it should be viewed as what it is, a tool —an *information processing tool*—of immense power and tremendous potential.

As people have been exploring ways of programming and utilizing computers for solutions to complex problems, they have tried to learn more about this process by investigating and studying the mechanics of the human brain. The desire to utilize the latent potential of the computer encourages research into the structural organization of the brain and into the operation of its individual components, because there is a good chance that as we learn how the brain accomplishes some of its less-understood feats we may make computers to duplicate them. But in the process of this research, people have been discovering how very subtle and complex their own processes of sensing and understanding are. At the Bell Laboratories, for example, a computer is being used to simulate the functions of the inner ear, but the computer takes about fifty times longer to do what the human ear can do. At Harvard University, a computer is programmed to analyze English sentences for grammatical structure; it does a fine job of it but at the rate of only two sentences per hour.

At present, although intellectual processes of a high order (in the sphere of cognition) can, when understood, be programmed for computers to duplicate, such processes run slowly and expensively. When we discover areas of mental work in which we can outperform computers, we tend to regard computers as sluggish or clumsy, but perhaps a more proper way of looking at it would be to realize that the particular task is extremely difficult and that our own ability in this respect is outstandingly high.

In the context of computer applications to business problems, where we may regard computers as crude and unsuitable for the handling of specific functions, the main reason is that such functions contain a constituent that we are careful to distill out of the work assigned to computers, namely, the part of problem solving that has to do with the formulation of the problem in the first place. Thus man continues to do the intellectually more difficult task and assigns the machine merely the execution of solution steps already decided upon. This division of labor makes the computer, of course, look extremely good.

Until we know more, then, about how we ourselves do mental work and how our brain actually operates, the principle that will guide the application of computers generally, and in business functions particularly, is to divide the job between man and machine in a way that will utilize the best talents of each. The more mundane but high-capacity tasks of information processing will be assigned to the computer, while the more contemplative, conclusion-drawing processes will be reserved for the human mind.

WHO MUST UNDERSTAND THE JOB: THE MAN OR THE MACHINE?

Some of the more complex modern machines are sometimes referred to as being "smart," and people who work with this type of machinery may discuss the merits of one piece of gear as against another in terms of their relative smartness. The characteristic of such smartness pertains not to the ability of the machine to do its work automatically (this being taken for granted) but to features such as recognizing a wrong material, rejecting a false coin, or stopping when some piece of machinery gets out of position or breaks down. Computer hardware, however, is often attributed also another kind of smartness by the uninitiated, tantamount to intelligence. This is a misconception, of course. At best it could be said that a computer has the ability to accommodate (accept, store, and execute) a *smart program.*

It is always the program that embodies the cleverness, decision-making ability, and control over the procedure, never the machinery itself. In the older view, the term "computer" was equated with the hardware, as the concept of a machine always applied to the equipment rather than to the instructions that control it. But a newer, and better, view holds that, although the computer is a machine, this machine consists of both hardware-supplied and programmed capabilities or functions. In a computer, the program (in the generic frame of reference) is an *integral* part of the machine. Figuratively speaking, a computer is a Golem of electronic clay, and the program that resides in it is its soul. Just as a person without life is no longer regarded as a person, a computer without a program is not a computer at all but a mere shell, an empty vessel.

As far as "smartness" is concerned, no computer can be better than its program. In the case of national election-night television coverage, when different makes of computers are used by the major networks to predict the outcome, the impression is sometimes given that the product of one or the other competitive computer manufacturer is better because his machine predicted the result closer, declared the winner sooner. This is nonsense. In such sweepstakes, it is the respective teams of statisticians and programmers (who decided in advance how the machines will be used) who are in competition, not the equipment. In actuality, it would be possible to pit competitive computer systems against each other in a race to determine which of them will complete *an identical job* in less time, or which of them will accomplish more of some set of diverse tasks in a given period of time. But this would be a different kind of race, because the merits of the hardware would not be judged on the basis of the *logic* of the program being executed.

The knowledgeable reader must wonder at this point why something so self-evident is being belabored. It is because the author has met all too many business executives who kept losing sight of this when expressing dissatisfaction with the way the computer they had installed was performing in this or the other application area. They were confusing the responsibility of their own system design and programming staff (and their personal responsibility) with that of the computer.

A computer does not possess innate intelligence, and it should therefore be understood that one does not just state a *problem* to the machine; rather, one states a *procedure* for solving that problem or that class of problems. Programming is the art of stating procedures for the machine to follow, and success in writing a program that is to accomplish some particular objective depends more on understanding the task and less on skill in programming technique. To prepare a program for the calculation of a rocket trajectory, for example, calls for only a few weeks' study of programming but several years' study of physics.

The same principle applies when it comes to business applications. We must remember at all times that *merely introducing a computer into some operational system of business controls that has not been soundly conceived in the first place cannot, by definition, transform it into a superior system.* We can, however, revamp and redesign a system the inadequacies of which have been, perhaps for the first time, brought into sharp focus through the attempt to achieve a successful computer application. If this is not done, the resultant disappointment can invariably be traced not to some lack of capabilities on the part of the computer, but to deficiencies of the system being automated.

A computer, unlike a human being, will function with absolute success only in what we might term a perfect environment, that is to say, it assumes that the logic of the procedure it is executing is unexceptionable, the instructions correct, file data valid, and input data error-free. When we remind ourselves that the inanimate computer has no intrinsic powers of reason and judgment, the above requirements are self-evident. It should therefore be self-evident also that if any of the areas supposed to be perfect is, in fact, imperfect, the computer system tends to fail. Such failure is reflected in the computer's output, which is then invalid, incomplete, or late, and at any rate less than fully useful to its recipients. The seriousness of the consequences will vary with the application. This does not imply that a computer cannot usefully function under less-than-perfect conditions, provided that the system's developers recognize and anticipate such imperfection, as we shall discuss in Chapter 8.

CONSIDERATIONS OF POLICY AND PROCEDURE

Because the computer can duplicate mental processes, i.e., mentally implementable procedures, it is obviously possible to *transfer* such procedures (more precisely: instructions for the execution of these procedures) from man to machine. Computer applications imply such a transfer and are the result of this transfer. Successful applications reflect the high quality of the transfer effort, including both the process of transfer and the *soundness of procedure* that has been transferred.

It depends not on the machine but on the human beings instructing it whether the application will prove to be successful, whether the computer system will "work." It is axiomatic that, just as the quality of music is primarily determined by the player rather than by his instrument, *the limitations of the computer lie not in the machine but in man.* What people who endeavor to apply computers may overlook, however, is the fact that there is a fundamental difference between transferring to, or instructing, a person and instructing a machine.

Today's computers solve only preformulated problems, in the sense that the solution procedure must be known to start with and that it must be possible to state it precisely enough for the computer to follow. For a computer to solve a problem, the latter is said to have to be a *well-structured problem.* A human being, on the other hand, has the ability to solve (at least some) ill-structured problems. If we define an operational system that controls some business function as a set of related, interacting, and interdependent procedures and decision rules, we must add an important qualification before the system can be judged suitable for transfer to a computer. This is the requirement of consistency, i.e., that the procedures be capable of being consistently followed.

The precept of consistency is highly significant, if for no other reason than because, once transferred to a computer, the machine *will* follow the procedures consistently. If the procedures being transferred do not meet this test, the system will fail in its purpose. This tells us something about the new, higher standard of quality of definition, logic, and structure required of systems that are to be automated with the aid of computers. In precomputer days, operating procedures of a business did not need to be, and usually were not, stated precisely. The people who followed these procedures would patch up the deficiencies, arbitrate the inconsistencies, and fill in the loopholes as they went along.

In fact, most of us, in our own managerial work, by necessity construct *ad hoc* procedures as we take the various steps called for in dealing with unplanned situations for which a formal procedure does not exist or is not known. To the extent that people are able to do this, it is because they understand the general *intent* of the procedure. A machine, on the other hand, obviously does not possess any similar understanding of the intent of its program.

A computer will follow its instructions blindly, faithfully, and to the last letter. It accepts no responsibility for the logic of its instructions nor for the validity of output which results from the execution of these instructions. When planning and developing applications in a business environment, the axiom *man improvises, a machine does not* can serve as a useful, constant reminder of the computer's limitations.

As we contemplate the sloppy procedure that men are able to follow more or less successfully, we come across the basic concept of what is known as *capturing logic,* i.e., determining and formally stating *how* men do what they do. If the computer has universal application potential, it can only mean that it can do anything—but there is a catch to it. A computer can indeed do anything provided we first tell it how. It is this telling it how, which in effect combines both problem definition and problem solution, that captures the logic of how *we* would go about doing the job. The principle of captured logic consists of being able to state solution methods precisely and unambiguously and documenting them in specific detail.

When planning and developing business applications for a computer, this ability to capture the logic of operating procedure will be crucial. The necessity of it will (it is hoped) force the business manager to sit back and rethink just exactly what he is trying to do in his function and to reevaluate why and whether he wants to continue doing it the same way. Usually the effort to capture the logic of a procedure (or system of procedures) leads to the discovery of its deficiencies, a better understanding of both the function and the system controlling it, and almost invariably, to a revision and improvement of the system itself.

This work calls for analyzing each function that is to be transferred to a computer and automated—and analyzing it all the way down to the elements of problem and solution. At times, this can lead to startling discoveries. Antiquated ways of doing things may come to light, and some traditional methods and habits may have to be discarded. *Gray areas* must be eliminated, and in areas of judgment and decision the basis for, and the elements of, the decision must be isolated and formally redefined. An incidental benefit of this process is the "deskilling" of jobs formerly difficult to supervise because of fuzziness of content.

The insistence of the computer on carrying out every last instruction with unquestioning obedience and its refusing to make up for our mistakes of procedure is forcing us to reformulate our procedures and to make them both sound and foolproof. One of the important lessons that the computer has taught us is the fact that in a business operation it is desirable and *practical* to discipline our operating activities, i.e., to formulate policies, procedures, and decision rules in a much more formal and rigorous fashion than we previously thought feasible.

As the computer program represents an implementation step derived from the procedure being automated, it follows that the completeness, logic, and soundness of that procedure is all-important. The soundness or appropriateness of operating procedure can, however, only be judged in relation to company policy. Thus the process of capturing the logic of procedure tends to force formulation—or at least formalization—of company policy. Questions of policy can be expected to arise at many points in the design of computer-based business systems:

1. Do we have a policy to cover this?
2. Is it formulated or is it "unwritten"?
3. Is it stated with sufficient clarity?
4. Is it being uniformly interpreted?
5. Is it appropriate?

Formulation and clarification of company policy is desirable in its own right, and one of the salutary effects of installing computers is that it receives fresh emphasis. From the point of view of the business executive, however, this may often be an uncomfortable, even annoying, aspect of trying to capture logic so that it may be transferred to a computer. But this is precisely the contribution the executive should be prepared to make, and it is important that he does make it.

Special Reminder

Beyond this point in the text, the discussion assumes that the reader has a familiarity with basic computer characteristics and functions, as well as with the most commonly used data processing terms. The layman is advised to read the Appendix (Fundamentals of Computer Design and Technology), or at least the first of its two parts, before proceeding with the next section. The background gained by reading the Appendix will make it easier to understand many subsequent points and arguments which, even when stated in nontechnical terms, assume this background.

PROGRAMMING

Programming, at present, is neither science nor art, as it lacks the essential attributes of either. It is something in between, which comes closest to being a craft—a highly skilled, intellectual craft. No two programmers may work exactly alike, as a great variety of approaches to the solution of a given problem is possible. There is an esthetic aspect to a given program, and to programming in general. This is often described as *elegance* in programming. In programming the implementation of a task, the selection of a particular programming procedure or technique can be a matter of taste.

Generally, an elegant program is one that is ingenious, clean, and sparse, in the sense that the objective is achieved with as few instructions as possible. Elegant programs have the dual advantage of occupying less space in computer memory and taking less time to execute, but they may take much longer to write than a workmanlike, pedestrian-type program that produces the same results with less efficiency.

A programmer whose incentive is to achieve elegance and to display flair in his work is often a source of frustration to management concerned with deadlines and programmer costs. The frustration stems from the fact that, at present, not enough is known about programming as a process, so that few standards (other than those of documentation, terminology, etc.) can be set for the programmer to adhere to. With the amount of programming now going on everywhere, and the investment in programming that this represents, the problem is of considerable concern to both computer users and computer manufacturers.

The latter are conducting, and sponsoring, research into the process of programming, hoping that a *science* of programming can be established. What is obviously needed are program mass-production principles and methods. When these are developed, relative efficiency of computer programs will most likely be subordinated to the objectives of low cost and speed of production, on the model of Detroit automobile manufacturing. The cars that come off the assembly lines are no Rolls Royces but are a very good value for the price.

There are three objective criteria of computer program quality, i.e.,

1. Program *size* (the number of instructions that will occupy computer memory), relative to the task the program must accomplish

2. Program *efficiency*, which is a function of how many instructions will have to be executed (how much time will elapse) before the desired result is obtained. On the surface, it may seem that small program size equals efficiency and vice versa, but that is not necessarily so, because in one iteration through a program, certain strings of instructions may be executed more than once and others bypassed, depending on how the program is structured.

3. Absence of *program error.*

The program error, commonly known as the *bug*, is an interesting phenomenon. The engineers and scientists who developed the first working models of computers believed that they would be able to write, the first time around, completely accurate programs of instructions for their machines. It was an infuriating—and humiliating—experience when they found out they could not do it. It appears that no one is capable of properly stringing together 200 or so instructions on the first try, if there is even a slight complexity to the program.

In today's practice, it is expected that no program will work right away, and the process of *program testing* and consequent *debugging* is an integral part of programming. Programs are tested by running them (or attempting to run them) on the computer, using some set of *test data* for which the result has been predetermined. If the computer does not come up with that result (it practically never does the first time), it is proof of bugs in the program, and the programmer has to go "back to the drawing board." He analyzes his instruction statements, finds the error (in this he is aided by computer printouts of memory contents and the like, from his test run), and fixes it. He is then ready for another test, and most likely, another round of debugging work.

The author, who once took a course in programming, can personally attest to the fact that by the time a program fails the fifth or sixth test, a novice programmer is thoroughly convinced that the machine is malfunctioning, which it, of course, is not. Based on a survey conducted by GUIDE, an association of IBM computer users, the average program of some scope (trivial programs excluded) takes about thirty tests before it works perfectly.

The actual process of programming consists of work on several levels and in several stages. First, a programmer determines a general strategy or approach to how the job in hand should be handled. Next, the method of attack is detailed by breaking it down into the major tasks and diagramming these according to their logical and precedence relationship. This is known as blocking out the logic or *block diagramming.*

The third step is the writing of individual instruction statements to carry out the functions of the respective blocks. This relatively menial work is typically farmed out, block by block, among junior programming personnel. It is known as *coding*, because it generates instructions expressed in a code acceptable to the computer. It is the code that is subsequently tested, but the faults of the program may also lie in the logic diagram or in the general approach to the job.

The work occurring on these different levels constitutes the so-called *programming hierarchy*, a hierarchy of programming functions that result in the production of code. The quantitative measure of this production is the number of *lines of code*, which is not necessarily the same as the number of instructions that the computer will eventually have to execute. This is because code can be written in different so-called programming languages, made up of broader, generalized statements that the computer can later translate into instructions proper.

PROGRAMMING LANGUAGES

Programming languages have been developed in order to make computer programming easier and less error-prone. Although the subject is admittedly strictly technical, nevertheless a business manager should understand the basic concept, as well as the fundamental differences between the main languages and the criteria by which to judge their applicability. After the management reader has read the following review, he will be better equipped to deal with questions of which language his company's programs should be written in and with controversies between the experts. If he knows the purpose of each of the few main languages, and their applicability, he may validly arbitrate disputes between specialists belonging to different schools of thought, because it is often the highly technical considerations that obscure the issue.

The subject of programming languages is important. It should be particularly important to the business executive whose company has a large programming staff and a large investment (present and future) in computer programs, when he considers that, according to some estimates, the shortage of system analysts and programmers may reach 250,000 by the end of 1970 and that salaries in this area doubled between 1963 and 1968.

To grasp the concept of programming languages (also called computer languages), one must keep in mind that a computer only understands its own *machine language,* i.e., instructions expressed in a code and format prespecified by the computer's manufacturer. Original computer programs were written by programmers in this code, and it can still be done, but it is extremely laborious because the typical machine language is complex, unnatural from the human point of view, difficult to memorize, and therefore particularly vulnerable to error.

To show what a machine language actually looks like (see Appendix for an explanation of how instructions are handled by the machine internally), the IBM 1401 computer code is chosen here even though the machine is now obsolete. For the current "generation" of computers, this language would have to be expressed in hexadecimal notation, which subject it is assumed the reader has no desire to go into. Assuming an imaginary (and oversimplified) payroll job where the employee's hours worked are punched in a card and his hourly pay rate plus the amount of his weekly savings bond deduction are recorded on magnetic tape, instructions stored in the 1401's memory might look like this:

IM%U3QOOR@OO4QO3SQO7QO3B?OO

This actually represents five instructions that mean the following:

1: Read a card into memory (location predetermined)

M%U3QOOR: Read a tape record from tape unit No. 3 into memory location beginning at address 2800

@OO4QO3: Multiply (hours worked) in memory location of address 001 through 004 by (pay rate) in memory location of address 2800 through 2803 and retain result in the latter location

SQO7QO3: Subtract (savings bond amount) in memory location at address 2804 through 2807 from (gross pay) in memory location at address 2800 through 2803

B?OO: Branch back to first instruction which is stored in memory location beginning at address 3000 (and work on the next employee's pay data)

The problem of someone's having to learn and use such an artificial scheme of expression (note that address 3000 is written as ?00, etc.) is obvious, and to overcome it, so-called "higher level languages" have been developed that more closely resemble human forms of expression. A language of the next higher level than machine language itself would be in the general category of *basic assembler languages,* also known as *symbolic* languages, and the five above instructions could be written this way:

R

M %U3 RATE R

M HOURS RATE

S BOND RATE

B START

This is quite a bit better than machine language, and it will make the programmer's job easier, even though he must write as many instructions, one for one, in this language as he would in machine language. The computer, however, cannot execute instructions written in this form. Therefore, each so-called programming language actually consists of

1. A *scheme* of expression (the language proper)
2. A *translator* program (or programs)

The program that will convert statements in a higher-level language into machine language is supplied by the computer's manufacturer, and it is geared to produce the code peculiar to the make and model of the machine in question which can then, *and only then*, execute it. Translator programs for languages in the basic assembler category are called *assemblers* or *processors*. They are characterized by the fact that they translate program statements (technically known as the *source* code) into machine instructions (technically known as the *object* code) one-for-one. Assuming a capable programmer, object code produced this way is always the most efficient one, but writing in an assembly language is usually deemed still too laborious relative to the efficiency it produces.

The laboriousness of writing computer programs can be further reduced—at the expense of some of the efficiency of the object code—by using programming languages of a still higher level than assembly languages. The best known of these, and the ones most widely used, are FORTRAN (FORmula TRANslator), which is particularly suitable for scientific and engineering computing, COBOL (COmmon Business Oriented Language), which is tailored for commercial applications, and PL/I, which combines the features of both. Less widely used are ALGOL, BASIC, etc. The important languages are those which are sponsored by the government as federal standards and those which are supported by computer manufacturers. This support takes the form of

1. Investment in improving the language itself
2. Investment in improving the performance of the translator programs
3. Supplying translator programs for new computer models being introduced

The above *procedural languages* are utilized to describe procedures for solving general problems. A number of *problem-oriented languages*, used for stating the problem rather than its solution procedure (which is preprogrammed), are also being supported. Examples of these might be APT and AUTOSPOT, languages for the preparation of part programs for numerically controlled machine tools, and RPG for producing reports. COGO, JOVIAL, etc., represent other examples of special-purpose languages. Programming languages in the FORTRAN, COBOL, and PL/I category are known as *compiler languages,* and their translating programs as *compilers,* because their statements do not have a one-for-one relationship to the object code they produce. Their statements are broader, i.e., one of them may be compiled into more than one machine instruction.

PL/I, developed in the early 1960s by IBM, is intended as a general-purpose programming language, and it is currently equal to FORTRAN and COBOL in object code efficiency. Assured the support of the largest computer manufacturer (but lacking government sponsorship at this time), PL/I may become the standard high-level programming language of the future. The five instructions in the preceding example stated in PL/I would require only four statements (the example is too trivial to display the many-for-few capability of such a language and its compiler) that would look as follows:

READ FILE (CARD) INTO INPUT;
READ FILE (TAPE) INTO WORK AREA;
NET PAY = HOURS*HOURLY RATE-BOND RATE;
GO TO START;

This example shows that, through the use of high-level languages, programming (or at least the coding portion of it) can be elevated from the antlike machine language labor to English-like statements where the logic of their use, rather than familiarity with a weird coding scheme, is of primary importance. Next to their ease of use, the important aspect of these languages is the fact that (computer manufacturers' future support being assumed), once a program is written in one of them, it can be recompiled for a different computer, likely a more powerful successor to the present one, in the future. High-level languages tend to solve the problem of *reprogramming.*

This is not the case with assembler-level languages, because they are (and have to be) tailored to a particular computer model or family. It should be noted that assemblers are relatively small programs that can be used with smaller, inexpensive machines. Compilers are large and require considerable computer memory capacity for that reason. In making a business judgment on this subject, the executive should weigh the cost of more memory, machine size, etc., against the value of gains in programmer productivity.

To evaluate the merits of a given programming language and its compiler, the following criteria apply:

1. Ease of use
2. Probability of language being perpetuated
3. Compilation speed
4. Size of memory required to accommodate compiler
5. Efficiency of the object code
6. Quality of diagnostics
7. Default options

The ease of use, obviously a very important characteristic, is self-explanatory. Language life expectancy—a question of continued support—is best judged in light of who stands behind it and what he has at stake in it. Compilation speed (how long does it take to convert to machine language instructions?) will be of high importance in engineering and scientific computing where a large volume of "one shot" programs will continually have to be compiled, but of no importance whatever for most commercial applications (for a fuller discussion of scientific and commercial computing, see next chapter). We have already commented on the memory capacity required, and the tradeoff considerations, as well as on the concept of object code efficiency.

The quality of the so-called "diagnostics," i.e., the capability of the compiler to detect and identify errors committed by the programmer and to inform him of them following the test run, is obviously of extreme value, as it increases programmer productivity. It should be noted, however, that more extensive diagnostics can only be performed at the expense of compilation speed. A fast compiler is not necessarily a good compiler, if it takes many test runs to compile properly! *Default options* is another feature found in some compilers, and it means that certain errors of form and syntax that the programmer made are "forgiven," i.e., corrected by the compiler itself. This also is valuable, as it saves test runs and debugging.

In judging the suitability of a particular language and compiler, the manager should (keeping the above criteria in mind) look at what kind of data processing shop he runs. Is it an *open shop* or job shop where user departments do their own programming and generate a multitude of small programs, using the computer center for compilation and testing more so than for the running of the tested-out programs? Is it a *production shop* where masses of data are being processed using the same programs repetitively? Is the work similar to what is found in a university environment, where execution speed (object code efficiency) is of no consideration? As in so many areas of data processing and computer system planning, looking first at what it is we are doing, or want to do, proves to be the best way of arriving at sound management decisions.

Chapter Three
Approaches and Methods for the Processing of Information

The advantage of significantly increasing the productivity of engineers, researchers, and programmers would seem certainly to offset even the most glaring inefficiency of a computer system they use.

In designing and implementing computer-based systems in a business environment, one of the principal problems is the difficulty of communication between data processing-oriented and business-oriented personnel. Systems analysts, computer specialists, programmers, and other technicians are typically highly skilled but usually (and understandably) lack the broad business background and experience required to supplement, and to guide, their technical skills so that these may be successfully applied.

Without positive, and intelligent, direction by business management, the technician often finds himself in a position of attempting to solve complex business problems that he does not fully understand. Consequently, his view of certain business functions may be distorted or simplistic, and lacking perspective, he will often recommend the adoption of approaches and methods for the processing of information that favor data processing efficiency, or elegance, at the expense of service to the business operation that is to be supported.

It is obviously desirable, therefore, that business management become more knowledgeable in the area of data processing concepts and methods than has been the rule in the past. Today, the business manager cannot escape the requirement of a reasonable understanding of certain technical matters in the area of data processing method and technique, because without such an understanding he will simply not be in a position to judge the suitability of systems approaches and methods proposed by the technicians.

In the following discussion, therefore, a review of some of the fundamental data processing philosophies and of the most important methods approaches may serve to acquaint management and other business-oriented personnel with concepts and terms, as well as with criteria for the applicability of the various methods, that should prove useful in their future systems-related activities.

TYPES OF COMPUTER USE

With a computer, or electronic data-processing system, several different types (*modes*) of use in an industrial environment are possible. The first distinction between systems, or categories of systems, can be made based on their mode of acquiring data. In one category, the computer's instrument extensions acquire and input data directly, i.e., such systems are data self-acquiring.

This type of computer use will be found where physical events and processes are computer controlled by means of monitoring through sensor instruments linked to the central processor and by the latter's originating signals to similarly linked control instruments. Typically, both types of instruments are remote from the central system, which, by definition, operates in *real time* (is continually and instantaneously responsive). Computers being utilized this way are called *data acquisition systems, sensor-oriented systems,* or *process control systems* and will be found where laboratory, process, test, etc., automation has been implemented.

In the other, broader category, data are being supplied (input) to the systems by human beings. Within this category we can distinguish among five principal types of use:

1. Scientific and engineering computing
2. Use of computer as analytical and simulation tool
3. Inquiry and information retrieval
4. Accounting-type applications
5. Operating support systems

Scientific computing is characterized by a high degree of calculation, i.e., high incidence of arithmetic operation as against *data han-*

dling, which is a term that covers the volume of input and output, posting to file records, etc. Programs tend to be nonrepetitive, as the system users write them to solve particular problems they encounter in the course of their work. Scientific computing is typified by a large number of diverse programs (often small in size, but not necessarily in the amount of processing) being run on computer systems geared to maximum data processing efficiency, with the speedy return of output data to the user (called *turn-around*) as the primary system objective.

The use of the computer as an **analytical tool** is probably always a part-time, or once-in-a-while, mode of utilization, which can take place in any of the other categories. In this mode, a limited area of the business (more exactly: data representing this area) is subjected to analysis through special calculation or simulation so as to obtain better insight into a problem and to permit management to evaluate alternative courses of action. Special programs are typically created for this purpose, and system response (the time of output availability) is usually not a critical consideration.

Inquiry and information retrieval represent a separate category of applications, which mainly utilize the computer's recordkeeping capability. Into this category fall such applications as personnel or warranty record maintenance (retrieval-oriented) and management information systems (inquiry-oriented). The most important of these will be separately reviewed later.

The accounting and operating support categories are known as *commercial computing* or commercial applications.

Accounting, administrative, and similar work is characterized by the recording of historical data for purposes of *measurement* of past performance. High volumes of data must be handled but calculating requirements are very slight. Although promptness of output is certainly desirable, its timing is not overly critical. Accounting-type reports are by nature periodic, and their frequency is often low by design, where longer spans of performance must be covered for these reports to be meaningful. Data processing methods of high economy—but permissive of the delays required to achieve this economy—are both suitable and appropriate for this type of work.

Operating support systems exist where the computer is used to aid, by various means, in the conduct of business operations. Applications for order entry, inventory control, purchasing, production scheduling, shop floor control, and the like are in this category. Such systems are employed to execute operating procedure, keep operating records, provide for file inquiry, and signal for specific action. In comparison with accounting systems that are *measurement-oriented,* operating support systems are *action-oriented.* They constitute part of the sinew and muscle of the operating arm of the company, and where they are improperly designed or used, business performance suffers directly and immediately.

The mix of data handling, calculating, and response requirements varies, but responsiveness is universally more critical than in accounting systems. Programs tend to be large, repetitive, and normally have long, continual use. In soundly conceived operating support systems, data processing efficiency is subordinated to the efficiency of the business operation the system serves or controls. Data processing methods compatible with the achievement of this objective—business performance first, data processing performance second—should obviously be employed, but in practice there is often confusion on this point and wrong system design decisions are made, particularly where the accounting or data processing viewpoint prevails.

BATCH PROCESSING AND IN-LINE PROCESSING

In commercial computing there exist two philosophies, two distinctly different approaches to the processing of information. One is *batch* or *periodic processing,* and the other is *in-line* or *continuous processing.* It is interesting to note that the latter, which today is considered advanced and sophisticated, actually preceded the former historically.

In the sphere of business or commercial information processing most of the data processing functions can be viewed as *file-updating* tasks, or more specifically, as the collection of transactions, posting to master records, evaluation of new status, and determining action indicated by the new status, as presented in output reports.

In the days of the bookkeeper with the green eyeshade, when strictly manual accounting methods were being used, clerks used the principle of in-line processing in that they posted each transaction to the ledgers as it occurred, or at least in the sequence in which it occurred, thus keeping records continually up-to-date (by the standards of their time) and the accounts in constant balance.

Once calculating machines, and particularly, punched-card equipment, were introduced into the accounting process, however, the bookkeeping approach changed. Machine accounting brought about batch processing, so as to utilize the limited capabilities of the machines. Instead of taking each transaction through all the logical steps of the accounting procedure (posting it to the various accounts, journals, etc.) before tackling the next transaction, records began to be updated on a periodic basis.

Like transactions were accumulated to economical quantities (batches) and taken through each step of the procedure as a group. The batch was first sorted to the sequence of the master file to which it was to be posted. Only then would the actual data processing, or *run,* begin by sequentially accessing file records and updating same. This made processing more efficient, but the former advantage of the files being at all times updated and in balance was lost.

Curiously enough, the batching principle has become so universal and business personnel so conditioned to it that today many people consider the fact that practically all records and reports are always out-of-date to be a normal, natural phenomenon. Yet it no longer need be so.

The batch processing approach is typically characterized by:

1. *Setup,* including the reading in of the appropriate program, loading of the card reader hopper, mounting of tape reels, etc. Setup, on the average, may add up to 20 percent of total data processing time.

2. Need for *completeness of input data* batch. All the transactions in question must be available, in *machine-readable form* (i.e., punched into cards, transcribed onto magnetic tape, etc.) before processing can begin.

3. A certain amount of *preauditing* of the input transaction group so as to:

a. Ensure completeness.

b. Minimize interruptions of the subsequent processing run due to detection of errors.

4. A certain amount of *preparatory processing* must take place prior to operating on the transactions:

a. Sorting, collating, sequence checking, comparing, control coding, etc.

b. Developing auxiliary records such as lookup tables, reference indices, etc.

5. Reading in and *handling of all file records,* i.e., also of records not subject to updating. This is a limitation inherent to sequential processing of card decks and tape.

6. Several processing *passes* (transaction batch being run through more than once), due to:

a. Preparatory processing, sorting of tapes, etc.

b. Intermediate results based on the complete data batch being required for further processing.

Batch processing is, by definition, periodic processing. Accumulation of data over periods of time and processing of data batches at specified intervals is appropriate and justified under the following conditions:

1. Where the period is fixed by law (quarterly tax reports) or custom (monthly accounts receivable statements).

2. The balance of efficiencies and inefficiencies inherent to batch processing is, in a specific instance, in favor of batch processing.

3. The period corresponds to the operating dynamics of the management level for which the output is being prepared, i.e., where data must be accumulated over a period of time before a report lends itself to meaningful evaluation.

4. The economy of periodic, batch processing outweighs the value of operational advantages obtainable with continuous processing and its nondelay outputs.

Generally speaking, batch processing proves quite satisfactory for most accounting and like work, which incidentally, was the first to be automated. From there, batch processing methods were carried over into other functions, including operating support systems. There, however, these methods turned out to be less satisfactory because records got out-of-date between processing cycles and reports showed status conditions *as of* some past point in time or summaries of activity *cut off* at (and reported only up to) some such point in the past.

These deficiencies, inherent to periodic processing of data in batches, can be overcome by continuous or nonbatch processing methods permitting transactions to be entered in random sequence and at more or less random times. Utilization of these methods has been made possible by developments in both the technology and the methodology of electronic data processing. The introduction of random-access secondary-storage devices and larger, as well as faster, main memories available in computers reduced dependence on sequential processing techniques, and advances in programming brought about new concepts of data processing operation.

The concept of principal importance is that of *in-line,* or continuous, processing. (The similar term *on-line* means something else. It denotes direct linkage of an outlying equipment unit to the central processor, and to its program.) In-line processing is not just a technique but rather a philosophy, the application of which has several grades or degrees. It is not a frequent batch. In-line processing is nonperiodic, and it is characterized by the fact that the prime-application program or programs are in control of the system throughout the workshift, accepting individual transactions for processing at random times in random sequence. How transaction data are provided to the central processor (whether in punched cards manually collected and fed through a reader, or by some form of transmission) is not relevant to the in-line concept.

The highest degree of application of this principle is exemplified by the so-called *real-time systems*, a special case of in-line processing. Such systems have *on-line* linkage of remote input-output devices, transaction data arriving at the central processor are receiving its immediate attention, and response (output) is instantaneous. Real-time operation is characterized by lack of delay in system response, but because a lack of delay is a relative concept (in reality, there must always be some delay, even though infinitesimal), there is some confusion in the use of this term. A useful definition of real-time response stipulates that it be *fast enough for the purpose intended.*

Thus a three-second response by an airline reservation system (such as used by major United States airlines) is considered satisfactory; a ten-second response might be suitable for on-line factory data collection or production monitoring, but anything more than a small fraction of a second would fail in an application where a computer guides a numerically controlled machine tool in contour milling, for example. Real-time, as has been mentioned, is a special case of in-line processing which, aside from system response, is distinguished by the fact that transaction-acceptance time not only is random but corresponds to the time of transaction occurrence.

In-line processing, as far as internal system operation at the central-processor level is concerned, means that each transaction is taken through all the logical steps of the appropriate procedure and all its processing is completed before another transaction is accepted. (Transactions arriving simultaneously through separate channels are entered into main memory, and in this sense they are being accepted; but processing is still, in most computers, done on a one-at-a-time basis.) All the file records affected by a given transaction are updated, but no other records are being accessed and handled. This is practical only with randomly accessible file records. Thus, on the hardware level, in-line processing is characterized by random-access secondary storage. The (potential) capability of response to inquiry into the status of any file record at any time is inherent to all in-line systems.

The processing efficiencies that such systems embody consist of the following:

1. Setup is minimal.
2. No need for batch completeness audit.
3. Preparatory processing does not exist, and the capacity of the system is used for operating on the data instead of preparing them for being operated on.
4. The need for a preaudit for invalid transactions is eliminated, as

the computer is typically programmed to detect and reject erroneous entries and to proceed to the next valid transaction without interrupting the processing run.

5. No handling of unaffected file records.

6. One-pass processing.

On the other hand, in-line systems have certain inherent processing inefficiencies, which can be listed as follows:

1. Multiple accessing, during a workshift, of a given file record, particularly where active file records are relatively few and where there are repetitive transactions of the same kind.

2. The same operation on data is repeated since the system is unable to summarize like transactions and to treat them as a group.

3. System tends to idle when the transaction stream temporarily dries up, unless it is programmed to share the processing capacity with batch jobs that stand by or to handle special, housekeeping-type work routines reserved for lulls and off-shift processing.

On balance, in-line processing is less efficient, from the data processing point of view, than batch processing. The question must be asked, then, when and under what circumstances an in-line approach is indicated. This will be the case either when the specifications of the job to be done dictate such approach regardless of processing economy (a batch-oriented airline reservation system would be inconceivable) or, in a specific case, the in-line approach would actually be more economical, or most importantly, when it affords an *operational advantage,* the value of which exceeds the extra cost of in-line processing. In operating support systems, as defined above, this will often be the case, and care should be taken that the selection of the processing approach not be based on the criterion of data processing efficiency alone.

The in-line approach generally invites the consolidation of files and thus facilitates integration of related business functions and their processing jobs. This means that several such jobs that would otherwise have to be done in separate runs and probably against different files can then be done simultaneously. Data-processing job integration creates its own processing economies, and the fact that files tend to become consolidated compensates, to some extent, for the multiple accessing of the in-line method.

Under the batch approach, when sequential processing methods are used, every file record is handled during a run and files tend not to get combined so they do not become too bulky and thus increase the processing time of each run. With in-line processing, combined files permit one transaction to update what otherwise would perhaps have been several different files. Thus in-line methods incorporate multiple accessing of a file record for like transactions but also multiple updating with each access.

But aside from the question of processing efficiency, the principal justification of the in-line approach lies in the operational advantage being gained, where this applies. Technically, the operational advantage is always derived from the *timeliness of output*. Only the type of output that can promptly be acted upon (purchase-order cancellation, work reassignment, expediting notice, etc.) is significant here. For other types of output (historical data, financial statements, etc.) the value of relative timeliness is probably quite low.

In a manufacturing enterprise, there are application areas in which premium value will be assigned to immediate collection, processing, and analysis of input data, as well as to nondelay system output. The most highly dynamic areas of rapid information generation and rapid change of conditions are the manufacturing activities proper and the control functions closely related to them. These are the most likely candidates for in-line processing. Prerequisite to a justifiable in-line processing application is a high volume of transactions being generated on a more or less continuous basis rather than in periodic bursts.

An in-line system can either exclusively utilize its own computer (a *stand-alone*, or *dedicated*, system) or share the equipment with other applications on either an off-shift or a sharing basis. Characteristically, an in-line system is transaction oriented, i.e., geared for the acceptance of individual input messages through card readers or transaction terminals, rather than through paper or magnetic tape. The latter, where used, is utilized for so-called housekeeping tasks (transaction journals, various logs, and periodic transcriptions of random-access file contents, for audit purposes, are good examples) and historical-data recording rather than for regular data input-output.

Where the computer is dedicated to the in-line application, the properly balanced system will typically utilize a relatively slow (inexpensive) central processor combined with relatively fast random-access file storage. Central processor speed need be no faster than as required for executing the necessary instructions per transaction pending total *seek time* (the time it takes to locate a record in the file and to read it into main memory) per transaction. Main-memory (core-storage) capacity requirements are relatively modest, as transaction data are being read in and out one at a time and program size (the number of instructions) tends to be small. Furthermore, program segments and *subroutines* (strings of instructions utilized at several points in the program, or common to several programs) can be kept in random-access storage and retrieved as required. These general observations do not apply to real-time systems, which must have extra-large central processor capacity in terms of both speed and main memory size, to guarantee the minimum response requirement even under the worst conditions (peak in transaction traffic).

Where common computer equipment is being shared with other (batch type) applications, a faster, more capacious, and more expensive central processor will most likely have to be used. *Multiprogramming* (for a fuller explanation, see below), i.e., multiple program execution, is required in such equipment-sharing operations. Only a central processor specifically designed for this type of processing can be used, and its main-memory capacity requirements will be high.

To sum up, the method for the processing of information should match the requirements of the environment the system is to control, the operation it is to support. Business in general, and manufacturing in particular, is a continuous activity, wherein events and transactions take place continually but irregularly, at random times. Some, but not all, of these events will require subsequent management and nonmanagement action, following their recognition and evaluation by the computer-based operating support system. Timeliness of such recognition is of the essence if maximum operational advantage is to be had.

An in-line system operates *in phase* with the activity it is intended to serve or to control, by being continually ready to accept random inputs while the activity lasts and thus being able to detect the need for action at the earliest point in time. In-line processing methods should be a strong candidate for selection when operating support systems are being designed, despite their relative lack of data processing economy.

COMMUNICATIONS-ORIENTED SYSTEMS

The history of rapid communication over distance, from smoke signals and jungle drums to radio signals, reflects the continual growth in man's ability to convey information beyond the range of the human voice. In less than a century, the communications industry has developed from the first manually keyed telegraph to television transmission and communications satellites.

In today's complex and competitive economy, business management has a need for the latest facts where and when they are needed. Centralized knowledge of widespread operations, improvements in service to customers, and close surveillance of critical activities taking place in remote areas are all highly desirable. Every organization with activities in more than one location (or complex activities in one location, for that matter) must provide for some sort of system of communications for management control of operations.

With the development of electronic data-processing systems, it became apparent that existing telephone and telegraph facilities could be utilized for the purpose of sending data to a central point for processing. Large volumes of detailed information, formerly delayed by distance, weather conditions, or traffic, could now be transmitted, processed, and acted upon earlier than ever before. This is *data communications*. Actually, the incorporation of data processing equipment and communications facilities in a data transmission network is not such a recent development. The first working prototype of such a system began to be used by the United States Army Air Corps as early as the 1940s.

From the computer application point of view, the crowning technological achievement occurred the day information in storage could not only be accessed randomly but also be retrieved, or forwarded, from a geographically remote point. This has been made possible by directly linking remotely located input-output units (putting them on-line) to the central processor of a computer system. In communications jargon, such units bear the collective name of *terminals* (they range from simple keyboard devices to small satellite computers), and they can be attached to the central system by means of private cabling or telephone lines if located in the plant, or utilizing leased lines provided by common carriers where greater geographical distances are involved. Such systems are said to be *communications-oriented*.

The on-line linkage implies *transmission* of data and immediate access between the outlying, or *peripheral*, device and the central processor without any form of intermediate transcription and/or storage of the transmitted data.

Once transmission of data to and from computers became technologically and economically feasible, many industrial computer systems users began taking advantage of this capability. The volume of transaction data transmission (in this context, transactions are called *data messages* in contrast to administrative or verbal messages) has been steadily increasing, and data traffic over common carrier lines is expected soon to exceed, or has already exceeded, that of voice or verbal text messages. The common carriers in the United States (AT&T, GT&E, IT&T, Western Union) now offer a variety of services for this purpose, such as WATS, INWATS, TWX, TELEX, TELPAK, and Dataphone.

Communications orientation is a natural extension of modern electronic data-processing systems capabilities, and more and more computer-based business systems will inevitably become communications-capable. Some of the important factors that must be considered in communications system design are

1. The purpose of the communications system
2. The number and size of the messages (message traffic considerations)
3. The relative urgency of the various messages (priority considerations)
4. The reliability and cost of the system

Specific objectives of data communications are as follows:

1. To reduce the time, effort, and expense required to convert information to a form suitable for entry into a data processing system. This is accomplished by capturing the data at their source.
2. To boost the performance of a computer-based system by a more rapid movement of information from its point of origin to the point of its processing.
3. To provide accurate and timely outputs for management information and operating decision making.

Assuming that adequate processing and random-access storage capacity is available at the central system level, the single most significant expense item is line cost. Criteria for the selection of terminals are speed, reliability, ease of maintenance, self-checking features, capability to *buffer*, or temporarily to store, a message before transmission, terminal operator efficiency achievable, and cost. Beyond this, the more technical considerations such as communications network design and the specific configuration of special devices are best left up to communications specialists. The term "communications-oriented systems" covers computers with applications in the following categories:

1. Message switching
2. Remote inquiry
3. Remote batch processing
4. Remote computing
5. On-line transaction systems
6. Time sharing
7. Management information systems (MIS), a special case of inquiry systems

Message switching systems exist where a centrally located computer is utilized to act as an administrative message exchange between points of message origination and destination. In many large corporations with far-flung, scattered operations, warehouses, dealerships, etc., this type of system is replacing, and is economically outperforming, the former *torn-tape* systems built around a central exchange equipped with paper tape punches (for arriving messages) and readers (for outgoing messages), with clerks manually carrying and feeding torn off pieces of tape containing individual messages from punch to reader.

Remote inquiry applications utilize terminals that are capable of both sending and receiving information. The terminal may be located on the same premises as the central processor, but is termed "remote" if it is outside the immediate central processing area or computer room. Inquiry systems imply prompt entry into random-access file storage and prompt attention by the central processor to the inquiring party at the terminal. By this definition, inquiry systems operate in the in-line mode and sometimes have real-time response capability, depending on the prime application.

Remote batch processing is no different from regular, or conventional, batch processing as described in the section above, except that programs (usually), as well as the data on which the programs are to operate (always), are entered into the central computer from a remote terminal. The output of the run is also transmitted back to the remote terminal location. The remote user may do his own programming but may then keep the programs in the program library of the central system, so as to save the time required for transmitting them every time the respective jobs are to be run. Examples of remote batch processing will be found where a company's small divisions, plants, etc., distant from the site of the parent operation, cannot afford their own computers but are instead "plugged in" through terminals to give them the benefit of computer services. Alternatively, even larger operations can similarly be linked to a large, central computer system for reasons of economy.

Remote computing is a term that applies to situations where distant users (such as engineering and research laboratories) are equipped with on-line terminals, so as to provide local personnel direct access to a central computer facility. Applications are typically in the scientific computing category, and the data processing work consists not of batches of business transactions but of a multitude of individual programs and problem data being entered by terminal users. Sometimes the remote users are afforded instant and sustained access to the central computer system, so that they can interact with it directly (modify their own programs as the work progresses, order additional iterations of the calculating routine, etc.). This mode of operation is possible with the so-called *time-sharing* systems, reviewed in the section below.

On-line transaction systems are based on the already described in-line processing approach. When the input-output units are both remotely located and directly linked to the central computer, they act as terminals in a communications-oriented system.

Management information systems (MIS) are a special case of remote inquiry systems discussed above. Designed for use by top management, they incorporate the access to all system files for the executive terminal user, as well as other programmed features discussed more fully in a separate section below.

MULTIPROGRAMMING AND TIME SHARING

Multiprogramming, or more precisely, multiprogram execution, is a technique of processing several unrelated jobs in parallel, i.e., executing several different programs "simultaneously." Actually, as only one instruction is being executed at a time, the simultaneity consists of the central processor working, in turn, on segments of the various programs in some priority order and turning over control from one program to another every time a lower-speed operation, such as the reading in of another block of data from magnetic tape or disk, would cause the central processor to wait, i.e., to be temporarily idle.

The significance of this can best be brought out by comparing the relative speeds of input-output and secondary-storage devices with those of central processors. A tape unit capable of transferring data at a rate of 50,000 characters per second enters 1 character into main memory every twenty microseconds; if the central processor operates at 1 microsecond speed (memory cycles 1 million times per second), it means that, during the reading in of the tape record, it would idle nineteen out of twenty microseconds, or 95 percent of the time, as only one cycle is used to enter each character of data into memory.

It is evident that computer utilization can be significantly boosted through the multiprogramming approach, which is aimed at getting the maximum amount of work per unit of time out of the central processor. Only computers expressly designed for multiprogramming, however, are capable of it. This mode of operation obviously requires much larger memories, to accommodate the multiple programs and related data, as well as the rather complex *control program*, or monitor, that permanently occupies a portion of memory.

It also requires circuitry for *interrupt* functions (after the last character of the tape record in the previous example has been read in, the processing of some other job must automatically be interrupted and control returned to the program, presumably of higher priority, that has temporarily been abandoned pending its tape read-in), as well as enhanced capabilities in some of the peripheral units.

Multiprogramming creates many internal system problems as far as the policing of the various programs and data, allocation of memory areas, scheduling of the work, handling of interrupts, etc., are concerned. Without a relatively large, complex, and sophisticated set of control and service programs collectively known as the *Operating System* (discussed under the heading of Software below), multiprogramming is inconceivable.

Time sharing differs from multiprogramming, although it is also a multiprogram execution technique, in that predetermined specific slices of time are allocated to the various programs, *in rotation,* and the basis for transferring control from one program to the next is elapsed time rather than the occurrence of a wait condition or an interrupt. Time-sharing systems are characterized by multiple users' working with the computer through remote terminals simultaneously. Each active user is being provided *sustained access,* i.e., is communicating with the system directly, without apparent time limitation.

Because of the difference between human speed and computer speed (which is on the order of 1 to 1 million), the user at the terminal is under the illusion that he has exclusive possession of the system which is responding to his inputs very fast indeed, although it is actually paying attention to him only periodically and is servicing other users in the interim.

Time-sharing systems are termed man/machine interactive, because the approach permits operation in the so-called *conversational mode,* man and machine "talking" to each other, back and forth, at a tempo set by the man. While the individual user ponders or evaluates a given reply by the system (message, report, image displayed) and is deciding what he will do next, the computer is not idle but is serving its other simultaneous users.

Computer hardware for time sharing must obviously be fast, have capacious memory, and be equipped with an internal electronic clock, or *interval timer,* capable of measuring the passage of time in very small increments. Other special hardware functions are also required, and it can generally be said that time sharing is feasible only with computer systems specially engineered for this purpose. A set of computer manufacturer-supplied programs that include special time-sharing control features is a necessity.

The general idea of time sharing is to establish a system that would be *application independent,* i.e., one that could service any kind of user and do all types of work after accepting any user-supplied program. The concept of time sharing is deceptively simple, but the implementation of a general-purpose time-sharing system (there are also applications of specialized purpose that can utilize the principle of time sharing with limited control program requirements) has, in practice, proved to be an enormously complex task. Programming requirements for a time-sharing system with all-round capability are of a magnitude that, at least at the present time, precludes the implementation of a full-blown, all-purpose system that would be economically feasible.

The time-sharing approach, in its more limited versions, lends itself to a variety of applications including MIS (see next section below) and other inquiry systems, on-line data collection, production monitoring systems, direct numerical control of machine tools, etc.

When evaluating the desirability of adopting the time-sharing approach in a given instance, business management should keep in mind that time-sharing systems are quite uneconomical and inefficient from the data processing point of view. All of the excess cost is borne for the sole purpose of providing maximum service to the individual users, whose productivity and contribution is thereby to be enhanced.

The general inefficiency of a time-sharing system derives from several factors, particularly underutilization (when some terminal stations are idle), processing inefficiency (caused mainly by the "round robin" method of jumping from program to program), a multitude of internal housekeeping and control procedures (execution of programs not related to the actual job) collectively known as *system overhead,* and the necessity for backup, i.e., a duplicate set of hardware to take over in cases of occasional but inevitable equipment failure.

The system inefficiency must, however, be weighed against user efficiency—the potential increase in his effectiveness and productivity. Is the user's talent highly valuable and, perhaps, rare? If so, the high cost of providing him with the best possible tools diminishes in importance. The advantages of significantly increasing the productivity of engineers, researchers, and programmers, for instance, would seem certainly to offset even the most glaring inefficiency, or underutilization, of a computer they use.

Although there are as yet no hard conclusive statistics on this, results of limited studies reported in data processing literature indicate, for example, that the productivity of programmers who are able to test and "debug" their work through on-line terminals increases from between *three* to *seven times!* This is not too difficult to believe, when we think of a busy executive's reduction in effectiveness if he were forced to use the telephone only during specified limited periods of the day instead of having full-time access to the instrument.

COMPUTER OUTPUTS AND MANAGEMENT INFORMATION SYSTEMS

Computer system outputs are directed at either of the following:

1. Other devices that are to perform a subsequent function
2. Files in secondary storage
3. The system's human users

The central processor will generate outputs, or *commands* (in the form of *machine-readable* signals), to activate other hardware, such as channels, input-output units, and other peripheral devices that are under its control. The whole system can be said to generate signals and commands directed at non-data-processing machines where the latter operate under computer control, such as in the sensor-oriented applications discussed earlier.

In commercial data processing, probably the bulk of the central processor output is directed to files in secondary storage (magnetic tape, disk, etc.). This is the function of file record updating, i.e., changing the contents of a record as a result of the last transaction processed. This type of output is not in man-readable form, as it consists of a transcription of digital data from main memory onto a magnetic-surface medium. This process is technically known as "writing," as contrasted with "reading," which is the reverse.

Of main interest are the outputs generated for use by the system's human users. (The wide range of man-readable, or usable, output possibilities is discussed in the Appendix.) The bulk of user-directed data is presented in alpha-numeric or graphic form, and it can be either displayed on screens of special devices or else printed (drawn) on paper. Printed outputs (technically known as *hard copy*) are in prevalent use, predominantly in the application areas of management, planning, and business controls.

Printed output categories are the following:

1. *Reports*
2. *Messages* (such as action notices, replies to inquiry, etc.)
3. *Documents* (such as paychecks, manufacturing process sheets, insurance policies, etc.)
4. *Special listings* (such as audit trails, diagnostic statements, printouts of memory contents at time of program malfunction, etc.)

As far as commercial applications are concerned, the trend has been somewhat away from traditional reports in favor of exception reporting (unsolicited) and replies to inquiry (solicited), both of which tend to be briefer than the conventional reports. This trend is a reaction to the general tendency of flooding the user with computer printouts. The people who control the computer system sometimes act as though the benefits, or utilization, of a computer consisted in producing the maximum quantity of user-directed output. Modern high-speed printers can spew out printed copy at incredible rates. A single such printer operating on-line can produce upwards of a million lines, or about 75,000 *individually composed* and printed pages each day. (This is *before* copying and reproducing machines enter the picture!)

Where the tendency toward report proliferation is not checked, the avalanche of paper can create, and in some companies has, in fact, created, really serious problems. Management and other users resent reams of detailed data, particularly when such data are being generated at a rate exceeding that of their conceivable assimilation. Under such conditions, the report recipients' attitude toward the system is likely to be adversely affected and general psychological damage can be great. The author has met business executives who refuse even to look at computer-printed reports and who make their secretaries summarize and *retype* the information that their job responsibility impels them to use! This is indeed a sad commentary on one of the forms of computer misuse. We do not want the computer to tell us all it knows. The fullest possible utilization of the individual equipment units that comprise a computer system is obviously desirable. Yet, as far as the production of reports is concerned, the effectiveness of the overall system is probably in direct proportion to the *underutilization* of high-speed printers.

Management Information Systems

In connection with human-user-directed computer outputs, so-called *Management Information Systems* (MIS), which have become the goal of many companies, merit a separate review. They hold out the promise of solving the report-proliferation problem by radically altering the whole philosophy of management information reporting.

The MIS concept has lately created considerable interest on the part of both business management and system-oriented personnel, as evidenced by the inclusion of the subject in many management seminars, data processing conferences, technical and trade literature, etc. It is the latest of the imagination-stirring concepts that seem periodically to emerge to foment enthusiasm, controversy, and confusion in the management and data processing communities. In this regard, MIS is the successor to the IDP (integrated data processing) of the 1950s and to the "total system" of the early 1960s.

It is customary for writers and speakers on the subject of MIS to begin with the proclamation that there is no agreement on what precisely constitutes an MIS. It is true that the mix of functions that make up a management information system can be conceptualized in different ways, but the various definitions of MIS have enough in common to permit a general discussion of the subject.

Implementation of the MIS concept aims at the creation of a comprehensive system of inquiry designed primarily for top management use. The system is based on the principle of direct user/data relationship by affording the user entry into the system files so that he may retrieve the exact data he needs. An MIS is defined as a system that makes any information in the data base (files) immediately available to the user, to satisfy his planned, as well as unplanned, information requirements.

By common consensus, the following essential attributes characterize a management information system:

1. A *data base,* as the foundation for the system
2. A good portion of the data in random-access file storage
3. Remote entry by the user through a terminal capable of two-way communication, and his direct access to file data
4. Prompt response by the system to the user's requests for information, i.e., the system's ability to retrieve and to present to him the data he needs
5. System flexibility, in the sense that both planned and unplanned information requirements can be met, as well as the system's ability to delimit the exact amount of data the user wants and to structure it into a format *he* specifies
6. The ability to provide, upon the user's request, successive layers of detail to trace a condition to its source
7. File security, to prevent unauthorized users from obtaining privileged information

One school of thought adds another attribute to the above, namely, the capability of furnishing the user *unsolicited* information, this type of message being triggered whenever the system detects that file data representing a critical condition in some area of the business warrant calling this to his attention.

Although the concept of MIS grew out of the information needs of the top executive, it obviously has application on the operating management level also. Thus a comprehensive MIS would consist of several such lower-level subsystems which, along with sources of privileged information available only to top management, would constitute a pyramid-like system structure through the apex of which the executive would have access to the MIS files and programs at all levels.

In a layered MIS of this type the lower-level manager, though provided with access to the system files, would likely be barred from retrieving certain higher-management-level information, such as the executive payroll or corporate personnel records. But the principle of file security can be applied in yet another way, by structuring the system so as to prevent his access to *some* of the files on his own level, thus restricting him to data that are within his jurisdiction.

In management information systems that are operational today, we find examples of such an arrangement in the case of a marketing MIS comprised of a number of sales district subsystems or a manufacturing MIS made up of several plant-level systems used by the individual plant managers. The marketing executive and the manufacturing executive can inquire directly into any sales district or plant files, respectively, but a district sales manager cannot, through his terminal, obtain data on another district's performance. The plant managers in our example are able to get some, but not all, of the information pertaining to sister plants.

The MIS approach, where successfully implemented, promises to become a superior management tool. The capability of this type of system to generate *customized reports,* in a departure from traditional reporting methods, and in general to provide the user with the information he needs at the time he needs it and in the form he wants it, would obviously be of great value to the executives of any company.

Present computer and communications technologies make implementation definitely feasible, and a number of such systems (in their limited version) are currently "on the air" in both industry and government. But certain implementation problems do exist, some of which are in the programming and *data base* or file organization realm and others that have to do with the executive user himself. Management personnel in organizations that either plan to have an MIS in the future or are in the process of developing one should know what the considerations and obstacles to successful implementation are.

One of the main MIS design problems is the structuring of the data base. The technical term "data base" covers, in essence, the set of the different files that are accessible to the system. The data base concept, its meaning, and the related problems are more fully discussed in Chapter 8. Suffice it to state here that to find a universally applicable formula for optimum file organization proved to be one of those information processing concepts that seem deceptively simple at first but are plagued by innumerable difficulties in implementation. Until good theory of data base organization is established, the individual MIS user will, at least to some extent, have to custom-design his own file organization scheme.

The next major problem of system design is to determine management's specific *information requirements*. What does the manager for whom the system is being designed need in the way of data, in order to run his business (or that portion of the business for which he is responsible) effectively? What are the essential elements of the information needed for decision making?

In practice, these questions are not always easy to answer. Many managers do not know, specifically, what they need or what they *might* need in the case of some future unanticipated developments. The typical executive is unable to answer this kind of question offhand, probably because he has not been thinking of his role and his function in a data context. Yet, most of his acts are exclusively based on information he is getting from various data sources. His essential function is that of evaluating information and processing it, converting it into action. Without data about the performance of his business he cannot plan, cannot exercise control over operations, cannot manage. He *needs* data without perhaps realizing *what* data he does or does not need.

When a management information system is being designed, the executive has a most important contribution to make, a job that cannot really be delegated to anyone else. He simply *must* determine what his own information requirements are, in terms of both contents and timing (response requirements). He has "homework" to do and should take adequate time to study, and make a conscious effort to define, what information he needs to function effectively in his job. If he does not realize that the determination of information requirements is *his* responsibility, someone else—most likely the systems specialist—will make the decision. The business executive will then be getting the information that the *technicians* think he should have.

The executive who avoids "homework" by specifying that he wants the system to be able to provide information about anything and everything, at any time and in any form he may specify, is setting an unrealistic goal which will cause unnecessary difficulties, project delays, and costs. With the proper effort, it *is* possible to establish the bounds of the information required. As an example, a marketing executive of the author's acquaintance, who now has a terminal in the office and is using his MIS very effectively, spent weeks in the initial stages of the system's design determining what information is essential for the performance of his function. He finally settled on eight categories, in varying depth of detail, of sales and sales-related performance data with which he now manages the marketing division of his company.

For the benefit of the manufacturing industry executive, the following MIS information requirements blueprint is being offered as an aid in getting started. The task should prove easier if the various types of information are first *classified* by category and if each category is studied separately with regard to the types of data required for the exercise of effective overall management control. The example below is not meant to be exhaustive but rather should be regarded as a skeleton to be fleshed out by the individual executive so as to fit his particular circumstances.

MIS INFORMATION REQUIREMENTS

PROGRESS OF ACTIVITIES
  1. Sales quota performance
  2. Shipments
  3. Performance to production schedules
  4. Cash receipts
  5. Project status

QUALITY
  1. Final test results
  2. Warranty claims
  3. Assembly defects
  4. Scrap and rework

COSTS
  1. Inventory investment
  2. Budget performance
  3. Production efficiency ratings
  4. Project costs

OTHER CRITERIA
  1. Staffing, recruiting
  2. Service departments performance indices

TREND ANALYSIS
  of the above

Once the information requirements are defined, it must next be determined how the data will be gathered, organized, stored, retrieved, processed, and presented. With the possible exception of the latter, these are technical system considerations. The executive should be concerned only about the requirement that the information, when the system eventually provides it, be *understandable* to him. He will then be expected to know how it relates to his business and to understand the *purpose* for which he requires it.

Another, rather interesting, problem in management information system design is the fact that the system tends to be tailored to the individual needs of specific executives and therefore might not prove suitable for their successors with perhaps different backgrounds and management styles. One difference between individual executives is the so-called "information threshold," which can be relatively high or low, depending on the person.

President Eisenhower, for instance, evidenced a very high information threshold, as he preferred problems to be summarized for him very succinctly, preferably on one page. Former Secretary of Defense McNamara, on the other hand, wanted his data in considerable detail and sometimes would dig deep into subsidiary reports and records before deciding an issue.

The business background of an executive is another factor that affects MIS design. Most managers have a natural tendency to seek more information about, and to exercise tighter control over, activities with which they are intimately familiar. Thus a company president who advanced to his position through the sales organization will likely use a mix of data quite different from that used by his successor with, say, an engineering background. Both men would need information about the performance of all the functional arms of their organization at some minimum level of detail, but beyond that, either one could be expected to wish to mine *different segments* of the data base for additional details.

For this reason, executives who participate in the design of a management information system that will outlast them should consider, when furnishing information requirements specifications to the system's implementers, that their successors may not have the same preferences. The system specialists, in turn, should provide for a reasonable amount of future system modification and evolutionary change, rather than "casting the system in concrete."

The executive MIS user himself typically constitutes a rather formidable obstacle to a truly effective functioning of the system. One of the principal goals of MIS is to establish direct user/data relationship, and the whole concept is based on the assumption that the business manager will have a terminal at his desk and will operate it himself. Any other way the usefulness and effectiveness of the system will be diminished, because of the break and delay in the flow of information between its source and the user. It is a fact that, when the executive has his assistant or secretary operate the terminal for him, he will tend to ask fewer questions of the system and will thus be less informed than he perhaps should be or would like to be. Aside from the question of the secretary's availability at any particular moment that the executive might wish for prompt information, a man simply will not make demands of another human being (more detail on the question already asked, or rearranging the data provided in response to a previous inquiry) that he would not hesitate to make of a machine.

Despite all this, the majority of higher-level business management personnel have no wish or inclination to operate inquiry terminals, for reasons that are largely psychological. In people's minds, the operation of a key-driven device is associated with a relatively menial clerical-type function, and an executive apparently cannot operate a terminal without damage to his self-image. Be that as it may, the fact is that in business organizations with currently functional management information systems no more than one out of ten managerial information recipients is willing to make the inquiries personally. There is a theory that this problem will disappear with the next generation of managers, who will have been differently conditioned and trained in the use of computers since their college days. They will have used terminals and otherwise interacted with computer systems as they were progressing through subordinate positions, and having once learned the power of the tool first-hand, are not likely to ever be willing to give it up.

Although this sounds plausible enough, the problem of the present remains, and in the organizations that have management information systems installed, a search for interim solutions through substitute measures is going on. One approach that is being experimented with is the interposition of an "information specialist" between the system and the executives.

In the actual case the author has seen, this specialist operates out of an "information center" equipped with system terminals, closed-circuit TV camera, and microphones. Executive offices contain video and voice gear, and the MIS users request information not from the system directly but by speaking to the specialist who, at the push of a button, materializes on their respective screens. The specialist operates the terminal and reports the reply either verbally or by training the TV camera at a visual display unit containing the data. This arrangement is intended to make the executive comfortable by letting him request information in his accustomed way, by speaking to a person he is familiar with.

Where the executive wishes to communicate with the system directly, a technical problem at the programming level must be considered, namely, the so-called *query language*. How is the user to pose his questions to the computer? Must he use many difficult-to-remember codes and formalized statements with their prescribed commas, dashes, and special characters, from which he better not deviate if he expects the computer to understand him? Or can the system specialists devise a set of English (or English-like) commands and then write programs that will translate these into the coding the computer understands?

This will mean more of a programming effort, of course, but will make it easier on the user who then can be expected to avail himself of the system's services more freely. In cases of such custom-designed query languages, it is even possible to program the computer so as to allow the user a reasonable leeway for errors of form. This means, in effect, that the system will understand the request even though the user committed a minor error in the way he stated it. A good query language is said to be *syntax insensitive,* and here again, the required extra programming cost should be weighed against the value to the user.

The value to the user is the paramount factor in the justification of a management information system. The same arguments apply here that have been advanced in the section on time sharing above. MIS criteria should be based on efficient use of management's time rather than the machine's time.

When planning and developing management information systems, it is recommended that the plans include a trial and design modification period following the launching of the new system that would span perhaps a year. The system and the philosophy of its operation should be evolved in a continuing dialogue between the system's designers and its management users, and this dialogue should be carried over into the first year of operation. No amount of systems analysis, operations research, methods studies, or direct interrogation will ever detect the need for some of the questions that will be asked in the first year of the system's operation.

MIS is a superstructure intended to straddle *existing working* systems in the commercial applications area on the level below it. Too many business executives are so intent on the results that they are impatient with, and discount, the effort and time that should be devoted to the building of sound accounting and operating support systems first.

A company whose order entry, inventory control, costing, production scheduling, or billing systems do not function satisfactorily would be well advised not to divert its systems development and programming resources into the implementation of a new management information system at a time when such resources should more properly be applied toward an overhaul of systems already installed.

To provide a business manager with a superior information tool so that he may easier find out that things are bad all over makes little sense. Problems are not solved through a better measurement of them nor necessarily by instant information to management.

SOFTWARE

The term "software" (one more of those semantic monstrosities invented by the data processing profession) and the slightly better term "programming systems" cover all the programs through which the power of the computer machinery (hardware) is enhanced. Programs written to do the actual productive data processing work (jobs) are known as *problem programs, user programs,* or *applications.* They are considered outside the scope of software, as they are not being supplied by the computer manufacturer, i.e., do not come with the machine. Software encompasses programs in the categories of so-called

1. Language translators
2. Control programs
3. Service programs

Language translator programs pertain to the subject of programming languages, which has already been covered in some depth. In the context of software, or computer-maker-supplied programs, what the user gets is the program or programs that *convert* statements expressed in a given language to machine language comprehensible to the computer hardware in question. Such programs are the various *compilers, assemblers, processors,* and *interpreters* mentioned above.

A control program is a package of instructions that relieves the computer user of organizing and allocating what is known as the system's resources (blocks of memory, registers, secondary storage, and input-output units) for each new job he wishes to run. Control programs have become a necessity with the advent of multiprogramming—their function is somewhat like that of scheduling and controlling work in a factory job shop. The control program automatically schedules and supervises the job flow through the system, controls the location and retrieval of data, etc., to assure the most efficient and uninterrupted processing of jobs. A control program consists of several subprograms, or *routines,* of which three are fundamental:

1. The *Supervisor*
2. The *Scheduler*
3. *Input-Output Control*

The Supervisor controls the other two, as well as the service programs (see below), language translators, and user programs. The basic function of the Scheduler is to communicate with the computer operator, and that of Input-Output Control to communicate with, and to control, the attached peripheral devices.

Service programs consist of

1. *Housekeeping* and *utility* routines
2. *Application* programs

Housekeeping instructions prepare data and programs for input, processing, and output operations, maintain and update files, and transfer data between files. Utility routines perform a variety of functions ranging from system testing or *diagnostics* (a computer self-checking feature) to sort/merge operations.

Application programs are oriented toward jobs and user programs, but they are generalized (to be useful to many different users) and typically are intended to assist with problems such as file data organization, linkage of file records, etc. Often they are made up of *modules*, i.e., standard functions, calculations, etc., that would be used in a given type of application. The user saves programming effort by selecting and incorporating pertinent modules into his program.

All the above programs are said to constitute the so-called **Operating System** that is part and parcel of modern computers of medium to large scale. The function of the Operating System is to exploit the full resources of a data processing system by enabling the user to move a wide variety of work through his computer with a minimum of external intervention and effort. For computer product lines consisting of several compatible models varying only in size (i.e., capacity and speed), the Operating System is offered in more than one version or program size and in modular form. The user is expected to select the version that fits his machine (a good portion of the Operating System permanently *resides* in main memory) and purpose, and to *configurate* from the available modules the specific Operating System he needs for his data processing work.

Although an Operating System is primarily intended for high efficiency of the machine, this is at least partially accomplished by increasing the efficiency of the personnel who instruct and operate the machine. An Operating System can take over many of the functions formerly performed by data processing personnel and in addition can provide special services for the benefit of the operators and the programmers.

Sometimes it is not clear to management whether, in a given situation, a smaller or a larger version of an Operating System should be selected, particularly where the latter would entail added investment in expanded main-memory capacity. The principal criterion here is not so much the type of data processing work to be done but the number of people who directly interact with the machine (this includes programmers but not system analysts). By rule of thumb, if this number is ten or more, a larger Operating System version should pay for itself by permitting a better utilization of these people.

Chapter Four
The
Commitment

Experience has demonstrated that the day-to-day problems that confront the Corporation's operating executives are so absorbing in their demand of time that too little opportunity is afforded for the development of a better operating technique, which requires much study and research. The importance of research work as contributing to the advancement of industry through scientific study is well established. The marvelous contribution that it has made to the progress of industry and the advancement of the standard of living is universally accepted. It is not so generally recognized, however, that research may equally well be applied—and it is important that it should be applied—to all functional activities of a business.

Alfred P. Sloan
(From a letter to stockholders of General Motors Corporation)

THE STUDY

It would seem self-evident that, just as products are developed and improved through research and study, business corporations could increase their effectiveness by conducting a sustained study of themselves. The machinery through which a business acts, i.e., the organization of people for planning, controlling, and managing, as well as the system of procedures that regulates and coordinates their activities, could be made subject to constant improvement, if only management would establish this as a main objective.

If management strove continuously to improve the functioning of the operating arms of the corporation with half the zeal normally directed toward improvement of products—if a fraction of the resources supporting product development were allocated to improving the company—the return on the investment, in terms of profitability and competitive strength, might well prove phenomenal. Conversely, companies typically get into difficulties or go out of business not so much because of poor products as because of poor management.

Although most corporations are not organized to study and conduct research into their own structure as a regular function, the prospective introduction of computers into business operations forces the issue, through the prerequisite of a *feasibility study*. This presents an opportunity for the company, or at least for one of its divisions, to take a look at itself.

The study itself, typically carried out over a period of several months by a team of individuals appointed for this purpose, is essentially a process of review, intended to yield a fuller understanding of the problem and to indicate its solution. The area or function to be automated is studied with a view toward improving its performance through the use of a computer system. In the course of this study, both the main features of the new system and the configuration of proposed computer equipment required for the implementation of the system are determined. The basic design of the new system takes place as part of the study which culminates in a proposal to management to authorize the expenditure and allocate the resources necessary for implementation.

The study, or as it is technically known, feasibility study, should answer three fundamental questions:

1. The *technical* question of whether the job *can* be done with existing computer technology
2. The *economic* question of whether the job *should* be done, i.e., whether resultant benefits warrant the expenditure required for achieving them
3. The *operational* question of whether the system, as proposed, *will* in fact work

The first question, although of some importance a few years ago, can nowadays almost always be answered in advance, affirmatively. The state of computer and communications technology is so advanced now that there is a large gap between it and our knowledge of how to utilize it. The technical question has consequently changed its original meaning from *whether* to *how*.

The second question of economic justification will be more fully dealt with in a separate section of this chapter below. In the context of the current discussion, however, two points need to be made. One has to do with the fact that the important question of economic feasibility is usually not given the type of management attention it deserves, and the job is therefore handled rather poorly. The standard method of weighing system development cost and the subsequent system operating cost against the benefits of the proposed application is too narrow-sighted, because it fails to take into account the foregone opportunity to apply system development talent and resources, which are always in short supply, to other areas of possibly much more importance to the company.

If, for instance, several system analysts and programmers are assigned to automate some bookkeeping procedure at a time when the company's inventory is out of control or when service to customers suffers because of parts shortages in the plant, the *real* cost of implementing the paperwork system is probably many times that which is indicated through the formal economic justification.

The second point has to do with the fact that those assigned to work out cost justification, usually accounting and technical personnel, are rarely qualified to place a value on the true potential benefits the new system could provide. These people are probably well equipped to estimate system development costs, and the level of service that will be achieved following this development, but they ought not to be expected to determine, say, the impact of the new system on inventory investment and its relation to production and customer service. This task belongs to an experienced business manager capable of evaluating the full potential effect that the new system can have on the business operation as a whole. Only such a manager can, if need be, attach a dollar-and-cent price tag to benefits that otherwise would be labeled intangible.

The third question the study should—but rarely does—answer is that of operational feasibility. Will the proposed system, in fact, work? Why will it work, or what will be done to assure that it does work? This all-important question is usually not dealt with in the management proposal, and it is possible that the people responsible for the conduct of the study and for the proposed system's basic architecture have not addressed themselves to this question at all.

And yet, questions such as whether the intended recipients of the system's output, the system's *users*, will actually use it and translate this use into superior performance, whether the users will be motivated and educated to use the system, and how effectively, are of crucial import. When looked at this way, it can hardly be argued that the question of operational feasibility is not more important than the other two. Top management, when assessing proposals for computer-based systems, should never forget to ask this question.

As there are three aspects to a feasibility study, there are also three general *methods* that can be employed in conducting the study. One such method—and it is frequently used—is the *survey*. Under this approach, the study consists largely of an intensive investigation, definition, and documentation of the present system, such as it is. The reader may have seen the results of such a survey in the shape of an impressive volume of documentation, exhibits of every single form in current use (the white, yellow, green, and salmon copies of the stock receipt ticket), plus extensive flowcharts, in minute detail, usually tacked up on all four walls of the survey team's workroom.

The objective of the survey method is to define the present system so that areas requiring improvement might become apparent, as well as to make certain that in the design of the new system no minor function or procedure is overlooked. This method of study, although apparently quite popular, has two drawbacks, of which one is major. First, the executives for whom the survey had presumably been done are likely to find the task of plowing through and digesting the documentation both distasteful and time-consuming.

Second, and far more important, is the likelihood that both system developers and management will become *biased*, i.e., conditioned to think in terms of the old system. If this happens, it might overly, and perhaps improperly, influence system design decisions affecting the new proposed system. One of the axioms of system development sums it up neatly: Don't automate the system the way *it is*, but the way *it should be*.

Another method of system study, also in frequent use, could be labeled *ask-them-what-they-want*. Under this method the future system users, i.e., the heads of the departments whose operation will in any way be affected by the proposed system, are solicited to specify their information requirements, to state what they wish the new system to do for them. Having obtained statements of all such requirements, the idea is to design a system that would provide everyone with what he said he wanted. The author must admit that he favors this approach even less than the survey because, in his experience, the parties thus consulted almost never knew what they wanted or, more precisely, what they wanted was not necessarily what they actually needed.

The general method of study that can be expected to yield the best results is to try to *determine the needs of the business*. This can be done by means of an investigation of the marketing and manufacturing environment in which the company must operate, coupled with a limited survey of current internal procedures. The study of the present system need be pursued only to the extent required to help gain a better understanding of the information requirements of the overall operation.

Obviously, the key individuals responsible for conducting the study this way must be broad-gauged enough to see beyond the particular function that is to be automated and capable of learning the significant characteristics of the business as a whole. They should also have the vision to appreciate not just the present but also the future needs of their company. Many computer-based systems have in the past failed to meet expectations because those conducting the study made the serious mistake of not taking into account future growth, diversification, and competitive factors. As a result, systems were implemented that would have been suitable at the time of the initial study but proved inadequate when the systems became operational a year or two later. The system should always be designed for the business of tomorrow.

It is characteristic of control and communications systems in business enterprises that the eventual system environment will be different from the one that exists at the time of original system design. It is interesting to note that, in addition to changes that will occur independently of the system, computer-based systems themselves have a way of inducing changes in their environment also. More on this topic will be explored in the next chapter.

Throughout this book, stress will be laid on the desirability of system user participation and management involvement. An attempt of proof will be made of the ultimate advantage of having those in the best position to make the most important system decisions, i.e., a company's internal talent, make them. The system study should *always* be conducted by company personnel, with capable business management representation on the study team.

This does not mean that outside expertise, especially in technical matters, should not be sought and used. But the procurement of outside services should be limited to obtaining the assistance of experts, not the fleshing out of study and system implementation teams by "bodies." Experts and specialists, whether retained for a fee or made available by the computer manufacturer free of charge, should act in a consultative, advisory capacity and should not play a decision-making, responsibility-assuming role. This belongs to the management of the company undertaking the expenditure and effort of implementing a computer-based system.

Management sometimes, in these cases, seeks to buy external help not so much because competent individuals do not exist within the company, but because they are engaged in critical functions of the business. In the operations that these individuals manage, or in the projects they are working on, they often appear as indispensable. "I don't see how I could spare George for this new project," an executive is apt to say. But to think in terms of *sparing* someone is to confuse the issue. The man in question is not being spared (in the sense that the company can temporarily afford to do without his services), but is being reassigned to a task of transcending importance that the company cannot afford to staff with second-best. The best advice might be to pick the man who can be spared least. And, oh yes, the assignment should be *full-time* for the duration of the study.

The following eight objectives, or general system criteria applicable to the basic system design done as part of the feasibility study, are offered for the reader's consideration:

1. Control by exception
2. Displacement of clerks not a primary objective, but rather the elimination of clerical work by nonclerks (analysts, buyers, engineers, foremen)
3. Automation of routine operating decision making
4. System to serve as a tool for the evaluation of information required for nonroutine decision making
5. A minimum of paper output
6. A high degree of information processing, i.e., output data to be of such quality, in such form, and at such time so as to require little or no reinterpretation, analysis, summarization, reconciliation, and re-recording.
7. Speed in the receiving, processing, and disseminating of information so as not to lessen its usefulness
8. Providing for system expansion and refinement without a need for fundamental resystemization and reprogramming.

Along with these specific criteria, system developers should always pursue the overall, and most important, goal of creating in the new system a superior tool for the conduct and management of the business. Not just a cheaper but a more *intelligent* operation should always be the principal objective.

> *The efficiency of a data processing system should be subordinated to the efficiency of the business it serves.*

THE PROPOSAL AND COMPUTER JUSTIFICATION

In the preceding section on the feasibility study, the statement was made that the study culminates in a *proposal* to management. It is the purpose of the study to produce such a management proposal, along with information required to support and defend it. The proposal is essentially a request that management authorize the expenditure and allocate the resources necessary for implementation of a new, computer-based system. In evaluating the proposal, the executive is called upon to make a business decision of considerable importance, as company funds and talent are to be committed to a project of far-reaching consequences. This may be a trying time for top management not sufficiently knowledgeable about computer systems to be able to exercise independent judgment.

It is not unusual for the situation to be in a state of some confusion at proposal time, when management listens to conflicting claims by representatives of competitive computer manufacturers, faces a possible controversy among operating managers, and tries to evaluate the arguments of its own technical advisers. So that the business management reader may in the future be better equipped to deal with questions of proposal and cost justification, this section is devoted to a discussion of these two mutually related subjects. Computer selection is discussed separately in the section immediately following.

THE MANAGEMENT PROPOSAL

The business executive should realize that representatives of computer manufacturers tend to take the initiative in making a study and submitting a proposal to management. Such proposals may be entirely sound, depending on the qualifications of the individuals who prepare them to judge the needs of the business, but better results will generally be obtained in the end if the proposal is prepared, and backed, by company personnel.

The computer vendor's representatives can participate and assist in all phases of study and management proposal preparation, but their principal role is that of working out and recommending the computer *configuration* (i.e., the specific set of related data processing machinery) required to handle the job in question.

The form of the management proposal is immaterial, as long as its contents enable the decision making executive to evaluate the proposal properly. The proposal should, however, cover the following ten points:

1. Objective
2. System outline
3. Equipment configuration and specifications
4. Equipment cost
5. System development project cost
6. An outline of project phases
7. Project organization
8. Project personnel/cost timetable

9. Justification
10. Means of assuring successful system operation

The *objective* of the new system shows how well the individuals proposing it know what they are doing. The *system outline* represents the basic design formulated during the study, as discussed in the previous section of the current chapter. Proposed data processing *equipment specs* and *cost* (whether rental or purchase price) are obviously essential to any such management proposal—and they are never missing. Depending on the job to be done, however, the cost of machinery may be minor compared to the *cost of developing*, programming, and installing the system. This cost should be calculated and included in proposal.

An outline of *project phases* demonstrates that the proposing party has assessed what it will take to get the system to its operational stage and that project cost estimates have a firm basis. *Project organization* addresses the very important question of how the new system will be implemented and by whom.

The *personnel/cost timetable* provides the dimension of time to the project cost figures, showing *when* the money will be spent and on what. It also shows the timing of personnel joining and leaving the project. Various network planning techniques, such as *PERT* or the *Critical Path Method* may be employed to fulfill the function of the timetable. They will yield added benefits in subsequent project control (as discussed in Chapter 6), but as far as the management proposal is concerned, an old-fashioned Gantt chart will do the essential job.

Such a timetable need only show the personnel and cost data by month, as at the time of the management proposal these data represent estimates, rather than specific project detail that will be developed only after, and if, management accepts the proposal. The personnel/cost timetable should not only cover the time span of the system development project itself, but extend several months beyond the conversion, or cutover, target date so as to show costs of the system's operational phase. To arrive at valid cost estimates in this phase, the individuals proposing the system will have to consider the impact that the new system is likely to have on the affected business functions, and their organization.

Justification, in some form, is part and parcel of the management proposal—the executive demands that it be included. It is a subject that is often problematic, but at any rate so interesting that it merits separate discussion (see below). The point about operational feasibility, or *why the system can be expected to function successfully,* has already been made in the section on the study, above. The business executive should insist that this all-important question be addressed, and answered, as part of the proposal and particularly so where technically oriented people prepare this proposal.

The top executive himself may not be especially interested in some of the ten proposal points reviewed above, but he will be wise to demand that all be covered nevertheless. Their inclusion and elaboration reflects the quality of planning done by the proposing party and tends to guarantee that the whole problem has been thought through. At any rate, if the proposal covers less, there is some doubt as to whether the people submitting it really know what they are doing.

COMPUTER JUSTIFICATION

Earlier we have touched on the subject of justification and pointed out that, where some mundane task is being automated, cost justification figures can be misleading, since they fail to take into account the foregone opportunity to apply system development resources to areas of more importance to the business. Another point made was that only an experienced business manager is capable of assessing the full potential of a computer system, in terms of its value to the business as a whole, and of attaching a price tag to benefits that technicians could only label intangible.

In the days of punched-card data processing, when strictly clerical tasks were being mechanized, justification rested on displaceable clerical costs, which often could be calculated to the last penny. In the case of a computer system this is no longer a valid approach *unless* the computer is intended to be used merely to speed up, or to reduce the cost of, existing procedure.

Where the proposed system is to be utilized as a superior tool for managing the business, i.e., to gain operational and competitive advantages by being able to do things *heretofore impractical* or *impossible*, the objective obviously has shifted. It has shifted from immediate cost displacement to goals such as reductions in inventory investment, improved response to customer demand, increased capability of reacting to changes, better utilization of labor, plant, etc. As the objective has changed, so should justification criteria.

In the past, particularly where a computer succeeded a punched-card equipment installation, it tended to continue to be used as a cost cutter. There can be no real objection to business cost cutting, of course, but the enormous potential of the computer is more profitably employed in making, rather than saving, money. Furthermore, many computer users today *already have* automated clerical and bookkeeping routines and have achieved the savings inherent therein. The computer's past role as a cost cutter, as against its present and future role as a profit maker, is more than just an interesting point of departure. It changes, or should change, the whole philosophy of computer system justification.

Many conservative business executives still demand that proposed computer systems be justified the traditional way, in terms of displaceable cost and "tangible" benefits. Many a computer system development project was aborted, or at least delayed, because of this, to the disadvantage of the company. Where a computer system holds out the promise of increasing the effectiveness of business operations and thus improving the company's competitive posture, there is an analogy between the investment in its development and that of introducing a new product into the market.

Business management, when a new product is being developed, cannot add up savings, measure or guarantee profits, yet authorizes huge expenditures nevertheless. By whose judgment, and by what criteria? Should the same type of judgment, and the same type of criterion, apply to computer system projects that cannot be cost-justified by conventional means? These are the questions the business executive should ask of himself.

The typical computer system proposal enumerates expected savings, quantifies the value of other "tangible" benefits, and lists "intangible" benefits without attaching any dollars-and-cents price tag to them. Yet these very "intangibles" often represent the most compelling reason for approving the proposal. Clearly, what is needed are new methods of quantifying the heretofore intangible benefits.

The decision-making executive should request that the proposing party go an extra step on these intangibles, dig deeper into them to try to measure the effect they will have on the conduct of the business. In the final analysis, there can be no truly intangible benefits in a business operation where eventually everything is converted into dollars and cents on the profit-and-loss statement.

There are no intangible benefits, only benefits difficult or impossible to *measure in advance*. The impossibility of advance precise measurement often derives from the fact that the new system will provide an *opportunity* to achieve benefits, but there is no assurance that this opportunity *will be taken advantage of*. If, for instance, the new computer system will relieve buyers in the purchasing department of clerical duties that may have accounted for 30 or 40 percent of a buyer's time in the past, the value of this benefit will entirely depend on what the buyers will do with the extra time.

One of Parkinson's "laws" states that work expands to fill the time available. If this is permitted to happen in the case in point, then the value of this benefit is zero. But if the manager of purchasing sees to it that the buyers' extra time is utilized for more extensive sourcing, more frequent requests for bids, more attention being paid to the quality of purchased materials, and more extensive price negotiation, the value of the system-created benefit can be considerable. The operating manager has the opportunity, but all depends on what he will do with it.

In line with this reasoning, the problem of computer justification can be approached by

1. Assigning a quantitative value to the intended advantages
2. Estimating the probability of attaining them

It should be noted that, under this approach, the value is *assigned*, not calculated or otherwise *determined* in advance. Operating managers, such as the purchasing agent in our example, who can reasonably be expected to benefit from the new system, can be called upon to promise or make a commitment to achieve certain specific results once the new system is operational. This will translate the so-called intangibles into dollars and cents.

If a plant manager who is proposing a computer system for his operation commits to running the plant with, say, 15 percent less inventory and half the expediting budget, no other formal justification may be necessary. The advantage of this approach lies in the fact that top management is in a position to pinpoint responsibility for the achievement of benefits to specific individuals, can hold them to their commitment, and can audit results with extreme ease. This is rarely so with a conventional cost justification, which is normally larded with qualifying statements and assumptions that the original justifiers can later always demonstrate as not having materialized. At any rate, justification figures developed by accounting and technical personnel are beyond effective recourse in case they later prove invalid.

The problem with this approach will be not so much in persuading top management to accept this philosophy as with the affected operating managers' willingness to make this type of commitment. If the purchasing or plant managers in the above examples prove reluctant to commit themselves, then an entirely new situation has arisen, and top management should question whether a new computer system is really needed when its direct beneficiaries show little confidence in attaining specific benefits.

Considering the impact that computers are having, or can have, on business operations, the problem of computer system cost justification can also be tackled by reversing the question that conventionally developed justifications attempt to answer; i.e., "Can we afford to do it?" If management asks instead, "Can we afford not to do it?" and conscientiously answers this question, it will, in many cases, dispose of the whole dilemma of cost justification.

Another aspect of the general question of computer justification is represented by progressive managements who authorize expenditures for novel computer applications that they believe herald the future, without regard for immediate payoff. Applications such as production monitoring or *direct digital control* (DDC), computer-driven machine tools or *direct numerical control* (DNC), automation of quality inspection and product test processes, computer-controlled warehouse operations, numerical control part programming via on-line visual display terminals, and many others, including probably all the time-sharing and management information systems (MIS) discussed in Chapter 3—these represent leading-edge computer applications that are not, and should not be, cost-justified through conventional methods.

Such computer systems, often used on a pilot scale, may not be paying for themselves, but their value lies in the knowledge and experience being gained by user personnel. Getting this experience under the company's belt, as it were, may constitute a significant competitive advantage for the future.

The future will bring extensive use of computers in all facets of business operations. The conservative businessman must weigh whether his insistence on conventional computer cost justification might not be denying, or postponing, this future to his company. The advent of the computer rendered many traditional ways of business operation obsolete; and so it has obsoleted old justification criteria for information processing systems.

In the future, the cost of such systems will have to be weighed not against direct savings but against the value to the user, the manager, the engineer, the technician. It is this talent that represents the most precious asset a business possesses. To the extent that computers can increase its effectiveness and productivity, they should and must be used.

While price is one of the considerations in determining cost effectiveness, it should be noted that price must be viewed in the light of the ability of a proposal to satisfy stated requirements. Therefore the price comparison is, in order of consideration, secondary to responsiveness to requirements.

The Office of the Secretary of Defense (*in explanation of why a 1967 computer award went to the high bidder*)

COMPUTER SELECTION

In the procurement of various machinery needed for the conduct of business, such as machine tools, transportation, and materials handling equipment, or office machines, management normally can rely on time-tested selection techniques. In these cases, objective selection criteria are, in fact, so well established that responsibility for specific decisions can safely be delegated to specialists. But a computer is not just another machine, and the process of selecting it cannot, and should not, be reduced to a formula.

This is primarily because of the complexity of the computer itself, but also because of the unique way computers are being marketed, and because of the implication of long-range effect on the business operation, which is attendant to the selection decision. A computer is complex not only in terms of its internal structure but in its open-endedness, i.e., variability of configuration which affords an almost endless number of different possible capability mixes. The total job the computer is to do in the future would have to be precisely defined—and this is seldom possible in a commercial application environment—for it to be even conceivable to determine the exact mix, no more and no less, of data-processing capabilities required.

This is the principal difficulty which hampers attempts at valid comparison among different computer makes and models. The way computers are being marketed also represents an important consideration in their selection, because the computer buyer is, in effect, entering into a rather intimate long-range relationship with the computer vendor. A computer user does not just buy or rent a machine, but depends on the computer manufacturer for assistance, support, and a long list of services.

The business manager needs to be better oriented in the principal considerations concerning computer selection, because he will be faced with conflicting claims of competitive computer sales personnel and possibly those of his own advisers. It is probably safe to assume that salesmen will not *volunteer* information they do not want the customer to have; but if the customer knows the right questions to ask, he can expect to get straight answers and be in a better position to make the decision. The average business executive will probably counter this argument by pointing out that his technical experts *know* which questions to ask.

True enough, as far as technical questions are concerned, but *computer selection also has a nontechnical, business aspect.*

The vision of the specialist is usually narrowed by his very expertise in matters technical, and he should not be expected to exercise broad business judgment. When selecting a computer for business applications, it is not the technical but the business view that should prevail.

To orient the business manager in the area of computer selection, specific considerations will be reviewed below, the discussion being organized as follows:

1. Outside assistance in computer selection
2. Vendor selection
3. Machine selection
4. Considerations of growth
   a. Compatibility
   b. Emulation and simulation
   c. Modularity
5. Economies of scale

OUTSIDE ASSISTANCE

Expert assistance in computer selection can be obtained from the computer manufacturer, from an independent consultant specializing in computers, from one of the major public accounting and/or management consulting firms, or from one of the new technical firms specializing in programming and other computer-related work.

When seeking outside assistance with computer selection, the business executive should be careful to distinguish between machine selection and vendor selection (see below). Choosing the vendor is essentially a matter of business judgment and the prerogative of exercising it should be *retained in-house*. In line with this argument, however, it must be pointed out that once management decides on a given vendor, the latter can be expected to provide competent counsel regarding all facets of machine selection. All reputable computer manufacturers can be counted upon to provide the services of qualified specialists to resolve any technical questions.

In cases where selection of the vendor will be subordinated to machine selection, outside advisers—provided they are qualified—will render a valuable service by bringing an element of objectivity to the issue. It would not be realistic to expect such objectivity from competing computer salesmen.

VENDOR SELECTION

In selecting a new computer, business management has the basic choice between *single source* versus *multisource* selection. This is the option of either preselecting the most desirable computer manufacturer or putting out invitations for bids.

Where an existing computer installation is to be replaced and the multisource selection approach is taken, the case against the switching of brands (assuming that there are no serious grounds for discontinuing the relationship with the original vendor) lies in its costliness. Switching back and forth between computer makes is always costly, whether or not the associated costs are immediate and evident.

Representatives of competitive computer manufacturers will, of course, minimize these costs, which mostly derive from the need to reprogram, to reorganize file records, and otherwise to adjust to the differences inherent in the "strange" machine. Some computer manufacturers developed special aids to facilitate such conversion. This is known as "emulation," "simulation" (for a fuller explanation of these terms, see *Considerations of Growth* below), and "liberation," i.e., termination of dependence on the original vendor due to the programs being expressed in a language uniquely suited to the installed machines.

Conversion programs often do quite an effective job of translating existing computer programs into the form that is required if they are to run on a different make of machine, but the practice is questionable because translated programs, by definition, cannot work as efficiently as they would, had they originally been written in the new machine's "native mode," i.e., with its specific features in mind. What this means is that many of these programs may eventually be (and should be) rewritten, at considerable cost, but this fact is probably obscured at the time of conversion.

Furthermore, the company that is changing allegiance should ask who will reconvert their future programs should they wish to return to the original vendor at a later date. In this connection, it should be noted that if programs are written in higher-level languages, problems of conversion will be lessened (but not entirely eliminated).

The point was already made that in selecting a computer vendor, his machine should not be the sole selection criterion. What the decision-making executive should look for, in addition to the capacity of the machine, and its cost, are factors such as the reputation of the computer manufacturer, software support, commitment to application development ("canned" programs meeting the needs of a specific industry), probability of future offerings, the computer manufacturer's research and development activity, and the various services offered with the machine.

The scope and quality of services provided as part of the package paid for by the computer user through the rental or purchase price are obviously important factors that should bear on vendor selection. Such services include system engineering assistance, machine maintenance, technical publications, application aids and education services ranging from the training of equipment operators and programmers to special classes for executives.

There are also other, less tangible qualities of a computer vendor's organization that it is wise to consider when selecting from among the competitors. Will the computer manufacturer be ready to come to the customer's assistance should things go wrong either with the machine, its software or with applications? Does he stand behind his product, and is he dependable? Can he be counted upon to make good on announced future products and services and other promises explicit or implied? What is the quality and *èsprit de corps* of his personnel? Is he dedicated to excellence not only in word but in deed? All of these are valid questions which should play some part in vendor selection.

In multidivision or multiplant companies, there is also the consideration of standardization of both computer equipment and programs, which is becoming the goal of more and more corporate managements. System standardization facilitates the relocation of both products and people from one plant or division to another and generally permits much better utilization of corporate systems resources. Where corporate policy calls for such standardization, the selection of the computer vendor will also be a matter of policy. A related question is that of computer equipment compatibility, i.e., the ability of a given program to run on several, or any and all, of the computers installed throughout the corporation. This is another valid objective, which will favor single source computer selection.

In cases of multisource selection, there are eight main criteria that can codetermine the final choice:

1. Availability and quality of software
2. Hardware performance
3. Manufacturer support
4. Compatibility among the various computer models offered
5. Cost
6. Capability of system growth
7. Delivery
8. Availability of application programs

These selection criteria are ranked here in the order of decreasing importance attached to them by commercial computer users. The above ranking is the result of a survey as reported in the February, 1967, issue of *Datamation* magazine. It should be noted that this reflects the practice, which does not necessarily make it right. Nor do responses of users to

a survey necessarily tell the whole story. Although the listed considerations undoubtedly carried weight in vendor selection, the other factors
discussed above were certain to have affected the decisions also.

MACHINE SELECTION

Here again, there are said to be objective versus subjective criteria of
selection, but they would probably be better labeled as *technical* compared to *business* considerations. The "objective" methods of machine
selection are as follows:

1. Published evaluation reports on the performance of hardware and
software
2. *Benchmark* problems
3. Programming and execution of test problems
4. Simulation and mathematical modeling

Assessments in data processing literature of performance of the various computer models represent the most frequently used guide to machine selection. Where specifications or performance evaluation data do
not afford an entirely clear picture of relative capability, resort can be
had to actual tests. This is the approach often used by private corporations, and always used by government, to decide among competitive
makes.

The essential difference between the two types of test, i.e., the
benchmark and the test problem, consists in the selection of the problems
and the purpose of the tests. The so-called benchmark problems are selected so as to represent the *job* to be done. The results of the benchmark test are judged on whether and how well the computer met the
requirements specified for the application. The technique of benchmark-
ing is only applicable where the full specific job the computer will do is
known in advance, of course.

The programming and execution of the so-called test problems is
aimed less at the job and more at the various *functional capabilities* of the
machine. The problems are selected with a view to testing out, and
measuring, such capabilities. The results achieved by the machines tested
can then be compared and price-performance judgments can be made,
but the limitations of this technique lie in the fact that weights have to
be assigned to the different aspects of the machine's capacity before any
comparisons can be made. Furthermore, performance data unrelated to
the actual task the machine will have to perform are not fully meaningful.

Simulation and mathematical modeling techniques are, at present, not frequently used for purposes of machine selection, although they can serve as valid evaluation tools, at least until better analytical techniques of computer cost-performance become available.

As far as computers are concerned, establishing a clear measure of cost-performance has so far proved to be a somewhat elusive goal. The problem does not lie in the element of cost, which is known, but in the expression of performance. Performance in relation to what? Even computer manufacturers lack a fully satisfactory method of determining cost-performance of their products for purposes of marketing strategy and pricing policy. The reason for the difficulty is the fact that a computer has simply too many different facets of capacity, too many separate capabilities, to permit meaningful capacity comparisons between similar machines.

The problem can be demonstrated on an example of two imaginary machines which are priced the same and are alike in all respects except four attributes of their central processor, as follows:

	Machine A	Machine B
Memory speed		
(Cycle time in microseconds)	1.5	2.5
Memory size		
(Thousands of characters)	40	50
Addressing format		
(Number of characters required		
to express one memory address)	3	4
Number of characters moved from		
memory to control unit, per cycle	1	2

The question is which of the two machines is bigger, faster, a better buy. Machine A cycles faster, but when transferring instructions from memory to the control unit takes 1.5 microseconds per character, whereas machine B only takes 1.25. Thus the latter is *effectively* faster when in the instruction state, but it is in this state only part of the time. The rest of the time it executes the instructions, and execution times vary with the type of instruction—multiplying takes longer than adding, for instance.

Machine B has the larger memory, but machine A needs less memory because of its more compact instruction format. Of course, instructions are not the only thing that occupies memory, and besides, different programs vary in size. This precludes an exact determination of which machine has more *effective* memory capacity.

Comparison between these two machines is inconclusive, even though the example is vastly oversimplified. Cost-performance can only be determined in relation to a specific task, but the machines would excel each other from one job to another. To make matters worse, if the mix of the jobs themselves varies, the true measure of cost-performance can only be had in retrospect. The problem is inherent in the "nature of the beast," and it is elaborated here merely to caution the business executive not always to accept at face value machine comparison data prepared by specialists, by whatever method.

The predominant characteristic of the computer, and the main measure of its power, is speed. But speed alone, as expressed in terms of memory cycles per second in the machine's specifications, is meaningless. Even when related to the other capabilities of the machine, it is all but meaningless if unrelated to the actual job the computer will have to do. The fastest computer is the one which has the greatest so-called "throughput," i.e., which performs the most work per week per dollar of rental. When evaluating two or more machines of roughly comparable capacity range, the only foolproof method would be to program, in advance, all the jobs for each one of them and then run these jobs in their proper mix, over a period of time. Short of this, all comparison data should be taken with a grain of salt.

From the above discussion it can be seen that job definition is the real key to machine selection. What is the job, and how do we want it done? This is the question that should be answered by the computer user, not by technical specialists. Incidentally, job requirements also reveal the other side of the cost-performance coin. If the computer will not do what you want it to do, then it does not overly matter how much or how little it costs. This is the message of the Defense Department statement quoted at the beginning of the current section.

The point was made earlier that there are business, and not only technical, considerations of machine selection. Among these should be listed equipment *reliability*, which, although it appears to be primarily related to the technology of the product, is actually also a function of maintenance service. *Effective* reliability derives from the zeal of the computer vendor's field personnel to keep the equipment operational at all times.

Another consideration of machine selection which has already been mentioned is equipment and program standardization within a given corporation. It will often be advisable to tailor or duplicate configurations so as to satisfy the objectives of standardization, even though a different, or smaller, machine would satisfy local requirements. When selecting a computer, management must also consider economies of scale. A larger machine is usually cheaper in terms of cost per task performed. This phenomenon, and its implications, will be separately reviewed below.

Business judgment should also be applied to machine selection as regards plans for future add-on's to the computer system. This is one dimension in which the system can grow, by adding additional (or more capacious) input-output devices, more secondary storage, more main memory, and/or special optional features. The longer-range growth of a computer system should be geared to corporate strategic and five-year planning, as otherwise information processing objectives are not likely to be realized. This is a serious matter that bears on the future performance of the company as a whole, and therefore merits serious executive attention.

CONSIDERATIONS OF GROWTH

A computer system grows as a result of growth of the job. The job the computer is to do can grow three different ways; i.e.,

1. Increase in work *volume*
2. *Additional* applications
3. Application refinement and *sophistication*

If the business, and its product line, expands, its growth will cause an increase in transaction volumes and file records. The capacity of the computer system will sooner or later have to be increased accordingly, if it is to handle the work load. This type of computer system growth should represent no problem, as long as more input-output units, file storage devices, blocks of main memory, and special speed-increasing features can be *added* to the same computer model. Problems that arise when job growth forces the *replacement* of the original computer will be discussed further below.

If job growth is the result of additional applications, it can take two directions. When the new applications do not affect previous applications and their programs, the solution is straightforward; i.e., capacity can be expanded the same way as in the case of an increase in work volume. If, on the other hand, the new applications are not independent of the ones already programmed, the programs will have to be related, and there will be some rework.

If computer system growth is the result of making the original applications more comprehensive, more effective, or more sophisticated, existing programs will obviously have to be revamped and perhaps drastically changed. The effect on computer system growth may also be profound, as the new approach to the job may call for a substantially different hardware configuration and a different set of software. As the growth of the information processing job establishes the need for increasing the capacity of the computer system, some special considerations apply in regard to both hardware and programs.

Compatibility is an important feature of modern computers, but its full meaning can often be elusive. In principle, compatibility among a series, or family, of computers means that the various models of a product line utilize the same basic design logic, sometimes called design *architecture*. Thus they have an identical *instruction set;* i.e., all models accept the same instructions and execute them to produce identical results, albeit at different speeds.

Because computer programs are made up of strings of such instructions, the conclusion can be drawn that a given program can run, without modification, on any of the "compatibles." The implication of compatibility is that growth can take place *without reprogramming.* This is not strictly so, however. Do we have to reprogram, then? It is perhaps vexing that this question must be answered yes and no. Without some knowledge of what compatibility is and what it is not, the business executive will have a confusing and frustrating time on the occasion of computer selection. He will be hearing both yes and no throughout the various presentations and reports preliminary to the decision.

The first thing about this subject that must be pointed out is the difference between *upward* and *downward compatibility.* A program written for a smaller model will always run on larger models (assuming that they contain the same special features, etc., as the small model), but not vice versa. A program cannot be used, without modification, downward if, for instance, it occupies more main memory than the small machine has, or if it utilizes both hardware and software facilities available *only* with larger models. This does not say that downward compatibility never exists—a small, simple program can be compatible up and down the line.

Upward compatibility is the more important factor, however, because computer systems typically expand rather than contract. Does this mean that as long as the computer system grows, original programs need not be modified? They do and they do not, depending on the software being used. This introduces the concept of *hardware* versus *software compatibility.* By and large, the hardware of a compatible computer family is truly and fully upward compatible; i.e., the circuitry will handle the program and will produce identical results. It is the software, the operating system and the compilers, that constitute the obstacle to full compatibility.

Different computer models use different software. The larger and more powerful versions of software require larger memories and more speed to make their utilization economically feasible. Does this mean that the larger software packages *must* be used on the larger models? It does not. Can we not, then, continue using the smaller versions of software on the larger model, to avoid the need for program modification? We can indeed, but we would not want to. Using the smaller, simpler software packages would preclude utilization of the larger machine's full potential.

This brings us to the very heart of the compatibility dilemma. To take literal advantage of the compatibility inherent in the hardware means not taking advantage of the machine. What is true for software is also true for all other programs. They *could* be left in their original state, but leaving them in it would *underutilize* the computer.

Depending on circumstances, such underutilization may be prohibitively costly. Although it will cost less per operation, instruction executed, or character stored when using a larger computer, the machine itself costs more, and if it is only partially utilized—if we, in effect, use only half of the machine—cost per operation may actually go up where it should have gone down. Theoretically, compatibility exists, but in practice we cannot afford to take full advantage of it.

Thus, as the computer system grows, at least some program modification and some reprogramming is indicated, *for reasons of economy.* The unfortunate effect of this situation is the fact that, under the existing conditions of rapid system expansion, a computer-using company can tie up its whole programming staff on conversion, program modification, and reprogramming work. Some companies have, in fact, gone two or three years without a single new application program being written. Utilization of the machine is certainly important, but it is not all-important.

Not *every* existing program need run with maximum efficiency. To do an intelligent job of determining what should be reprogrammed from scratch, what should be modified, and what should be left alone, the author recommends the well-known technique used in inventory control, called ABC analysis. Commercial application programs can be ranked by how frequently they are being run. The large, daily jobs should be made to run with maximum efficiency, for which the program may have to be rewritten. Small programs and medium-frequency programs may merit some modification, whereas the infrequently used, or once-in-a-while, program should, if possible, be left as is.

Compatibility still is a valuable attribute of modern computers. Because of practical considerations, *effective* compatibility is only partial, but even so it saves reprogramming dollars and facilitates computer system growth. Compatibility is of great aid at the time of converting from a smaller to a larger computer model, but it should not be a way of life.

Modularity is an extensively publicized attribute of modern computers. These computers are indeed designed so as to enable the user to configurate his system, and later to expand it, in terms of "building blocks," as required. Thus there is a range of main memory available for a given model that can be built up in several blocks. Channels, input-output devices, file units, etc., can be added to the system one at a time. When the computer system reaches the saturation point, a larger central processor can be substituted for the previous one. Thus the system can be upgraded, and because the equipment is compatible and modular, it can generally just be added to, rather than completely replaced.

Modularity conveys the impression of gradual, smooth, pain-free computer system growth. This is true as long as additional devices and features are being added to a given central processor. But central processors grow, within a product line, in discrete steps, and as a computer system is upgraded from one model to another, larger one, the smoothness of growth is interrupted and certain problems do arise. These problems, and the related considerations, are quite similar to those of compatibility. Modularity exists in principle, but in practice the user cannot take, and would not wish to take, full advantage of its implications.

As with compatibility, the limitation lies not in the hardware, which is truly modular, but in the software. With a larger model of the computer the user gets, and can use, the larger versions of compilers and of the Operating System, which is all to his great advantage. But it creates problems of conversion. Computer system growth is not, and should not be, completely gradual. It occurs in steps.

If the small user graduates from a model for which programs have been written in a basic assembler language and now wishes to use, say, COBOL, his new computer *must* have at least the minimum size of memory specified by the computer manufacturer who developed the compiler. The most advanced version of FORTRAN, for instance, requires a memory size of about 100,000 character positions and can function only with the largest versions of Operating Systems. This is called "paying the minimum entrance fee" to reach a new plateau of data processing power.

If the business executive understands the advantages, as well as the limitations, of the concept of computer modularity, he will be in a better position to evaluate claims of computer manufacturers regarding modularity. He will know how to ask questions about what modularity is and *what it is not* and will be able to reach a sound decision at computer selection time.

Emulation and simulation are terms used to describe two different conversion aids, or more precisely, the techniques used to implement these aids. They are offered by computer manufacturers to facilitate the transition between a computer and its successor when they are *not compatible*. As was mentioned above, competitive manufacturers also sometimes use these tools to induce a switch in computer brands.

The distinction between emulators and simulators is that an emulator is a piece of *hardware*, whereas a simulator is a *program*. Both serve the same purpose, which is to make it possible for programs expressed in the language of the machine being replaced to run on the new machine. This obviates the need for reprogramming.

An emulator is a unit of machinery whose function can perhaps be best understood if one thinks of it as a second, alternative control unit of the central processor to which it is linked. The "foreign" program's instructions are channeled through the emulator, which, in effect, causes the circuitry of the central processor to act the same way the emulated machine would act in executing such instructions. This, then, produces the same results as the machine that is being emulated would yield.

A simulator, which is a special program that resides in the successor computer's memory, treats the "foreign" instructions as data, which it operates on and translates into instructions in the "native" language of the new computer. They can then, and only then, be executed. Thus the operation of the machine that has been replaced is simulated. It is somewhat as if the old smaller machine were contained within the new larger one, because the simulated program deals only with those hardware devices and facilities that are functionally the same as those of the replaced machine, and is unaware of the rest.

Programs that are either emulated or simulated fail to utilize the full resources of the new computer, and again, as in the case of compatibility, the degree of such underutilization can be significant. For example, the IBM 1401 has three so-called index registers which perform certain valuable functions within the central processor. The successor to the 1401, the IBM System/360 has sixteen such registers, but if a 1401 program is emulated or simulated on the 360, it will use only three of the sixteen.

Another example might be a disk storage unit of the new computer that has twice the capacity—double the number of tracks—as that of the replaced computer. Original programs, if simulated or emulated, "think" that the disk file they work with has only half the number of tracks it actually has, and therefore utilize only those. Such waste can, of course, be quite costly.

These conversion aids serve a useful purpose as a temporary arrangement to ease conversion by avoiding the necessity for mass reprogramming. These devices permit productive operation of the new computer system throughout the conversion period. The paychecks, reports, etc., go out—but at a cost. Some companies, however, continue to operate their new computers in emulation or simulation mode virtually for years. They pay rental for the whole computer but are actually using only part of it, thus wasting money that could pay for reprogramming, which eventually will have to be done anyhow.

ECONOMIES OF SCALE

The fact is widely known that it is cheaper to use a bigger rather than a smaller computer—cheaper per job processed. It costs less to execute an instruction, to add two numbers, to store a character in memory or to keep a record in random-access file with a large computer system. This phenomenon is not some marketing tactic of computer manufacturers but is a natural consequence of computer design and structure.

To grasp the reason for this, the business manager may want to think of it in terms of fixed and variable cost. A computer, whatever its size, must have one of each of certain things. Examples are the arithmetic unit, the interval timer, and a set of control registers internal to the central processor, as well as external devices such as a file control unit which can handle a number of file devices but is required even if only one such device is used.

Software has a similar effect in that a control program permanently occupies a fixed portion of main memory. Thus if memory is expanded, the added block is fully available for application programs and data, whereas the first one was not. In this case, cost per character of data stored in main memory will decline as more memory is added. Larger machines simply provide equivalent computation at considerably less cost.

The problem is compounded when special peripheral devices, such as visual display (cathode-ray-tube screen) units are attached to the computer system for purposes of special applications. These units have their own "one of" hardware which is required whether one or more are used, and they also require special software of their own, in addition to the general-purpose software that services the whole computer system. Thus the use of only one visual display device for graphic applications work is prohibitively costly. Several such units, plus a larger main memory, will permit more application programs to run at the same time, and these jobs then share the fixed cost of hardware and system overhead.

In addition to considerations of hardware and software economy, a larger computer with larger memory will permit the use of larger and more powerful compilers and of the more sophisticated control programs, which, in turn, will increase the effectiveness of programmers, computer-room personnel, and users. This may be more important that computer economies.

The knowledgeable business executive will take economies of scale, and their implications, into account when deciding on what computer to select. Obviously, the size of the computer selected is a function of the scope of the information processing job, present and future. Will the job grow, and will the computer system grow? The business manager should give growth the benefit of every doubt. Computer systems *will* grow.

Computer selection is a difficult and very complex task. The best basis for an intelligent decision is the fullest possible job definition coupled with job growth projection based on corporate long-range planning. Without these prerequisites, computer selection is a gamble. When the (present and future) job is defined, the decision-making executive should ask:

1. Does the proposal or bid meet the requirements of the job?
2. At what cost?
3. What other considerations are there?

The computer selection decision is a complex one, not unlike many other major business decisions. Both technical and business considerations bear on it, and because of its very complexity, it calls for the application of broad business judgment. That is why the business executive should not entirely delegate, but rather involve himself personally in computer selection.

Chapter Five
System Design

In Chapter 3 we classified the uses a computer can be put to into six categories: driving and controlling other machines or processes, serving as an analytical and simulation tool, doing scientific and engineering computations, performing accounting-type work, acting as a repository of management information, and finally, serving to support business operations directly. Computer applications in the latter category, or *operating support systems,* are the most difficult to design and implement. At the same time, they have the most direct and profound effect on the performance of the business as a whole. The following discussion will therefore focus mainly on computer-based operating support systems and their design.

System design (reference is to business procedures, not to computer hardware) is, without question, *the* crucial function in the development of systems intended to support business operations. Design takes place in two successive stages and on three levels of resolution. First, the basic system must be designed in one of the steps preceding a proposal to management.

In this first stage, the system is outlined as an approach, with only the essential aspects of its architecture completed, as the expense of a detailed design effort is not warranted until and unless management accepts the proposal. But where, specifically, do we draw a line between preliminary and detailed design? The question is self-answering: Basic design must be carried out to a level of resolution that will yield the information required to make—and defend—the management proposal.

In the second system design stage, following management approval of the project, the proposed system's architecture is implemented and the design is detailed in the first step of this implementation process. This brings the design into a second, and higher, resolution level. In subsequent steps of procedure writing and programming, which often also contain elements of system design, the latter reaches its third and highest level of resolution.

To design the system well—and this is a prerequisite for eventual successful system operation—many factors should be considered, the most important ones being as follows:

1. The framework
2. System design process
3. The black-box design principle

> *The investment in time is often least acceptable to management. Taking the time to draw up a master blueprint first probably means a postponement of keenly desired results.*

THE FRAMEWORK

Soon after computers began to be introduced into the commercial environment, there sprang up the dream of the "total system." In brief, the total system concept envisions that computer technology will be used not just to automate the obviously suitable, but not necessarily related, individual procedures and functions; rather, the business as a whole would be treated as the unit of automation under this concept. The computer system then would serve as a

1. *Universal data repository* in which would be stored all product specifications, operating records, and financial records
2. *Universal data receiver* accepting data from all sources both internal and external, through various media of data input and transmittal
3. *Universal data processor* that would evaluate received data, store them, and relate them to other input data and data from storage
4. *Universal data producer,* creating all messages, reports, and documents that are based on its data coverage

The early proponents of the total system idea predicted that the computer system would one day have direct (on-line) linkage to both data sources (sales offices, plant offices, factory, and warehouses) and data recipients (management, control personnel, suppliers, and customers). It was also expected that systems of cooperating companies would be coordinated in a sort of vertical EDP integration of vendor, manufacturer, and customer with possibly standardized forms, documents, and message formats, which today we would describe as computers talking to each other, directly.

That is the way it was supposed to happen. In many respects, the total system advocates predicted current trends quite accurately, and perhaps the whole idea will eventually become a reality. But that is not the way the vast majority of business computer users have gone about the job. What has happened was typically a start in a quick payoff area such as payroll and some accounting functions, followed by haphazard growth of electronic data-processing applications into sundry other areas. The direction these efforts took has often been determined solely by the relative enthusiasm for computers of individuals in the respective areas of the business.

Thus a patchwork structure without a master blueprint was permitted gradually to develop, in the form of unrelated and perhaps incompatible subsystems. Autonomous departments and divisions have gone ahead devising their own systems approaches, resulting in different treatments of jobs basically the same, individualistic file structures, unlinked files, nonstandard documentation, impaired communication links between different organizations within the same company, redundancy of effort and data, and generally a waste of corporate resources. As computer-based systems became more and more pervasive, it became difficult to move a product (and people!) from one plant to another because of the differences in the systems. Rarely could a computer program written by one plant or division be used in another plant or division.

The sad picture painted above actually fits so many companies that one is amazed (with benefit of hindsight, of course) that corporate managements have let this happen. The explanation must be that management failed to realize early enough what scope electronic data processing would reach in their companies, what investment this new way of life would represent, and how direct an impact it would have on the operation of the business.

At any rate, some large corporations are now undertaking massive efforts, at a cost of millions of dollars, to correct the situation by means of overhauling, unifying, and standardizing their systems. In many cases this is also reflected in organizational changes, quite typically the establishment of new high-level coordinating positions with considerable authority, including that of corporate vice-president responsible for systems throughout the organization.

The case for working to a long-range master plan has been proved. The desirability of having a more comprehensive system blueprint actually becomes apparent as soon as the first function of an operating support system is automated, particularly to those who are most directly concerned with how the new application or subsystem functions. Experience has shown that once you have successfully automated one job or function, the need for revamping, cleaning up, and automating contiguous functions suddenly becomes very obvious.

For instance, when a materials control system is installed that functions truly well, it is painful to see what poor quality inputs this fine new mechanism is being fed from the forecasting system, and what shabby treatment its outputs receive from the production scheduling and purchasing systems into which they flow. The urge to fix this stems from the realization that a new, strong link has been forged in a chain still otherwise weak. Obviously, the effective linking together of neighboring functions will be facilitated through a well-thought-out system master plan.

Operating support systems are developed and implemented one limited application or job at a time, eventually meant to result in a more or less comprehensive computer-based system that would be part of a company-wide information system. In order to succeed in the construction of such a complex structure, each new application must fit into some overall framework—the master plan for a total information system.

So much has been said and written over the past few years about integrated data processing, total systems, and information systems that by now it must sound like a collection of "blue sky" ideas and platitudes. Nevertheless, there is one total system aspect that remains eternally valid —the idea of working to a *grand scheme*. This is a *practical* concept, very useful in operating support system development and implementation. The grand scheme can have a flexible, even indeterminate, time base. It need not represent a plan of what is to be accomplished two years from now, or five years from now. It should show what is to be accomplished *eventually.* The time dimension may be changed one way or another as we go along, but the essential system specifications (assuming the plan is soundly conceived to begin with) should remain firm, to guide systems work along the proper path.

The point of the discussion is that management should make the investment of *time, effort,* and *expense* required to develop a sound long-range system plan which will facilitate a smooth fitting in of successive applications. It should particularly be noted that an investment in time is called for (three, six, even twelve months, depending on the talent assigned to the task), which is often least acceptable to management. Taking the time to draw up a master blueprint first probably means a postponement of keenly desired results and restraint of eagerness to forge ahead.

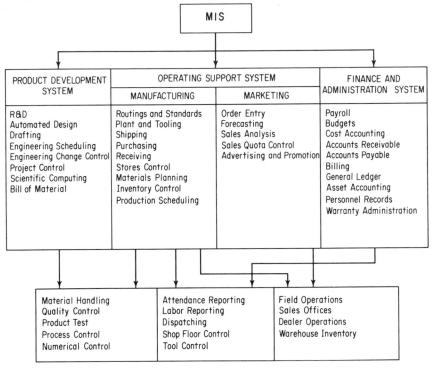

FIGURE 1

But the discipline will pay off over the long pull. In companies where the work of developing a master system plan was originally done poorly or not at all, it might be a wise move to do it now, even though computer applications may already be extensive. This may mean perhaps considerable and costly rework of existing subsystems and programs, but chances are that the job will have to be done sooner or later—and the later, the more expensive it will be, as those companies that are doing it now after years of erratic progress have found out.

The total information system can obviously be conceptualized and charted many different ways, but for purposes of this discussion let us consider a concept of subsystems on three levels that could be labeled either of the following ways:

1. Management	1. Management
2. Office	2. Planning and control
3. Factory and field	3. Execution

At the bottom of this system structure (Figure 1) are the three execution subsystems covering the areas of physical process within the factory (sensor-oriented computers would be utilized here), control over the progress of these processes, and control over field operations. On the middle level are systems of planning and management controls, comprising product development and engineering, manufacturing, marketing, and financial plus administrative functions. On the top level, the management information system represents a superstructure straddling all planning and control systems and having direct information pipelines into the files of subsystems on the execution level.

One function of the system master plan is to aid management in determining what sequence system development work should follow so as to achieve a rational and orderly system buildup. A question often asked is where to start and in which direction to continue from there. No pat answer can be given that would have general validity. Actually, there are two schools of thought on this, one advocating the building of a system from the "ground floor" up and the other favoring progress from top to bottom.

Both arguments seem to have some merit, because the first approach stresses the importance of foundation work (file data, as well as the capture and control over operating transactions) at the execution system level, whereas the opposing philosophy maintains that management information requirements must be determined (and tested out through the development of systems) first, before the lower-level system structures can be built so as to yield the information management needs in order to manage.

The purists' arguments receive little heed in practice, however, as most business computer users typically begin somewhere in the middle, usually in the areas of accounting (because it is easy) and materials logistics (because it usually badly needs improving). Picking a level to start at can be a matter of taste, but the choice is usually made on the basis of payoff, i.e., where the highest benefits can be obtained for the least system effort. There is nothing necessarily wrong with this, provided that such a decision is made within the context of a master system blueprint and provided that precedence relationships of functions being automated are recognized and followed in subsequent system implementation steps.

The precedence relationship is given by the time sequence in which related functions take place. In manufacturing applications there is, for instance, this sequence:

1. Forecasting
2. Materials planning
3. Inventory control
4. Manufacturing operations scheduling
5. Shop order release
6. Dispatching
7. Collection of production (feedback) data

If, for example, materials planning (the explosion of bills of material and calculation of net requirements) is chosen to be the first function to be automated, the next project should not be, say, dispatching, but either forecasting or inventory control. A computer-based system should be implemented by tackling adjacent functions in successive project steps, because this will assure the most orderly growth with minimum of system rework. Whether system growth takes the direction of up or down the ladder from the point of departure should make little difference, and the decision can be made based on greatest need or highest payoff.

Thus far we have been discussing the *level* (the vertical scale of the system chart) at which computer application work can best begin, but the other dimension (the horizontal scale of the system chart) must also be considered. Given limited system development resources, to which of the four principal planning and control system areas (see total system chart above) should they be applied first, and what should the longer-range scheme of priority be? We have mentioned the criterion of payoff, but the reader should not assume that true payoff is always self-evident. In fact, companies have tended to automate the "obvious" or "natural" areas (bookkeeping and clerical functions) first, and thus have often assigned their scarce system development talent to projects that proved to have a relatively marginal impact on the company's operation. When attempting to determine which way the initial system development effort should be bent, executives should ask themselves questions such as: What are the most important decisions we make? How could they be improved with better information? Which functions of our business are performing below par? Where do we have the least amount of control? What are our most important resources? In which area would an improvement contribute the most to profits or competitive survival?

If this type of question is asked, management will tend to select the truly most profitable (highest payoff) areas for their computer applications, rather than the easiest and most obvious. Although clerical displacement cost savings can be measured with ease and accuracy, the greatest benefits of using a computer in a business lie in the area of management planning and control, where these benefits often appear as intangible. They are, in fact, very tangible but difficult to measure in advance.

In industry, three areas, when successfully automated, consistently yield the greatest benefits:

1. Planning and control of finished goods in the distribution network
2. Planning and control of the use of materials, machines, and labor in manufacturing operations
3. Planning and control of the material procurement function

These are the real payoff areas that should receive management attention and primary emphasis, when computer-based systems are being planned. Accounting and financial reporting deserve lower priority and should be viewed as byproducts of the main system development thrust.

Systems in the area of process control, numerical control of machine tools, quality control, product test, and materials handling can be implemented in parallel with systems of planning and management controls, as the stress with such systems will be on instrumentation, and different computer equipment, as well as different system implementation talent, will be utilized. An area that requires special attention when operating support systems, particularly those on the manufacturing side, are being developed, are the product specifications–related functions of the product development system. For best results, one of the first (if not *the* first) applications should cover product specifications of all forms, but particularly the bill of material. These functions should be systemized and made subject to rigorous discipline.

If this is not done, the effectiveness of systems in the area of materials logistics and production is bound to be seriously impaired no matter how well designed and implemented these systems might be, because of their heavy dependence on the accuracy and up-to-dateness of product specifications. Where engineering executives are either reluctant or refuse to join in the early stages of operating support system development (there are still many, unfortunately, who take this position where the system under development is not primarily intended to aid in the engineering functions directly), it is up to top management to insist. Designers and sponsors of operating support systems in the manufacturing area would be well advised to think twice before going ahead under such circumstances, as without engineering cooperation at least partial failure is practically guaranteed.

Other subjects relevant to the successful development of comprehensive systems in a business environment are considerations of system complexity, level of automation, data base or file management, and system standards. These topics will be more fully reviewed in their proper place within the subsequent sections of this book. One more question remains to be answered, however, as regards total information systems. Many business managers would like to know when the job will finally be finished, when system development activities will be completed. The best answer is *never*, because human striving for further improvement is eternal.

The user should be coddled by the system—after all, he is human and the computer is only a machine.

IMPLEMENTING SYSTEM DESIGN

As noted earlier, system design occurs in two successive stages. In the first one, preceding the proposal to management, the basic approach to the new system and its outline are worked out. Following management's acceptance of the proposal there follows a detailing of the design, which represents the first system *implementation* phase.

In all computer-based system development projects the goal is always to fashion a successful system. Let us therefore first briefly examine what constitutes a successful computer application. It is sometimes not at all clear whether or not a given application is actually successful, i.e., whether the potential of the computer has really been utilized for providing a superior solution to the problem in question, as contrasted with previous methods.

In evaluating the quality of any computer application, one should start with the premise that a mere speedup of a job still basically the same as when performed under older methods is suspect and probably indicates underutilization. Success is not necessarily equivalent to making the computer do work. Underutilization of computer systems is a rather common phenomenon, which manifests itself not in hours of running the equipment or in the volume of paper output, but in the degree of usefulness (timeliness, meaningfulness, actionability) of the information being produced.

The success of a computer application will largely be determined by the quality of the system that is being automated. Automation of business functions with the aid of a computer means, in essence, that procedures are being transferred to a machine for execution. In this sense, automation is an implementation concept and as such cannot be discussed meaningfully in its own right, because there is always *something* being automated, in our case an operating support system, as defined in a preceding chapter. The results of such automation, and their value, will derive predominantly from *what* has been, rather than from *how* (or how well) it has been, automated. The real problem is the system itself, not its transfer to a computer.

Contrary to common belief, formulation of a good system is difficult, its automation is easy. Yet, many people direct all of their attention to, and are exclusively intrigued by, the techniques and technological trappings—the bells and whistles—of computer-aided automation, instead of the system that is being automated. This is a trap to be avoided because it assigns more importance to the method than to the goal and thus lets *means* dominate over *ends*.

Creating a good system is analogous to constructing a building. Architecture and design come first, and it is here where the soundness, beauty, and utility of the structure is irrevocably determined. Flaws in the basic architecture will not, and cannot, be overcome through superior workmanship on the part of bricklayers and carpenters—implementers. Similarly, system design is of paramount importance, because if done improperly, no amount of technically excellent programming and other systems work can correct the basic deficiencies of the system itself. System design is the first of several implementation phases, but the outcome of the whole system development project is often decided here.

The best available talent and the most extensive effort should be expended on designing the system. Of all the system development phases, this is the last that should ever be economized on. It should never be pressed to premature conclusion, regardless of planned deadlines. To assist in the design of operating support systems (for a point of reference, assumption is made that a system in the general area of manufacturing and materials controls is to be implemented), the following twelve pointers are offered as a guideline:

1. Make certain that upstream requirements are met.
2. Develop clear and explicit program specs.
3. Automate the function itself, not just its procedures.
4. Integrate, but avoid complexity.
5. Design a system that is modular.

6. Establish what the proper level of automation should be.
7. Avoid need for informal system.
8. Provide for auxiliary system functions.
9. Make system organization-independent.
10. Anticipate the system's effect on its environment.
11. Provide for system growth.
12. Keep service to user uppermost in mind.

1. Make certain that upstream requirements are met. Some time ago the author visited a prominent manufacturing company. At the time of the call, this company was spending several million dollars a year in computer equipment rental alone, but top management and operating executives were bitterly dissatisfied with the performance of their computer-based systems. The main characteristic of the trouble was that system outputs were glaringly invalid, particularly in manufacturing and marketing application areas related to the product, which, incidentally, embodies an advanced technology and is therefore of unstable design. Computer systems in these areas were giving the company "wrong answers" and causing them to do "the wrong things."

In an interview with the engineering vice president, the author learned that this executive had previously declined to allow the engineering organization to participate in computer system development activities aimed at creating a so-called data base (a scheme of file structure and central file maintenance) that would serve as a common foundation for all commercial applications. It was these applications that were now in trouble, and the engineering executive was congratulating himself that his division was the only one not "fouled up." In fact, the main reason he originally decided not to join in the system development effort was that he feared the engineering operation would get into just such a "foul up" as occurred. He was very happy that he stuck with his 3-by-5 cards and "did not have anything to do with those guys." Besides, he had his own computer for engineering work of the "giant slide-rule" variety.

What this executive failed to grasp was that one of the main reasons for the commercial divisions' being in trouble was precisely *because* he refused to "get mixed up" in a common system effort. The result cannot be described as anything but a disaster. Yet it could have been predicted, and one cannot help wondering why the company president let this happen. He alone had the authority to *direct* the VP of Engineering to participate, but since he had stayed aloof from all data processing activity, he did not even know that there had been a dispute. This does not absolve him from principal responsibility for a massive failure, very costly to the company.

In a manufacturing company, the engineer designs a product and furnishes its specifications to the rest of the organization, whose major activities are almost all related, in one way or another, to these specifications. Functions such as forecasting the requirements for components of variable, or optional, product features, net parts requirements calculation, inventory control, procurement of raw materials and purchased parts, spare parts requirements, catalogs and field service, assembly instructions, quality control and product test, cost accounting, and through it the general ledger and financial statements, warranty administration, many facets of industrial engineering—all of these are directly related to the specifications of the product structure, or bill of material.

When these specifications are either inaccurate, out-of-date, or organized in a fashion not suitable for convenient use in commercial and accounting departments and in their computer systems, the performance of these departments (and the performance of the whole company) will suffer. The problem will, of course, be most acute where the technology of the product is advancing rapidly and the resultant volume of engineering changes is high. Under such conditions, computer-based systems simply will not "work" unless

1. Central (i.e., not just Engineering) control is exercised over the organization and format of product-structure specifications.

2. Product specifications functions and their procedures are made an integral part of the system.

3. A well-developed foolproof engineering change procedure exists and is rigorously adhered to.

The question that sometimes may baffle a business manager is why, when computers are introduced into commercial operations, it seems to aggravate this situation which previously had been acceptably, if not entirely satisfactorily, handled. The reason for this is the fact that the machines which now execute product-related procedures, are, of course, incapable of independent judgment, cannot operate on information external to the system (unlike Charlie in Purchasing who used to get tipped off by George in Engineering over the telephone), and the system is designed and programmed to *assume* that product specifications data are correct.

In light of the heavy dependence of a computer-based system in almost any application within the commercial area on product specifications, the business executive should question how much sense it makes (and what the chances for success are) to attempt automating the respective functions if the "upstream" situation cannot first be fixed. The author would always favor the postponement, if need be, of other system projects and the allocation of system development resources for a fixup of upstream functions. Because of their paramount relevance to the success of "downstream" systems, they are given first place on our list of twelve system design pointers.

2. Develop clear and explicit program specs. In Chapter 2 we pointed out that a computer is capable of solving only *well-structured problems*, i.e., cases where both the problem and its solution are sufficiently well known to permit their explicit definition. In system design, this point is worth remembering. In the stage of system design that follows the acceptance of the proposal, we are implementing, *detailing* the design. What the system is intended to do, and *how* it is to do it, must be spelled out unambiguously, specifically, and with utmost clarity.

All the possible circumstances under which the system can be expected to have to operate should be considered, and the appropriate system responses resolved. We have mentioned earlier that only procedures that can be followed consistently should be transferred to a machine for execution. Provisions for the handling of exceptions, unusual conditions, etc., are part of any well-thought-out system design. The system designer should determine *how* the system is to deal with each type of exception, whether through a special program or by turning to people for help and resolution. It is good practice to test system design against the principle of consistency before the design job is declared complete.

When implementing system design, one encounters several strata, or layers, of detail. It is somewhat like peeling an onion, as for each layer removed there appears to be another layer of detail underneath. In this connection, the question may arise as to how much of the detail should be worked out as part of system design, or where does design end and programming begin. The answer really depends on how many elements of system design or *problem definition*, i.e., other than strictly programming tasks, are to be left for the programmers to perform. For best overall results, the system designer should always follow the practice of trying to reduce the programmers' system design responsibility to zero.

This means that system design work will take longer to finish than it would otherwise, but it also means that subsequent programming will take less time and be much easier. In fact, a common mistake typically committed by most companies engaged in computer-based system development is to allow, in the project timetable, too little time for system design and too much time for programming. For best results, system design detailing by the design team should stop just short of programming proper, i.e., block diagramming. Only in this way can truly explicit *program specifications* be established. The responsibility for program specs belongs, of course, to the system designer, and he should be prepared to bear it.

The objective of explicitness and clarity is reflected in the requirement of *design documentation*. It is not enough to figure out the design without formally defining it. In this type of work, if a solution is not, or cannot be, stated on a piece of paper, it is no solution at all. There are recommended disciplines, methods, and standards of system design documentation, but in principle the form and format in which design is documented are not important. In the absence of corporate documentation standards, "putting it down on paper" in plain English will do the essential job.

Is there a practical quality standard applicable to system design and its documentation, i.e., program specs? Yes, there is, and it can best be stated this way: *The quality of program specs is in inverse proportion to the number of times that a programmer will have to come back to the system designer for a system design decision, explanation, or clarification.* Ideal program specs are fully self-explanatory.

3. Automate the function itself, not just its procedures. Our desire to take advantage, in business operations, of the availability of computers is forcing us, and will continue to force us more and more, to review our general approaches to the solution of our operating problems. It tends to make us reappraise the way in which we operate our departments and our companies. As we come to grips with the task of designing a successful computer-based system, we realize that it may not be enough to automate individual procedures separately, but rather that the sum total of all procedures comprising a system (within the boundaries specified in the management proposal) should be automated as an entity.

When system design is approached from this point of view, it often becomes apparent that the organization, responsibilities, and the general method of operation of the functional area for which the system is being designed should be critically reviewed and reevaluated. This is a beneficial byproduct of computer-based system design, if it is oriented toward automating and improving the function itself and not merely its procedures.

The time of system design is the time of opportunity for a true and, if need be, drastic overhaul of the function the system is to support. The existence of any traditional division of labor within the function (which was probably caused by the low information-processing capacity of the system, whatever it may be, that is being replaced) or of any customary ways of going about the job should not be permitted to stand in the way of the best system design achievable. A well-designed system has a total tangible and intangible value which is substantially greater than the sum of the values of each of its parts installed and operated independently.

Designing a comprehensive system means encompassing and linking together all procedures pertinent to the function being automated. The computer's capability of handling and processing information should be exploited by means of restructuring the set of procedures that constitute the system. The set of automated procedures may, and most likely should, differ from the set being superseded, as dictated by the purpose of the computer-based system to optimize the performance of the business function in question. Again: Design for the automation of the *function*, not its *procedures*.

4. Integrate but avoid complexity. The objective of comprehensiveness expressed in system design pointer 3 addresses the *scope* of intended automation, but there are two other dimensions present in the picture. One is *integration*, and the other is the *level* of automation; they will be defined in this and the sixth system design pointers, respectively.

There is some confusion about the meaning of the term "system integration." Strictly speaking, integrating means making whole, making one out of many, fusing several functions or procedures into a single one. In system design this, per se, is not necessarily desirable, while integration in the sense as used by systems personnel to describe an automatic *linkage* of related procedures is always desirable.

It is true that some business functions can be effectively and advantageously integrated, i.e., fused, as a result of the superior information-handling power of a computer-based system. An example might be combining the materials planning and inventory control functions into a single job, as some companies have done. Another example would be a fusing of dispatching, expediting, and timekeeping functions on the factory floor, which many companies have implemented. Such combining is indicated where two or more functions naturally complement one another and where integrating them will result in economy or increased efficiency.

But whether or not the actual functions can be fused, it is possible to design an integrated computer-based system in which related procedures are linked so that the output of one procedure is used as input by another, without a break in the information flow.

A fine example of such system integration is a final assembly scheduling program which "consults" the backlog file of the order entry program, then works out a preliminary schedule, turns it over to the materials planning program for a breakdown into major assembly requirements, and then tests these against the records of the inventory control system for availability; the results of this test serve again as input to the assembly scheduling program, which modifies the original schedule and makes it final.

In this example, the individual programs, or procedures, are linked but not fused. The system is integrated, but the procedures are not. There are good reasons sometimes for combining several procedures into a sin-

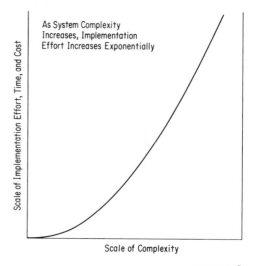

As System Complexity Increases, Implementation Effort Increases Exponentially

Scale of Implementation Effort, Time, and Cost

Scale of Complexity

FIGURE 2

gle program, but the results should be sufficiently better to outweigh the disadvantage of this type of integration, i.e., complexity. An integrated function is more complex than the sum total of the functions from which it had been combined. A system integrated this way is more difficult to implement, to maintain, and mainly, to modify.

System complexity is always undesirable and is tolerated only as a necessary evil. An interesting aspect of system complexity is its relationship to the implementation effort (cost, time) required. A system that is twice as complex as another will require considerably more than twice the implementation effort. This has been proved so many times in practice (underestimated requirements, overexpenditure, and overoptimistic target dates) that it is possible to formulate a "law" on system complexity, as represented by Figure 2.

Although this, of course, is merely a conceptual expression, without mathematical proof, of a general observation, it is nevertheless interesting to note that the relationship of the line of maximum complexity to the implementation effort curve is asymptotic; i.e., the point of contact between them recedes indefinitely. Thus work on a system sufficiently complex will never get completed at all.

Cost and delay are but one of several problems attendant to system complexity. Another is the extreme difficulty of modifying a complex system once it has been completed. Another still is the question of how successors of the people working with the system at present will be made to understand the makeup of the system. How will the next generation know "what's in the box"? A good question indeed, as only those individuals who stood at the cradle of a complex system *really* understand its structure.

One answer to the problem of system complexity (and every computer-based system is complex in some degree) is documentation of its design, logic, and programs. This is a technical requirement so well understood generally that we need not dwell on it here. Another answer, one that attempts to deal with the root of the problem, is *modular system design.*

5. Design a system that is modular. If a system, and its programs, can be fashioned out of linked modules, practically all problems of complexity disappear. There is no specific formula for how to design a system in modular fashion. Rather, the system designer must approach his task in a certain frame of mind. He should try not to make the system all of a piece, and he will succeed in this if, from the very beginning, he conceptualizes the system in terms of modules or building blocks rather than as an entity. Each module must then be designed to stand, as it were, on its own feet, i.e., to provide specific system functions without having to leave its own boundaries. To the extent that this is successfully accomplished, the various system modules can then be linked together in accordance with the logic of their mutual input-output relationship. They can subsequently be modified, substituted for, or even removed without the whole system structure collapsing like a house of cards.

In relation to the requirement of comprehensiveness, modularity of design is the other side of the coin. Carry out the design concept of system integration via linkable system modules. Avoid complexity like the plague.

6. Establish what the proper level of automation should be. If scope and integration are viewed as two different dimensions of automation, a third dimension is its degree or *level.* A fully automated system is defined as one that functions without any human intervention whatever.

The typical computer-based operating support system today is only semi-automated, in that intermediate outputs of its procedures or subsystems are being submitted to people for evaluation, "override," and other types of action. This indicates that only part—and most likely the simpler part—of the system logic has been captured.

As we observe any system currently installed in the commercial applications area, whatever its level of automation, we can always discern a layer of higher-level logic, i.e., procedures generating input to the system, being performed by people. This stratum of logic could conceivably be captured, and the procedures transferred to the computer also. Usually there exist several strata of such higher-level logic, which represent the potential for further automation. Most of our current systems still lean heavily on their human elements, even for relatively trivial tasks, and there is room in all of them for achieving a higher level of automation.

Here again, however, as in the case of integration, trying to achieve a high level of automation for its own sake is not necessarily a wise course of action. It should only be attempted where the result (usually speed) is clearly advantageous and where this advantage is worth more than the cost of capturing and storing the logic. There will be cases in which such cost, as well as the effort required, would be excessive. If a skeptical executive asks, "Does the computer know about the impending strike at Ford and the trend in the price of copper?" and the answer is that it does indeed and also knows what to do about it, the system's designers have clearly achieved a brilliant technical feat—but probably at an exorbitant cost.

How *much* do we really want to automate? This is a question a wise system designer will ask himself throughout the design process. Programming for all the possible events that may occur reaches a *point of diminishing returns*. Do not automate what people can do better, and remember that in many areas, people are still the best, and the most economical, system element.

7. Avoid need for informal system. What the system designer is creating we shall consider to be a *formal* system. It reflects the "official" way in which the business operation is supposed to be conducted. It is represented by the internal system logic and by system outputs, particularly those which instruct operating people in their actions. Purchase and factory orders, schedules, and other instructions are examples of such outputs. The documented, authorized procedures that support the system are also part of the formal system.

Operating support systems that function in manufacturing companies are almost always accompanied by corollary *informal*, or "unofficial" systems. The informal system consists of the practices used by operating people to overcome the deficiencies of the formal system with which they must work. An informal system can be defined as a set of loose unwritten procedures followed by individuals in the gathering of information from informal sources, in the commonsense processing of all information, and in supplementing, working "around," and overriding the actions of the formal system.

It is the informal system that enables individuals in a computer-using company to live with the formal system, by compensating for its crudeness, inflexibility, and imperfection. Today, everyone has an informal system in operation. Manufacturing organizations that spend hundreds of thousands of dollars per month for computer-system rental employ, at the same time, hundreds of expediters who literally walk information from source to recipient. A common example in factories are the published schedules and dispatch lists which are being ignored by production personnel who know, through sources of their own, what is *really* needed.

The formal system always represents what we *thought, planned, forecast* we would need, whereas the informal system establishes what we *actually do* need. The concept of the informal system is being introduced here as a tool useful to the system designer. The existence, and scope, of an informal system represents the *measure of (formal) system imperfection.* An important criterion of a truly well-designed and well-implemented computer-based system is whether operating personnel are able to, and want to, work according to the formal system. The good system is the one that people must and are willing to work to, because it represents the source of the best possible operating information at all times.

8. Provide for auxiliary system functions. A well-designed system of the type in question should, in addition to its primary mission of supporting or controlling the day-by-day operations of the business, have built into itself certain other auxiliary capabilities. Three such capabilities are suggested here:

1. System acts as a simulator.
2. System acts as a diagnostician.
3. System acts as a watchdog.

A soundly designed and integrated system is really an *operating simulator* of portions of the basic work flow of the business. It should be capable of answering "what if" questions, by accepting and processing fictitious input data resulting in reports which, in effect, say, "If these were real inputs, then here's what would happen." After such simulated inputs have been run through the system and its files, there must, of course, be a way of returning the system to its original status. Often this can be accomplished simply by entering transactions that will reverse, or cancel, the previous ones.

Although the system would act as a simulator only upon request, its *diagnostic outputs* can be programmed to be unsolicited. This is accomplished by designing the system so that it will go through certain routines (usually file scans) automatically on a regular basis and generate messages about what appears to it to be wrong, or about to become wrong. Error-checking capabilities programmed into the system also belong in the category of diagnostics. They will be separately discussed in the section on input data integrity of Chapter 8.

The third auxiliary system capability is to *police the performance* of the human system-output recipients. This is not difficult to implement provided that in the system design stage the required user responses are predetermined and their form and timing prespecified. The computer is then simply programmed to check up on this and report to management.

The above auxiliary system capabilities are obviously of great value to the direct user generally, and to management particularly. The best example known to the author is a random-access-oriented materials control system installed by a heavy machinery manufacturer. This system, in its simulator role, accepts fictitious inputs at the forecasting level, processes them all the way down to purchase requisitions and shop order action notices, and then "backs out" the simulated transactions by processing a set of corresponding canceling entries.

In its diagnostic function, this system tests each inventory record, every time it operates on it, for conditions such as excess current and projected inventory, expired need for an outstanding purchase order or the validity of a due date scheduled for a factory order, and prints diagnostic outputs once a day. It also polices operations in that it scans all its files once a week and produces a report for management in which it "squeals" on individual buyers and inventory analysts who either took order action without the system asking them to or failed to take the action the system recommended. It also lists all vendors who made premature deliveries during the past week.

9. Make system organization-independent. The system designer should, to the best of his ability, guard against system obsolescence. Unfortunately, many factors can render obsolete a system that, to all appearances, had been well designed initially. This system design pointer, and the next two, relate to the problem of system obsolescence.

One of the factors that can cause system obsolescence is organizational change. The system designer should strive to create a system whose internal operation is independent of the existing organization structure provided, of course, that the basic work the business does remains essentially the same.

A system will be organization-independent to the extent that its design is not *tailored* to the organization, and to the particular division of human labor, that prevails in the area that the system covers. This may sometimes prove to be a difficult requirement, as there is no specific recipe for designing an organization-independent system. Rather, the system designer should keep asking himself the question whether redesign and reprogramming will be necessary if this or that business function becomes combined with, or split away from, another one or if this or that type of change in organization takes place.

10. Anticipate the system's effect on its environment. A computer-based system can be expected to cause certain changes in its operating environment which, in turn, may affect its performance to such an extent that it will have to be modified or redesigned unless the original design anticipates such changes.

One type of change in the system environment occurs particularly in communications-oriented systems and is best expressed by the maxim: *Once new communication capability is provided, traffic increases significantly.* This lesson was first learned following the installation of SABRE, the pioneer reservation system of American Airlines. The volume of messages between the central computer and the ticket agents' terminals proved to have been seriously underestimated, which caused rework of the system and delay in the completion of the project.

It turned out that the agents, once they satisfied themselves that "the thing really works," suddenly realized that they had a powerful new tool at their disposal—and *really* began using it. They would make several inquiries where one had been anticipated, perhaps offering unsolicited information about other flights, connections, etc., to their customers so as to give better service. This, of course, is precisely what the system *should* enable them to do.

The same sort of thing is certain to happen when a new computer-based system in a manufacturing company provides for inquiry into the status of part numbers, or the location of open shop orders. If the new tool works effectively, it will be used extensively. The system designer should not base message traffic capacity on the number of inquiries operating people *say* they would make, because they think in terms of their current setup, which *discourages* inquiry, whereas the new system will encourage it.

System availability affects the way business is being run is another axiom that expresses a type of change caused by the very availability of a new computer system. The limited information-handling capability inherent to the old system acted as an effective brake on many types of change. For instance, if the new computer system easily handles engineering changes, there will be *more* engineering changes as a result. If changes in production schedules can now be implemented without the traditional confusion and disruption, the schedules are bound to get changed more often. These types of change are desirable—the new system simply enables the user to operate the way he always would have liked.

11. Provide for system growth. The most common cause of system design obsolescence is system growth, which has proved the most difficult to anticipate and plan for. Business management has in the past consistently underestimated information processing needs and thus the extent of future computer usage. Unanticipated system growth, in terms of both computer hardware and its application, will tend to render original system design inadequate, ineffectual, or inefficient. The system designer who appreciates this fact will particularly favor, and value, the existence of a long-range system master plan which can guide him in this difficult area.

Considerations of computer system growth have already been reviewed, at some depth, in the preceding chapter. The advice to the system designer at this point is simply to anticipate, and plan for, future growth to the best of his ability.

12. Keep service to user uppermost in mind. Last but definitely not least, we list the system design objective of serving the user. Service to the user is, after all, what the whole thing is about. If the system is to prove *truly* successful, once "on the air" it will need the user's cooperation and support. That is why the system designer should have the user's needs on his mind, in whatever he does. Service to the user should always be the overriding, primary system objective. The user should be coddled by the system—after all, he is human and the computer is only a machine.

This would seem so self-evident that even mentioning it might appear superfluous and unnecessary. Yet systems designed for computer room efficiency, not for maximum service to the user, are legion. The machine load report that is produced Wednesday afternoon showing the load *as of* Monday morning belongs in this category. The report to the vice president that he must first summarize and abstract from to get its meaning belongs in this category. The so-called shop floor control system built around a tape-oriented computer without data collection terminals, under which transaction *cutoff* time is at three o'clock in the afternoon (before the second shift in the factory even begins to work), belongs in this category also. The early cutoff permits key punching, sorting, and tape preparation for the nightly computer run, but results in reports and schedules for shop supervision that have to be updated with pencils the next morning.

(The machines really have taken over in these instances, because the systems were evidently designed to please and make it easy on the computer, certainly not to help the user.)

Unless the system is ambitiously designed for a high degree of automation and is to capture and execute higher-level logic, carefully planned exits from the system for manual review and approval, override, etc., should be part of the design. System output should be designed to make it easy for the user to recognize problems and exceptions and to make it easy for him to analyze and resolve them.

Wherever possible, "handles" for the user should be designed into the system. These are features of the system that permit the user to manipulate the performance of the system in certain areas. The user must not have the feeling that an impenetrable wall separates him from the system. Avenues should be provided to him for access into the very bowels of the system, to assure that he sees the system as his own, as *belonging* to him. Examples of this type of "handle" are the system which permits the purchasing agent to specify (and respecify at any time) what value a premature vendor delivery should have before it is reported to him, or the system which permits scrap factor constants in the scrap allowance formula to be freely varied from part number to part number, as specified by the production control manager at any particular time.

The system should be designed to be *usable* as well as *useful*. Avoid using codes instead of English titles on output reports. Translate, by means of a simple lookup table programmed into the system, the artificial calendar used for ease of calculation, into calendar terms to which people are accustomed. Coddle the user, not the computer, and remember that the primary goal is not the efficiency of the computer system but the efficiency of the business.

> *Design the system* from the outside in, *in a series of tests of feasibility as to the attainment of the original system objective.*

THE "BLACK-BOX" DESIGN PRINCIPLE

When a new operating support system is being developed, people who are charged with designing the system during the study and in the early stages of system implementation frequently have the impulse simply to speed up and to reduce the cost of existing procedure. Where a computer is replacing a punched-card installation, for instance, it is possible merely to transfer existing sorting, punching, tabulating, and similar routines to the computer and have it, in effect, imitate a sorter, punch, tabulator, collator, and calculator. This will make for a quick conversion, but it will hardly take advantage of the special capabilities of a computer.

In order to exploit these capabilities, the opposite approach should be taken, and the system designer, instead of asking, "How *are* we doing

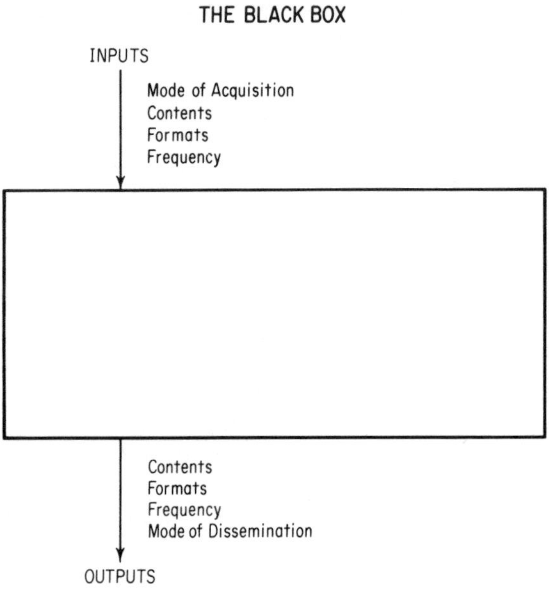

THE BLACK BOX

INPUTS

> Mode of Acquisition
> Contents
> Formats
> Frequency

> Contents
> Formats
> Frequency
> Mode of Dissemination

OUTPUTS

FIGURE 3

it?" should ask himself, "How *should* we be doing it?" Many people find it difficult to execute this type of mental switch without some formula to guide them. This is the question of system design technique. How do we actually go about it, and what do we do first?

In designing a computer-based system for the support of business operations, the first thing system designers should do is to find a quiet room, lock the door, roll up their sleeves, and start designing. At the outset, they should cease to be practical, down-to-earth businessmen and be dreamers for a while. The *black-box* method, which is used as a standard design technique by engineers who develop complex electronic hardware but which lends itself to the designing of systems of any kind, can guide them.

Before applying the black-box principle to an operating support system, let us examine the concept itself. Actually, it is quite simple, because *a black box does everything we want it to do.* It is a device whose performance we simply postulate by defining its inputs and outputs or, as a system designer would say, its environment. In this way, we specify what the black box will do without knowing how it will do it, or whether it *can* do it (see Figure 3).

Determining whether the black box can do it and how it would

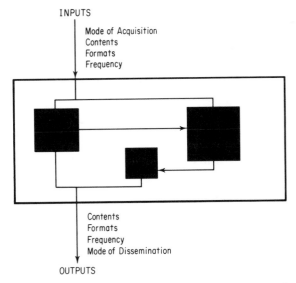

INPUTS

Mode of Acquisition
Contents
Formats
Frequency

Contents
Formats
Frequency
Mode of Dissemination

OUTPUTS

FIGURE 4

have to do it is the next step in the process of design (Figure 4). Once the environment is fully defined, it is time for taking the lid off the box and figuring out what would *have to be inside* to enable it to function as stipulated. The internal makeup of a big black box is, in turn, specified in terms of several smaller black boxes which would have to handle the various subfunctions dictated by their mutual input-output relationships. Each smaller black box has its own external environment which is being defined in this second step of the design process.

This process of defining the functional environment first and then determining what would have to be inside each black box is progressively carried down to individual system components and elements. The technique is iterative, and each successive iteration leads to a higher level of system resolution. Needless to say, this process will reveal impracticalities or impossibilities of implementation, and their specific reasons, where the performance of the first black box had been postulated too ambitiously. When using the black-box idea, we *design the system from the outside in*, in a series of tests of feasibility as to the attainment of the original system objective.

For best results, the system designer should similarly at first treat the new system as a black box. He should start out by defining the external performance of the *ideal* system—a system ideally suited to the needs of the business. For instance, the system designer could describe an ambitious production scheduling and dispatching system by defining its inputs (as shown in the first of the following tables) and by similarly specifying the desired outputs (as shown in the second of the following tables).

This example, which we are merely pretending to be ideal for discussion's sake, is incomplete, and the system's external performance is still not fully defined (specific formats and contents of both input entries and output reports and messages would have to be explicitly defined, for instance), but it serves to describe *external* system performance fairly well and suggests some of the things that will have to be determined or decided as we start looking inside the black box.

What *would* have to be inside the black box? For one thing, there is the question of terminals. How many are needed, of what type, and where should they be located? The Receiving department only needs a terminal with input capability, while the Tool Crib must have two-way communication. Can Inventory Control and Production Control share one input-output terminal? The factory manager is listed for terminal output only, but frequency is random—how will messages to him be triggered? How many terminals do we need for the machine operators? Must they be of the same type as the others? The black box leads the system designer straight to the areas that require resolution.

From the specified inputs and outputs it is evident that routings, standards, and open shop orders, as well as tooling data for each operation, will have to be stored by the system and these files will have to be randomly accessible. If we are to furnish machine load and production performance information at random frequency, what will have to be stored for this purpose, where, and how? How will the tooling data be maintained up-to-date? How many different programs will have to be written to provide all the specified services? How large will these programs be? Where will they be stored? As we answer these questions, we are moving from the outside into the viscera of the system and are designing its internal structure in the process.

With a system no further specified than in our example, many peo-

Source	Type of Input	Frequency	Form
Inventory Control	Part order quantities and due dates	Daily Random	Tape Terminal
Inventory Control	Changes to the above	As above	As above
Receiving	Arrival of short materials	Random	Terminal
Engineering	Notices to hold for engineering change	Random	Terminal
Industrial Engineering	Routing, standards changes, and releases	Daily Random	Tape Terminal
Assembly expediters	Priority codes	Random	Terminal
Tool Crib	Tooling availability messages	Random	Terminal
Etc.	Etc.	Etc.	Etc.

Recipient	Type of Output	Frequency	Form
Production Control	Machine load and production perform- ance data	Weekly Random	Report Terminal
Factory manager	Same as above	As above	As above
Production Control and expediters	Order location and status	Random	Terminal
Tool Crib	Tooling requisitions	Random	Terminal
Foremen	Notice to forward job reported complete	Random	Terminal
Foremen	Departmental work load analysis	Daily	Report
Machine operators	Next work assignment, always highest priority	Random, on request	Terminal
Etc.	Etc.	Etc.	Etc.

ple immediately raise objections, concluding that the system is too complex, too expensive ("we cannot afford terminals for machine operators") and that the computer on order is too small to handle it anyhow. This may be true, *but we do not know yet!* Let the black-box technique *prove* that the goal is unfeasible. What if we attached an audio response unit to the computer and put on-line touch-tone telephones into the shop? Then we could afford hundreds of them. Let us explore this. Will programming be too extensive and difficult? Let us find out.

At the first black-box stage, system designers should think boldly and should reach as far out as their imagination will let them. After all, they are defining the ideal system! At that stage, there should be no constraints. Cost, technology, or any other limiting factors should be disregarded. Again, many individuals cannot seem to free their thought process from practical constraint considerations, even temporarily. But it is important that the system designer be able to do this. He need not worry, the black-box process will keep him honest.

Start with the ideal and then *back down* as the black-box design technique will dictate, but *only* as it will dictate. Modify, tone down your original goals only as you have to. You will go farther this way and will end up with a system more advanced and more useful than had you used the present system as a point of departure, with the objective of improving its performance.

Chapter Six
Organizing for the Job

Being hopelessly behind schedule in providing service to users has become a way of life for Systems and Programming in most companies.

DATA PROCESSING AND DEPARTMENTAL ORGANIZATION

The introduction, and growth, of a computer system affects company organization. Because of the newness of electronic data processing in business and because of its rapid expansion from modest origins of a mere few years ago, there is still much groping throughout industry concerning the proper organizational accommodation of this function.

In this section we shall review considerations of organization and assignment of responsibilities among the various departments or groups concerned with the information processing system. The discussion will focus on local (division, branch, plant) relationships, as corporate systems considerations are reviewed separately in Chapter 9.

The functional and organizational units within a business that are related, in some degree, to the information system generally and to the computer system particularly, are the following:

1. Data processing
2. System development
3. Programming

4. Operating procedure development
5. System users

These functions, and their respective staffs, exist in every computer-using company but are organizationally combined in various ways. Historically, the directly system-related functions had their organizational origin in the formation of a Data Processing or Tabulating department and typically a nucleus of a systems-and-procedures staff. Following the transition from punched-card to computer data processing, programming became a separate function. In most companies, the programmers and systems analysts have been organized into a Systems department independent of data processing (computer room) operations. In some cases, the Systems department retained responsibility for operating procedures, and in other cases, this responsibility was made to rest with user departments.

Other organizational variations also exist. Some companies took what is known as the *open shop* (i.e., data-processing shop) approach, whereby systems and programming capability is decentralized and maintained by the respective user departments who then use the data processing facility as a service center. This arrangement has some merit in a scientific or engineering environment, but is rare and largely impractical for computer-based systems that support business operations. In a commercial environment, the *closed shop*, i.e., a central department in which programming and system development resources are concentrated, is the rule and will be so assumed for purposes of subsequent discussion.

The closed shop has many important advantages that recommend it as an organizational solution for business data processing. Among these advantages are better utilization of equipment and of systems and programming manpower, but more importantly, standardization of data processing procedure and documentation, plus central system planning, which is the only sound approach in a business. But the closed shop, by its nature of centralized service, also presents particular problems. These should be compensated for through management action on the level of organization and system responsibility assignment, as discussed below.

One difficulty with the closed shop arises when a major system development effort is undertaken which normally calls for a formation of a special project team or task force. Such a team should be staffed with talent from various departments, including *Systems and Programming*. From the latter's point of view, this does not fit in with the normal scheme of things, causes disruption of regular systems services, and raises questions of project organization, leadership, and responsibility.

These questions will be examined separately in the next section on project organization and control. For purposes of the current discussion, major system projects will be disregarded and only the regular function of the Systems and Programming department, i.e., the development and modification of individual applications, will be considered. There are two principal considerations pertaining to the overall data processing function in a business enterprise:

1. The *problem of communication,* both internal and external, as regards the staffs directly related to the data processing system
2. The *productivity* of systems and programming talent

The first is a function of organization of the directly system-related departments. The second, strangely enough, is primarily determined by how the *user* departments are organized and how they interface with the systems and data processing functions.

THE SYSTEMS AND DATA PROCESSING ORGANIZATION

The functions directly related to a computer system are

1. Data processing operations, consisting of key punching, punched-card equipment, and computer operations
2. Systems development and programming

These functions are normally split into two organizational units, as indicated. The first question that arises is to whom these units should report. It is best to have both report to a *common* superior, as otherwise considerable problems of communication and cooperation are certain to be created. Should this common superior be a full-time technical manager or one of the business managers such as the controller, plant manager, etc.? Assuming that these functions are of some scope, they warrant being managed by a technical manager on a full-time basis. They should not report directly to, say, the controller, because if he were to do justice to managing the data processing and systems functions, he would not have time to be controller. The reasons that recommend data processing operations and systems-and-programming being made a part of the same organization are

1. The high degree of *mutual impact* of these two functions, in terms of the use of hardware, documentation, and cross-communication
2. Presenting *one face* to the user, who does not care whether a problem or system failure was caused by the hardware or its operator,

by the programmer, or by the documentation that flows between the latter two

The next question that is often asked is to whom should the common head of the computer system–related functions report in the company organization. In most companies, these functions initially were made to report to the controller or to some other financial executive, because of the historical accident of accounting and payroll applications having been the first to be implemented. The first data processing installations were of modest scope and functioned essentially as an extension of other, conventional accounting machinery, such as desk calculators, ledger posting machines, etc. In fact, data processing used to be called *machine accounting*, and for a time, in the 1950s, there existed a professional society of so-called machine accountants.

But we are now a long way from "machine accounting," and in the average computer-using company, there is no longer any logical reason for treating computer system–related functions organizationally as being part of the accounting operation. Computer applications now extend to many nonaccounting functions of the business and in the typical company constitute—or should constitute—the majority of applications. Accounting and financial applications are becoming, and in fact have already become, of less relative importance. This trend will continue.

In light of this development, many companies have already separated computer system–related functions from the accounting organization. In such companies, the head of the systems and data processing organization reports to the "second in command," where such a position exists (i.e., assistant general manager of a local operation, or executive vice-president of a single-location company), or to an executive responsible for one of the business operating functions (e.g., manufacturing manager or vice president), or to the chief operating executive himself.

As the computer system becomes more and more general-purpose, from an applications point of view, and as it gains increasing importance to the conduct of the business as a whole, the organizational trend mentioned above will inexorably continue. That the systems and data processing organization must eventually report directly to the "second" or "first in command" (whose most important tool for managing is bound to become the computer system) is, in the author's opinion, inevitable. When this happens—and it is gradually happening in industry already—the head of this organization will attain executive (or local top management) status.

Another question which should be examined here is the internal organization of the Systems and Programming department. There are three principal alternatives of organization:

1. Organization by project
2. Organization by internal function
3. Organization by application area

ORGANIZATION BY PROJECT

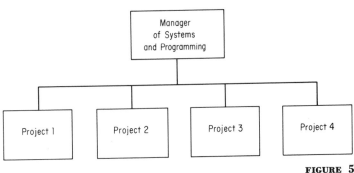

FIGURE 5

ORGANIZATION BY FUNCTION

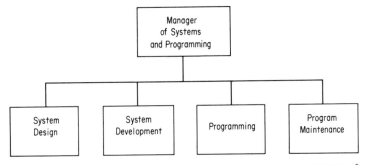

FIGURE 6

The concept of organizing by project is self-explanatory (see Figure 5). Where this type of organization has been tried, it has generally not worked out well. The main reason for this is the fact that projects come and go, which calls for perpetual reorganization with its attendant problems. Reassignment of personnel from project to project also means that no one can specialize and gain depth in the understanding of any one major function of the business.

The organization by internal function (Figure 6) slices up the systems and programming task horizontally, along the lines of the programming hierarchy mentioned in Chapter 2. Under this approach, personnel specialize in systems and programming function but not in an application category. Because of the way the job is sliced up, severe communications problems arise between system designers, system developers, programmers, coders, and program maintainers. This leads to an *excess of documentation* in terms of both its volume and resolution level. Time is wasted, responsibility is hard to pinpoint, and the users never know exactly whom to contact about their problems. This is not a very good organization.

Organizing by application area (Figure 7) represents the third basic alternative. Its main advantages lie in the specialization of systems and programming personnel by business function, which increases their

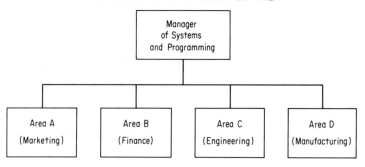

ORGANIZATION BY APPLICATION AREA

FIGURE 7

productivity, and in the relative ease of communication, both internal and external. Responsibility for applications and programs is well fixed, documentation can be kept to a reasonable level, and effective liaison with the various user groups is established naturally. The only real drawback of this type of organization is that it is not geared to projects that cross the boundaries of several business functions and consequently, application areas. Under this organizational pattern, projects are best assigned semiarbitrarily to one of the application area teams. This tends to cause somewhat of a problem of communication with users. But it can be overcome by the appointment of several official liaison men, for the duration of the project.

The overall organization chart for the systems, programming, and data processing functions (Figure 8) reflects the concept of organizing by application area. The organization tree has three branches or lines, and it is interesting to note that the department is organized rather like a manufacturing company. Thus if we think of information as being the basic material, or product, of the computer system–related functions, we can view Operations as the factory, Systems and Programming as product development, industrial engineering, and manufacturing en-

ORGANIZATION OF COMPUTER SYSTEM—RELATED FUNCTIONS

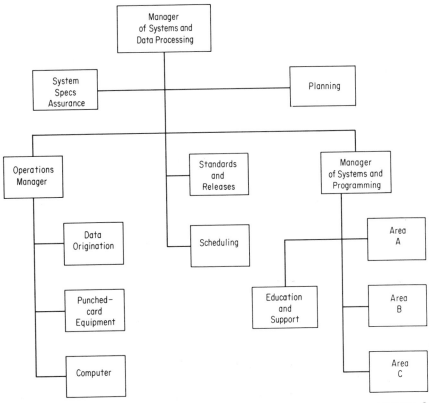

FIGURE 8

gineering, and the middle branch as quality control and production control.

Speaking of production control, it must be noted that in most actual organizations the computer-room scheduling function is performed by Operations. This is tantamount to a factory organization's being responsible for production control. But the objectives of a shop, or of a Data Processing Operations department, conflict somewhat with the objectives of the customer, or system user. The Operations department is not in the best position to evaluate job priorities, and therefore a smoother, more effective performance can be had if scheduling comes from an impartial source that can balance the needs of the customer and those of the producer.

The function of system specs assurance represents a form of high-level quality control, and the position would be staffed with the most competent and knowledgeable individual available, so as to spread the benefit of his contribution over all the application area teams. The function of planning would particularly include hardware planning.

Standards and Releases acts as a channel for documentation and new programs in their flow between Systems and Programming and Data Processing Operations. This will assure that the work submitted by the former conforms to the standards of quality required by the latter, which will minimize internal communications problems. The functions of education and system support (i.e., software-oriented work) are segregated from the application areas in the Systems and Programming organization, for maximum effectiveness. The essence of effective organization is to minimize lines of communication—this applies with special force to Systems and Data Processing organization.

USER DEPARTMENTS' ORGANIZATION AND SYSTEM RESPONSIBILITY

We have discussed earlier the user's role in system design and his responsibility for program specs. The fact is that the way user departments are organized, charged with responsibility for application specs, and the way they are made to interface with Systems and Programming has direct and significant bearing on the latter's productivity.

This productivity of systems and programming personnel should be of serious concern to the business executive, because qualified people in these categories are, and *will continue to be,* in critical short supply, as well as expensive. There is probably considerable room for increases in systems analyst and programmer productivity in every computer-using commercial establishment that exists.

The fact is that data-processing-oriented systems men, but particularly programmers, spend most of their time on problem definition, as was pointed out earlier. The people in the best position to define the problems, i.e., the functions to be automated by computer, are the users. They can do so with the most overall efficiency, as they do not have to *learn* the business function first. But in order to take advantage of this, their charter must include such responsibility, and they must be organized to discharge it.

Computer system user departments of a business enterprise should establish data-processing-oriented positions staffed with individuals who have a *business background* but who have some training in the computer-associated arts. Thus if a computer-based quality control system is planned, for instance, there should be at least one qualified quality control engineer with some competence in data processing, to work out, or to review, the system specs and to act as the Quality Control department's interface to Systems and Programming.

The channeling of all demands, proposals, and requests directed at Systems and Programming by the users, through a qualified "in-department" person will alleviate the problem of a job logjam in the Systems and Programming department. Being hopelessly behind schedule in providing service to users has become a way of life for Systems and Programming in most companies.

This backlog of projects and requests for additional service (in some cases numbering several hundreds of such requests) results from the complete freedom that users enjoy in most companies, to bombard Systems and Programming with a stream of ill-thought-through half-baked proposals. The latter department then spends a lot of time and effort evaluating, investigating, and passing judgment on the quality and reasonableness of such proposals, thus squandering away their precious talent and other resources.

In a situation where significant logjams have developed, the problem probably cannot be resolved by hiring additional programmers, or even by doubling the capacity of the systems and programming organization, because users can always generate half-baked proposals at a higher rate than any given Systems and Programming department can handle. It is simply *too easy* for the users to make requests without having to do their homework first, and thus to shift work that should by rights be theirs unto Systems and Programming.

If such requests and proposals must first pass technical "in-house" inspection, this will tend to stem the flow of projects into Systems and Programming. Those requests that will reach the latter are likely to be realistic and well enough defined to permit efficient implementation without backlog-caused delays.

Serious problems or cases of failure in this area examined by the author always contained a common element: the lack of user participation (as against mere collaboration). Companies that have dealt with service bureaus rather than writing their own programs or operating their own equipment have had the salutary experience of being pinned down by the service bureau to the explicit job specs that the customer must always provide, of course.

User departments should do business with Systems and Programming in their own company somewhat as they would do—would *have to* do—with an outside service bureau.

If users would approach the job this way, or more precisely, if management would *make them* approach it this way, they would perforce develop skills in defining their own information needs and thus become better "customers" for systems and programming specialists. The latters' contribution should consist in supporting the users' progress in increasing their grasp and control over business operations they are responsible for. In the final analysis, Systems and Programming can lead only by supporting.

> *The quality of project management is more important than the quality of technical talent used.*

PROJECT ORGANIZATION AND CONTROL

To develop and install a computer-based system of some scope, particularly one that cuts across departmental lines, is a multiphase project that will take many months of concerted participation by a number of individuals of diverse skill and background. The prevalent method of gearing up to implement such a project is the task force approach, under which a special project team is assembled and charged with the responsibility for all preinstallation planning.

This will consist of the various activities that must take place following approval of the management proposal, including the detailed system design discussed in the preceding chapter, and the tasks of miscellaneous planning, procedure development, programming, testing, and education, as discussed in Chapter 7. When organizing a system project team, management should be ready not only to assign people for the job, but to choose high-caliber people.

Although each such project will require that a mixture of diverse talent be brought together, the scope of user representation will obviously vary depending on the particular application. But active user participation is highly desirable in all cases. The project should not be staffed with specialists and technicians exclusively. Rather, user departments should have the strongest possible representation in as many project activities as is practical.

Departments whose jobs will go on the computer should, in turn, free up their top talent to represent them on the system development task force—the opposite of the practice by too many operating department heads of fulfilling this obligation by releasing whomever they can spare with the least inconvenience. To succeed with the project task in terms of the quality of the job, its cost, and timely completion, two considerations are of main importance. They are good *organization* and effective *control* over project progress.

PROJECT ORGANIZATION

Experience with many past computer-based system development projects indicates that good organization is prerequisite to the success of the project. The relative effectiveness of a team made up of the most highly qualified individuals imaginable will still largely depend on how well the project is organized and managed. Lack of proper organization is certain to result in underutilization of project resources, missed deadlines, difficulty in arriving at decisions, increased project cost, and general confusion. The quality of project management is more important than the quality of technical talent used.

For best results, project organization should be *monolithic*, with clean lines of responsibility and decision-making authority—the opposite of the committee approach. A single individual should be responsible for project progress and all system-related decisions, and he, in turn, should delegate responsibility to specific individuals and group leaders serving under him. As project team members can be expected to work in a spirit of cooperation, formal authority will actually prove less important than the feeling of clearly defined responsibility on the part of specific individuals.

For purposes of developing and installing a computer system that will support business operations, the basic organization shown in Figure 9 would be ideal.

At the top is a small management committee charged with the overall responsibility for the progress and cost of the project. Its chairman—not necessarily the senior executive—acts as liaison with the project team, serving in a dual capacity, i.e.,

1. Exerting general supervision over the project, *on behalf of top management*

2. Expediting management decisions, as required, *on behalf of the project team*

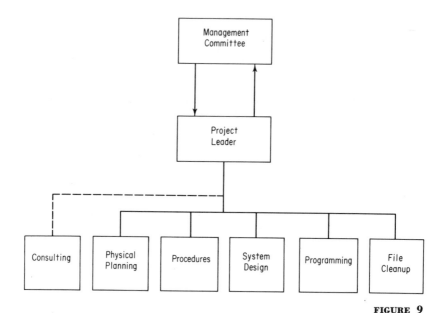

FIGURE 9

Reporting to the chairman is a single project leader. The person and competence of this individual will be of extreme importance to the success of the project. Who should he be? Here we must distinguish between two cases: that of the pioneering effort of developing a new, comprehensive system, and that of implementing subsequent individual subsystems and applications that have to fit in with other systems already installed.

In the first case, an experienced business manager, preferably one representing the prime function that is to be automated (a production control man in the case of a production control system, a quality control engineer in the case of a quality control system, etc.) would be the best choice for project leader. In the second case, the Systems and Programming department will normally supply the leader who, however, should then be backed up by a representative of the business function in question. In either case, the appointment should be full-time for the duration of the project.

Six groups or functions should report to the project leader, as indicated in Figure 9. Depending on the scope of the project, these groups may be large or small, perhaps as small as one man. They need not necessarily exist simultaneously, because they carry out tasks that represent different system development phases in different time frames.

System design implementation comes first, and in very small projects can be manned by the project leader himself. This function ends with the documentation of program specs.

Programming takes place somewhat later in the project, hence need not necessarily be staffed at the outset.

Procedure development will run roughly in parallel with programming, but normally at least some of these people will participate in system design implementation also.

File cleanup is a task that must not be overlooked and should be adequately staffed toward the end of the project. It will be more fully discussed below.

Physical planning concerns the preparation of the physical environment (air conditioning, cabling, site preparation, etc.) for the computer equipment.

System engineering and/or consulting represents the technical and programming assistance supplied by the computer manufacturer or procured from a commercial consulting firm.

Several points need to be made regarding this organization. First, it is an ideal pattern that it may not always be possible to achieve in practice, perhaps for reasons of company politics. Computer-based systems can successfully be developed by project teams organized differently, but the closer the actual organization is to the recommended blueprint, the better the odds for success will be.

The organization is not static and changes over time, with groups and individuals coming on board, and leaving the project, as required. It is much better to staff this organization with fewer people on a full-time basis than with many part-time contributors. The latter approach would defeat the principle of pinpointing responsibility and would make management of the project extremely difficult.

For best results, all the groups or individuals making up the project team should report directly, and without reservations, to the project leader for the duration of their association with the project. If the leader is charged with responsibility for bringing the system in on target, he must have full control over work assignment and attendance of project personnel. Where this principle is not honored, individuals "on loan" to the project tend to get recalled in cases of home-department crises, thus jeopardizing the outcome of the whole system development project.

Finally, the ever-present problem of communication, both between intraproject groups and between the project and the rest of the company organization, must be solved. In a computer system development project, communication equates with effectiveness. Regular project meetings serving to appraise team personnel of each other's progress and problems are recommended. In cases of major projects affecting multiple user organizations, it is often advisable to designate certain team members as official liaison men to the respective user departments.

PROJECT CONTROLS

A controlled project tends to succeed. The reason for establishing some type of project control machinery is not only the fact that talent, facilities, computer test time, and money are in limited supply and must therefore be managed. A formal process of management control, i.e., progress reporting and review, serves both as one more communication channel and as a motivating factor, and thus directly contributes to the success of the effort.

The control procedure that will be instituted can be geared to one or more of the following three elements:

1. Activity or progress, against time
2. Cost
3. Resources expended (e.g., programmer time)

Although all three can be controlled, it may be advisable to focus on only one or two of these factors, whichever are the most critical in a given case, for the sake of simplicity, ease, and the *cost* of control.

Prerequisite to effective control in any of these cases are the following:

1. A *plan*
2. A means of *feedback*
3. The ability to *analyze* progress in relation to plan, and vice versa, in order to *evaluate* status
4. Flexibility of *response*. Because of the dynamic nature of a computer system development effort, caused both by the imperfection in the original estimate of requirements and by changes occuring in the project environment, control response may have to take the form of one of the following
   a. Corrective action toward the activity
   b. Modification of the plan

On the practical level, it is always necessary to represent *planned* progress in some tangible form, so that *actual* progress can be measured against it. Before the various project activities can be meaningfully represented, first their respective times and then their precedence relationship must be determined. The best authority for the time requirements and other data pertaining to activities are the parties who will perform these activities.

Once all the required project activities, and their time values, are related to each other, taking into account their mutual precedence relationship (e.g., program specs documentation must be completed before programming can begin, and a program must be coded before it can be tested), the allocability of the required resources must be evaluated. In the management proposal, it was assumed that resources (people, facilities, computer time, etc.) required for the implementation of the system will be available in certain quantity at certain times. This assumption must now be tested.

The necessary resources may not, in fact, be available in the required quantity at the required time. For instance, the plan as originally conceived bunches up programmer time in a period that conflicts with another project that may be going on. Programmer manpower sufficient for both projects may be available, but it will have to be allocated over a longer span of time. The allocation of limited resources has to be *leveled*. This may affect the time frame of the project.

Many techniques are available for relating the various planned events and activities, and their precedence relationships, on a time scale. The old fashioned *Gantt chart* will, in most cases, still do the essential job. There is available a variety of so-called *network planning* techniques such as:

Critical Path Method (CPM)
Project Evaluation and Review Technique (PERT)
Line of Balance (LOB)

They are well described in literature and well understood, thus requiring no elaboration here. The reader should note, however, that computer manufacturers can make available "canned" PERT programs and others.

If a company undertaking a system development project already has a computer installed, it may be able to take advantage of this and obtain a very effective ready-made tool for project planning and control. It should be pointed out also that, although manual techniques can be used, the more complex the project the more costly they become, and beyond a certain point in project complexity, using one of the network planning computer programs is the only efficient and reliable means of mapping out the relationships of all the project activities and of updating the latter.

Using a technique such as PERT, for instance, has the following advantages:

1. Minimizes the cost of planning (and replanning!) the project.
2. Provides a means of quick replanning.
3. Both activity progress and project cost information are easily handled.
4. The program has the capability of allocating resources, as discussed above.
5. Reporting by several levels of detail, so that the executive can get a summary report from the same computer run that produces detailed reports for project personnel.
6. Creates discipline and aids communication by acting as a common language of project control.

Feedback is another element of project control. A feedback procedure must be established to serve as a reporting means for the updating of the plan. As far as progress reporting is concerned, the tendency is for too many people to want too much information too soon. We must remember that feedback can be expensive. The frequency of feedback reporting should be geared to the so-called *corrective action turnaround;* i.e., the faster corrective action can be taken, the more frequent feedback should be, and vice versa.

Project cost should be reported in terms of standard rather than actual cost, and dependence should be placed on project-generated cost reporting rather than on the regular accounting reports which introduce delay and even distortion (an invoice did not clear, etc.). We want these reports *fast,* because their *purpose* is corrective action and not accounting for the last dollar.

For purposes of reporting progress, the best unit of measure is *percentage of completion* of a given activity or task. This is the only statement of progress that does not require further interpretation to get at its full meaning. The *form* of feedback is of little importance—do it the cheapest, fastest way.

Feedback serves to enable management to review progress, cost, etc., against the plan. The timing and frequency of reviews should be predetermined and form part of the project control procedure. The timing should be geared to the so-called *milestones,* i.e., significant points of achievement. Completion of program specs, development of the education program, computer equipment arrival, etc., represent natural milestones of progress.

One more point needs to be made concerning reviews and evaluation of progress, and that is the so-called *intensity* of progress, which varies from activity to activity. People tend to assume that progress is linear, i.e., that something planned to take two months should be half finished after one month, but in reality it does not happen that way. Consider how a home-building project progresses versus how an engineering project progresses. In the former case, construction gets off to a fast start and a lot of progress is being made in erecting the supporting members, putting a roof on, etc. But then, as everyone who has had a home built knows, activity peters out to the point where the owner fears that the job will never get finished.

The opposite pattern exists in an engineering project, where considerable research and make-ready activity takes place first, and most of the productive progress is made toward the end of the project. For purposes of controlling the progress of a computer system development project, some preassessment of intensity of the various activities that will be subject to review should be made, to permit valid evaluation. Of the project control techniques mentioned above, LOB embodies this capability; in fact, it is the intensity factor that mainly distinguishes it from PERT.

In closing, it should be stressed that fascination with control technique should not obscure the understanding that the *fact* of control is more important than the particular control technique being used.

Chapter Seven
System
Development
Phases

The advantages of the "cold turkey" method of conversion are mostly psychological. It provides a powerful incentive for all system user personnel to swim hard to keep from sinking.

The overall effort of computer-based system planning, including design, development, and installation, progresses through several time-related phases which are interdependent and which have a precedence relationship. The success of the system that is to result from this effort is directly dependent on the amount and *quality* of planning that will precede its installation. This chapter is devoted to a review of system development phases, and its objective is to help the management reader achieve an orderly, well-scheduled, and generally efficient execution of preinstallation activities.

The purely *technical* considerations pertaining to computer preinstallation planning, such as physical site preparation, tape library organization, computer operator training, etc., are well known and have been spelled out, in fine detail, in technical manuals supplied by computer manufacturers. Therefore we need not dwell on them here. Instead, we shall concentrate on *management* considerations, which, as a rule, are not equally well documented in technical literature.

The ten system development phases of management interest are as follows:

1. The study
2. Proposal evaluation
3. System design
4. Programming
5. Development of new operating procedures to support system
6. Education
7. Conversion planning and development of auxiliary procedures
8. File cleanup activities
9. Program testing
10. Conversion

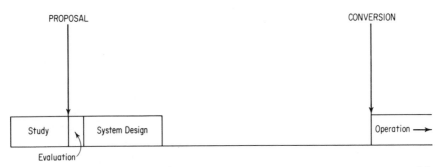

FIGURE 10

Because of their special importance, the phases of study, proposal evaluation, and system design have already been covered in preceding chapters. The three mileposts of computer system development are the start of the study, the proposal, and conversion (Figure 10).

The time span between these points will vary from several months to several years, depending on the scope of the project, as well as on the resources and talent that can be brought to bear on it. System development manpower requirements are usually expressed in terms of *man-months* of effort, and this is a reasonably objective measure, except for the fact that the overall time span cannot be much shortened by over-staffing the project. One of the axioms of computer system development is that *Doubling "bodies" won't cut project lead time in half.*

Unfortunately, there is no dependable formula for determining the precise overall time requirement for a major project of this kind, nor is it always possible to estimate, in advance, the exact number of man-months required. The more ambitious, comprehensive, and complex the system, the less reliable the initial estimates are likely to be. Past industry experience indicates that in the case of complex systems, particularly in the area of communications and real-time response, initial estimates of time and manpower requirements tend to be understated.

The best-known method of arriving at these requirements is to prepare, during the feasibility study, a detailed layout of all the development phases leading up to actual installation, and rely on educated estimates of competent individuals. The computer vendor's people can be of considerable assistance here, as they can draw on their experience with similar projects of their other customers. If the planned system is fairly complex, realistic planning will not target on a fixed-time, fixed-

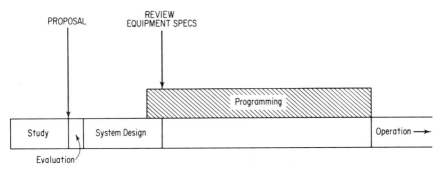

FIGURE 11

manpower basis. To avoid disappointment, the completion target should be set with a proviso that the effort will be X times reviewed (at specified times or when specific milestones are reached), reevaluated, and manpower or targets adjusted accordingly.

THE PROGRAMMING PHASE

For a review of the *technique* of computer programming, the reader is referred to Chapter 2. At this point, we are concerned about the *role* of programming in a computer-based system development project. In such a project, programming constitutes the fourth phase, following system design implementation, which it typically somewhat overlaps (see Figure 11). This is because programming can begin as soon as some of the modules of system design are sufficiently firmed up to permit preparation of final program specs.

Programming should proceed smoothly if the job of system design detailing was done well and completely. It is said that a programmer normally spends 90 percent of his time on problem definition and only 10 percent on programming for the solution, which is essentially the writing of instructions for the computer to follow. To the extent that programmers do not have to puzzle out what to do before doing it, their productivity can be increased *several times over*.

This phase should be the easiest and the most trouble-free, provided that the program specs developed during the system design phase are thorough and explicit. Another point to be made is that programming is the *only* phase that can be compressed without any penalty of final system impairment and the only one where lost time can be made up. Programming can be *bought!*

There are three approaches to organizing the work of a programming group, three ways of assigning programming responsibility. One approach is to assign each procedure to be automated, or each program, to one person to follow through from start to finish. This means chopping up the overall programming job into rather fine slices. A second method is to assign a larger portion of the task to two or three programmers, a team whose members will work together to develop the program. Where this approach is chosen, one man in each group should be appointed as team leader. The third method is to cut up the job horizontally, as it were, and have different personnel do the choosing of the programming strategy, the block diagramming, and the coding and testing.

All three of these methods are legitimate. The first one might be most appropriate for small projects, the second one for efforts of larger scope where individual programmers are assigned to serve full-time on the project task force, and the third one where the project team contains no programmers but relies on the services of an (organizationally independent) Systems and Programming department which is organized by programming function. Under method two there is a definite advantage in having more than one individual completely familiar with any given program during the testing and conversion phases.

As the programming phase gets under way, the specifications of the computer hardware that had been placed on order at proposal time will automatically be reviewed and, typically, revised to some extent. This should be expected, as the specific characteristics of the job will become fully known only as system development work progresses. The equipment capabilities should then be modified accordingly, as necessary.

DEVELOPMENT OF SUPPORTING PROCEDURES

This phase, which usually starts a little later than programming but for the most part runs parallel with it, is the development, and documentation, of new operating procedures that will support the system after it becomes operational (Figure 12).

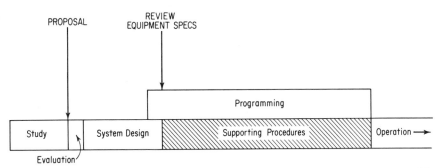

FIGURE 12

These procedures, sometimes documented in the form of a *user's manual*, will fall into two categories, i.e.,

1. Operating procedures
2. System and file maintenance procedures

The extent of procedure development will vary with the application, but it should be noted that usually both *new* data-processing-related procedural steps and modifications of *previous* procedures that the new system will impact will be encompassed.

Operating personnel from departments that will have to follow the new procedures should participate actively in their development. Although the structuring and documentation of these procedures must be done by trained systems analysts, user personnel should be in agreement with the substantive contents of procedures that they will later be called upon to adhere to. This will ensure that the operating procedures are realistic and that their users are motivated to follow them. Both points are important to a successful system operation.

Where practical, these new procedures should be *tested*, in the form of dry runs, for example, prior to conversion to the new system. The cost and laboriousness of such precautionary steps are preferable to the demoralizing confusion and procedure debugging under panic conditions which will ensue if errors of procedure are revealed only after the system goes "on the air." Considerations of system and file maintenance will be more fully reviewed below.

EDUCATION

The importance of this system development phase logically follows from the point already made but worth repeating here: *It takes the cooperation of users to make a computer-based system function successfully.* Depending on who these users will be, an appropriate program of education and training should be devised for them and implemented as an integral part of the system development effort. When the education job is done poorly or not at all, when *the logic of the system is not clearly understood by the man who must use it,* the new system is certain to encounter very rough going in its operational phase.

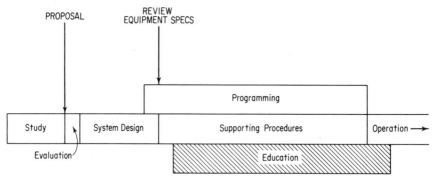

FIGURE 13

The employee education phase should normally begin sometime after the start of procedure development and should continue up to, and perhaps overlap, the system operational phase (Figure 13), depending on the conversion method employed (see below). It is a good idea to expose to education, in some degree, not only the people immediately affected but also the rest of the organization so that they are ready, psychologically and otherwise, when the new system goes into effect. The measure of success the new system will enjoy will be directly correlated to the amount and quality of education given to the individuals who will work with it.

To assure effective system operation, it is necessary to develop and administer a methodical program of education for all the classes of personnel affected, from operating management to the relatively unskilled clerical and production worker levels, as required. Such a program should cover the objectives of the system, the techniques employed to arrive at the desired output information, and most importantly, the new operating procedures that will go into effect once the system becomes operational.

There is a decided psychological advantage in having employees exposed to the new computer-based system before it takes final form. They are thus given the opportunity to look at it critically and make suggestions. This gives them a feeling that they had some part in the creation of the system, or at least that their importance as individuals vis-à-vis the computer is being acknowledged.

It should be the project team's responsibility to define the educational requirements, to prepare educational materials, and to conduct the various training sessions. This series of sessions or classes can be conducted on or off company premises, during working hours or after, but always at company expense, including overtime pay for non-exempt personnel, as required.

The costs of such training should be looked at as part of the necessary investment required to get the new system successfully "on the air." As a matter of fact, this part of the overall investment will likely return the biggest dividend of all. The important thing is to *include the education plan in the original management proposal,* to assure allocation of resources and management support. The inexperienced system planner who overlooks this may find himself short of capacity and without funds required to support the education phase—an extremely serious situation spelling inevitable trouble ahead. If management will not allocate funds for education as part of the system development project, the company would be better off to abort the whole effort.

A special aspect of employee education is the question of how new employees, hired *after* the system has become operational, will be trained. This problem is not nearly so acute as the education of employees "on board" at system startup time. Future employees will tend to get educated by their managers and coworkers. To assure consistency and ease of such training, however, this problem should be anticipated and appropriate educational aids prepared during the initial education planning phase.

Another important point is to start the education program early enough to ensure that everyone is adequately trained by the time conversion to the new system takes place. Education in these cases cannot be overdone. One can never do enough educating, and with the exception of projects with extremely long lead times, it is never too early to start the employee education program. *Start educating as soon as you have something to educate about* is a good rule to follow.

Special training aids and techniques for particular situations, such as the use of data collection and communications terminals by the rank and file, exist and can be made available by most computer manufacturers. The use of specially prepared brochures and booklets with questions and answers, illustrations, etc., is popular and effective. Management of a computer-using company should investigate the amount of assistance with the development of the internal education program, as well as other education services, available from their computer supplier.

Some computer manufacturers support extensive customer education programs, ranging from executive seminars conducted at country-club-like facilities to middle management and technical personnel classes offered at field education centers located in metropolitan areas. Customers of such computer manufacturers are entitled to these valuable services and should take extensive advantage of them.

In the final analysis, education is the one all-important key to successful computer use. There is no saturation point in education. Neither is there a shortcut to it. The business executive who wishes his computer investment really to pay off should always keep this in mind.

CONVERSION PLANNING AND DEVELOPMENT
OF AUXILIARY PROCEDURES

This phase encompasses the planning for conversion to the new computer-based system, including the development of *conversion procedures* and other nonregular procedures (Figure 14). Conversion procedures, which will go into effect just before cutting over to the new system, are gen-

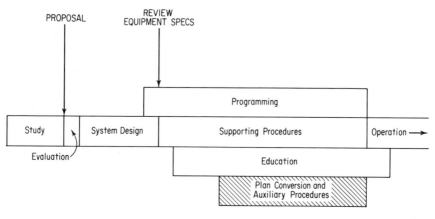

FIGURE 14

erally "one-shot" procedures that will expire as the system enters its operational phase. Some of these procedures will be in effect for perhaps only one day, others for several days or weeks. The intent of these procedures is to assure an orderly and smooth transition to the new system. They will cover activities such as the change, and its timing, from old to new methods of transaction processing, transition to new methods of file maintenance, etc.

Conversion may be planned to coincide with the start of a new fiscal year, or with physical inventory taking, or with a plant vacation shutdown. In such cases, the regular procedures which govern these situations must be coordinated with conversion procedures, and perhaps modified. A number of data processing procedures leading to system startup also belong in this category. Planning for conversion normally takes place toward the end of the programming and operating procedure development phases, when the specific requirements of conversion become fully known. In the cases of systems that are intended to support and control business operations, the organizational setup of the departments in question will often be affected. Conversion planning thus includes, or should include, the planning of *post-conversion organization*.

In addition to conversion procedures, other auxiliary procedures are developed during this phase. They cover the three areas of *backup*, *recovery*, and *audit trail*. Backup procedures deal with anticipated system and hardware failures. They provide a means for surviving such situations either by switching to a backup system or by temporarily falling back on more primitive methods, including manual data handling. Typical examples are the switching of real-time systems to a backup computer when the regular central processor goes down, the switching of on-line data collection terminals to off-line output card punches, or the substitution of batch processing for in-line methods when the system fails or falls too far behind. In most of these cases system performance is temporarily lowered and service to users degraded, but backup procedures permit business operations to go on.

System recovery procedures provide the means for resumption of normal system performance and service once the equipment is repaired. Various *restart*, file *regeneration*, and *updating* procedures fall in this category. The accounting term "audit trail" denotes auxiliary procedures for saving past transaction data for purposes of audit, as well as for reconstructing current status in cases of various failures or errors. The so-called periodic *file dumps*, i.e., recording of the contents of files on some off-line medium, are part of audit trail procedures, as the known past status, plus the saved transaction data, permits reconstruction of the current status.

FILE CLEANUP

Another system development phase that merits separate recognition is file cleanup. Files of operating records, such as bills of materials, routings, vendor records, inventory records, open orders, etc., normally need to be converted to a new format preparatory to their introduction into a computer-based system. Such conversion may include an audit for accuracy, as well as a reorganization, restructuring, recoding, and updating of the records in question (Figure 15).

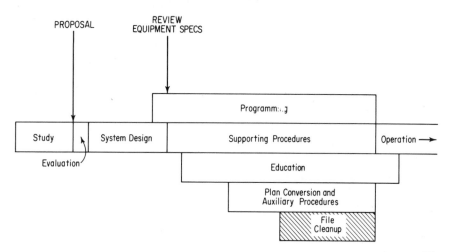

FIGURE 15

Where such records have previously been mechanized and exist in the form of punched-card decks, magnetic tape, etc., this will be only a minor problem. But where transition is being made from manual methods to a computer, the task may be extensive and its scope must not be underestimated. The effort of file record conversion can normally be quite accurately estimated and expressed in man-months of clerical work required. The system planner must not, however, overlook the fact that the newly converted records will have to be (probably manually) *maintained* until the time of cutover to the computer system. Where the rate of change affecting these records is significant, such as in the case of product specifications–related records, a surprise may be in store if the planning is done strictly on a man-month basis.

If the file cleanup job represents, for instance, six man-months of work, quite different results will be obtained if one individual is assigned for six months as against three individuals for two months. The difference derives from the amount of maintenance necessary under each of the alternative approaches. The phenomenon of maintenance consuming conversion resources is best illustrated by an example. Assuming a task of converting 3,500 records, with a rate of change affecting 25 percent of the records each month, and a clerk's capacity of handling 1,000 per month, we get the results shown in the following table.

| | Staffing: One Clerk | | Staffing: Two Clerks | |
	Maintain	Convert	Maintain	Convert
Month 1	0	1,000		
Month 2	250	750		
Month 3	438	562		
Month 4	578	422		
Month 5	684	316		
Month 6	751	249	0	2,000
Month 7	811	189	500	1,500
Total		3,488	Total	3,500

This example (which is exaggerated for purposes of illustration) shows that the same file cleanup job can require either seven or four man-months of work, depending on how it is staffed and also on its timing —obviously, if the team of two clerks starts the task in month 1, the converted file will have to be maintained for five months after completion. It is evident that to minimize the waste of effort in record maintenance, file cleanup should be planned to start close to the system conversion target date and should be adequately staffed to permit swift completion of the job.

Discussion of other aspects of file organization and maintenance is deferred until the section entitled The Problem of Data, in Chapter 8.

PROGRAM TESTING AND DEBUGGING

This is really a subphase of programming, because program test and debugging are integral parts of it. We list it separately because it takes place in its own time slot and because certain special considerations pertain to it.

Tests will begin during the latter part of the programming phase (Figure 16), and the first ones will be conducted on equipment made available by the computer supplier in one of his so-called data centers or test centers. The data center equipment will, however, rarely be identical with the equipment that is on order. It will therefore be probably possible only to test out individual program segments, or programs, but not necessarily the whole group of programs that constitutes the new system.

As far as methods of computer program testing are concerned, it is interesting to note that in the early computer days a programmer would load his program into the memory of the central processor, sit down at the console, and then operate the machine so that his program was *stepped through,* one instruction at a time. As bugs were discovered, the programmer was often able to make a correction on the spot and then proceed to the next instruction.

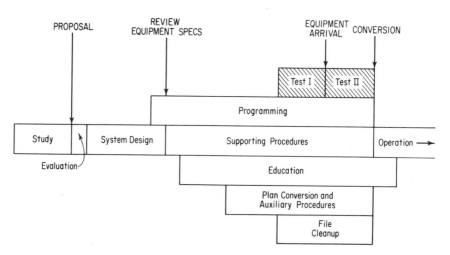

FIGURE 16

This method of testing and debugging, where the programmer plays the computer somewhat like a piano, is no longer practical, because present-day programs tend to be much more complex, i.e., contain thousands of instructions, and also because this method would now be considered prohibitively costly. With modern intermediate-to-large computer systems renting for hundreds of dollars per hour, a test program can only be permitted to stay on the computer until it "hangs up," i.e., stops functioning because of a bug.

Typically, this takes only seconds or minutes. Program testers should therefore bring along to the data center several more programs than they expect to test, to utilize the machine time allotted to them in case the first tests "flunk out" rapidly. It is also a good idea to test programs in the sequence of their importance and complexity, so that programs that can be expected to require the most tests are always at the head of the queue.

After the arrival of the equipment that had been on order, final testing can take place with fewer time constraints. All the new programs can be test-run as a group, and a special aspect of this test is the running of user-written programs in conjunction with the software, or *Operating System*, programs supplied by the computer manufacturer. Thus the whole system, including the equipment itself, is tested out prior to conversion.

A final comment on program testing and debugging pertains to large and complex programs. Earlier we discussed the phenomenon of complexity and its relation to the cost and scope of required implementation effort. The "law" on system complexity is confirmed in practice, where it might virtually take forever to debug a sufficiently complex program (actually, a multitude of interacting programs) completely.

Highly complex programs are *undebuggable,* because the practically infinite number of possible program paths (alternate instruction sequences) defies a full testing out. Some of the most sophisticated computer systems that are operational today, such as the large airline reservation systems, for example, operate with programs that still have bugs in them. The same is true for large software packages. Some *Operating Systems* are made up of hundreds of thousands, even millions, of instructions and will therefore always contain some bugs. In view of this problem, new so-called *self-repairing* techniques of programming are being used. These techniques, in essence, instead of hunting for bugs repair their *effect.* Their objective is to make a system, though imperfect, still useful.

CONVERSION

The final milepost in computer-based systems planning is the conversion or cutover from the old to the new system. This is obviously a critical point in the whole effort, and it must be planned very carefully and completely if risks are to be avoided. By D day, all computer programs should be tested out and operational, new procedures written, people trained, and the post-conversion organization ready to go into effect. The ship should be ready for its shakedown cruise. If the ship, however, is not in fact ready, it may founder or even sink. Management should never insist that conversion take place exactly on the planned target date if the entire system-planning job has not quite been completed. One of the truisms of computer-based systems development is *Don't go if you are not ready!* Otherwise, the company may be courting disaster.

At conversion time, a good idea is to organize a temporary "fire-fighting" group made up of people trained during system development, whose mission is to assist operating personnel in the initial stages of new system operation, which is always a trying time. One of these individuals should be assigned to each department affected, to trouble-shoot, to instruct, and generally to mother operating people as they struggle to adjust to the new system.

There are four basic methods that can be employed to effect conversion. The first one is known as *parallel systems,* and the idea is to operate the new system side by side with the old one, the objective being maximum security (see Figure 17). This method is suitable for those jobs,

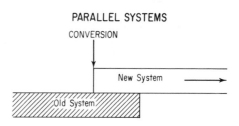

PARALLEL SYSTEMS

CONVERSION

New System

Old System

FIGURE 17

such as payroll, that must produce outputs exactly the same as before and where the outputs of the parallel systems can be validly compared. This will rarely be the case with systems that support and control business operations, because these systems, it is hoped, will be designed to do things previously impractical in terms of both output timing and output contents.

Furthermore, if post-conversion organization has been planned and implemented properly, operating personnel have been redeployed and trained to carry out new functions. It is hard to see how, unless additional people are brought in, they could effectively do their old jobs *and* their new jobs at the same time. Another general disadvantage of the parallel systems approach is the proven fact that parallel operations tend to drag on interminably, as people lean on the old familiar system and lack the incentive to make a go of the new one.

Another conversion method is the so-called *pilot system* (Figure 18). This is a fine method which should be employed wherever it is practical. Under this approach, only a small piece of the business, or of the function to be automated, is converted to the new system, while the old system is temporarily retained for the balance. An example might be a system of statistical (order-point) inventory control, where only a representative group of parts is given to the computer to handle. Performance of the pilot operation can then be observed, and any faults of the system revealed thereby can be corrected before total conversion is effected. Pilot systems remove the risk of disruption, confusion, and significant damage to the business caused by poor system planning and other system imperfections.

Unfortunately, this method cannot always be employed, because in many operating support applications such as materials planning or factory scheduling such a partial system would be either undesirable or completely impractical. Scheduling of shop operations, for instance, if done only on selected orders, would be meaningless, and the performance of the new system could not be evaluated, thus defeating the objective of the pilot system concept.

A very effective conversion method is the so-called *phase-in/phase-*

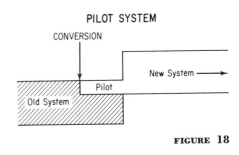

PILOT SYSTEM

FIGURE 18

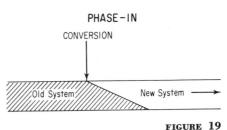

PHASE–IN

FIGURE 19

out, whereby the old system is permitted gradually to expire while the new system is phased in (Figure 19). An example of the application of this method is the introduction of new labor and production-reporting procedure into the factory, perhaps phasing-in data collection terminals to replace previous prepunched-card reporting. Instead of replacing thousands of outstanding shop packets or travelers containing the old-format cards, it is possible to institute the new procedure on top of the old one, as it were. Following conversion, all newly released packets would contain the new paperwork, and shop personnel would follow a different procedure when working on these orders. As the original shop orders are being completed, the old system is gradually washing out until it is fully replaced by the new one.

Where practical, gradual conversion methods are always preferable. Their obvious main advantage is the relative "painlessness." But in many cases these methods will not be suitable, and conversion must take place abruptly, overnight. This method is popularly known as *burning the bridges* (also "cold turkey"), and it has both disadvantages and advantages of its own (Figure 20).

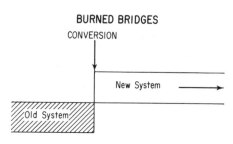

FIGURE 20

Obviously, this method of conversion requires more careful planning, with particular stress laid on well-developed fallback procedures to preclude the possibility of a major disaster such as a plant shutdown (it has happened) or invoices going out forty days late (this has happened also). The advantage of burning all bridges to the old system is mostly psychological. It provides a powerful incentive for all system user personnel to make the new system work. They realize that this is a "swim or sink" proposition, and everyone tends to swim hard to keep from drowning. This is exactly the effect that it may be desirable to create for the system shakedown period.

Chapter Eight
System
Operation

Throughout the various phases of system planning and development, it was implicitly assumed that the newly written computer programs will process valid data. The unhappy fact is that considerable effort is required to make this assumption a reality.

THE PROBLEM OF DATA

Many of the steps, decisions, and activities that take place in the time period between proposal and conversion codetermine, and set the stage for, the eventual success of a computer-based system. In the preceding chapters we reviewed and discussed many aspects of preinstallation planning. But the proof of the pudding is in the eating—and the proof of success of a computer system lies in how effectively it functions in its *operational* phase. The best system development efforts will go for naught if preinstallation planning fails to anticipate potential problems of system operation. The first and most common of these is the problem of data.

Data that the computer programs will operate on come from two sources, i.e., from files and from transactions. The discussion that follows is organized accordingly, for separate reviews of the subjects of

1. Files and data base
2. Input data integrity

FILES, DATA BASE

In a computer-based system, data files constitute the foundation on which the superstructure of applications is built. As with any foundation supporting a structure, it codetermines the soundness and utility of such a structure. The effective operation and cost efficiency of an automated comprehensive system (as against isolated applications) is, to a considerable degree, a function of *system file quality*. This quality, in turn, is reflected in the relative accuracy, up-to-dateness, and accessibility of file record information.

The business management reader may perhaps view the subject of system files as being too pedestrian and technical to merit his attention. In reality, however, the importance of file organization and file management to the success of a computer-based system is so great and its organizational, political, technical, and cost implications are such that the subject deserves a separate review. This is particularly so because of a universal tendency on the part of management to *underestimate* both the importance and the *requirements* of this part of the system planning job. The discussion that follows is conducted on two levels:

1. The general problem of *file integrity*
2. *Data base* considerations

File integrity (more precisely, the lack of same) is one important reason why many computer-based systems installed in business enterprises have failed to live up to expectations. Recent emphasis has, therefore, been focused on system files, their organization, maintenance, and accessibility. Both computer manufacturers and business computer users have realized that ambitious schemes for sophisticated information systems are unrealistic without doing some fundamental work on system foundations first. In the computer systems field, this has become known as the *back-to-basics movement.* Computer manufacturers are now investing heavily in the development of so-called file management software, and many a computer-using corporation is engaged in a system overhaul effort in which files, as well as the procedural and organizational machinery of their maintenance, are being revamped.

Something we knew all along, but tended to discount, is being forcibly brought home to us, i.e., that computer-based systems in a business will not work satisfactorily with poor files and that in the average company, files normally *are* in a rather poor condition. This seems invariably true particularly with manually maintained files of records related to product specifications (bills of material) and to the manufacturing process proper (routings, operation sheets). It is due to the fact that the rate of change affecting these—and similar—records is typically not matched by a corresponding capacity of the responsible departments to incorporate the changes into the files fully and properly.

When business functions that utilize the information contained in these files are to be automated, the respective files typically must be overhauled, restructured, recoded, and updated. This is usually recognized, and file cleanup is carried out as a subproject of the system implementation effort. But *fixing* something is one thing and *keeping it fixed* is another. Files tend to deteriorate following the conclusion of the fixup effort. The reason for this is the extreme difficulty of maintaining any file that contains other than static information. This difficulty is indeed the real cause of the original sad state of file data.

The task of file maintenance not only is difficult but requires such a large effort that it becomes, in practice, virtually impossible to keep a voluminous file complete and updated under manual methods, with the meager resources normally allocated for this function. A classic example is the average manufacturing routing file, which consists of several tens of thousands of records encompassing active, inactive, semiobsolete, and obsolete parts. Each of these records carries the prescribed sequence of operations, their descriptions, the routing to the various departments and machine tools within these, job standards, and the required tooling, not to mention part master data in the record header.

This file is constantly affected by so many changes in manufacturing method, standards, tooling, engineering changes, machine tool procurement, downgrading and retirement, shop reorganizations, etc., that true file maintenance becomes a nightmare. This is so because many types of change (such as the adoption of a new class of cutting tools, changes in departmental boundaries, or the acquisition of new productive equipment) literally explode throughout the file. A single such change may call for hundreds, or even thousands, of parts to be rerouted, operations to be added or deleted, and methods, standards, and tooling revised accordingly. The magnitude of the file maintenance job, in relation to its staffing, is simply such that it precludes anything much better than hit-or-miss maintenance.

The key to this problem is the staffing and budget provided for file maintenance, which, in most cases, is simply insufficient. The planners of computer-based systems usually recognize that files must be reorganized and updated, that in some cases the complexity of their structure must be *increased,* and that these files will have to be rigorously maintained in the future if the new system is to function properly.

Such demands often run into strong opposition by the heads of departments responsible for maintaining these files, because they foresee the increase in file maintenance cost, which *has not been budgeted*. Furthermore, since these department heads are being measured on the cost-performance of their functions, they will be reluctant to request additional funds for the maintenance of files to new, higher standards, particularly when they themselves are not the primary beneficiaries of increased file data integrity. Even when forced to augment their capacity for file maintenance, they may tend to bleed it at times of various departmental crises and, particularly, during cost-cutting drives. File maintenance may be economized on without the consequences becoming immediately apparent—but it may eventually prove fatal to the computer system.

It is interesting to reflect on our apparent blindness as to the true scope of the file maintenance task, which we *prejudge to be trivial*, perhaps because it is so routine and uninteresting. Business management has traditionally been reluctant to face up to this problem, yet even the old manual systems were built around the implicit assumption of file data integrity, and violations of this assumption impaired the effectiveness of such systems. Because these systems were entirely people-based, they got by without rigorous file maintenance thanks to the ability of human beings to improvise and to make up for deficiencies of procedure and file information. Because a machine lacks this ability, rigorous file maintenance is *imperative* in computer-based systems.

There is more to file maintenance than meets the eye. If there is one thing that people learn, sometimes painfully, from developing computer-based systems, it is that original file data are of unacceptably low quality, that therefore files must be fixed, that they must be *kept* fixed, and that keeping them fixed will take more cost and effort than anyone would have expected. In computer-based systems planning, it would be well to consider the axiom that *File maintenance cost will significantly exceed original estimates.*

In the future, either we have to be prepared to live with the high cost of file maintenance and look at it as one of the prices we pay for having a computer-based system, or we must find ways of transferring at least part of this burden to the computer itself. Fortunately, as computer manufacturers now realize that data files constitute system foundations, they are developing and furnishing various aids for file management. The philosophy of system file management and the pertinent techniques are embodied in the so-called *data base* concept.

The data base consists of one or more data files, and the various functions pertaining thereto are collectively known under such labels as "data management," "data base management," "file management," and "information management" systems. There are two classes of data that computer programs operate on, i.e., *input data* (transactions) and *file data*. In the current data processing terminology, terms such as "data control," "data management," "data base," etc., pertain to file data alone.

The term "data base" (sometimes also "data bank") is not merely a fancy name for a set of system files. It has some special connotations as to the characteristics of such files. The most significant attribute of a data base is its *commonness*, i.e., system files serving as a common base for a variety of applications and subsystems. Under older methods, the various departments and functional groups of a business maintained their own files, with file record information being organized so as to suit the particular needs of each individual department. This included a considerable amount of redundancy and data duplication.

For example, a typical inventory control record contained data such as the following:

1. Part number
2. Part description
3. Standard cost
4. Raw material used (for manufactured parts)
5. Purchase-order quantity or quantity discounts (for purchased parts)
6. Where-used information

All the above data was duplicated in at least one, and sometimes all, of the following different record files:

1. Cost sheets
2. Purchased parts records
3. Routings
4. Engineering drawings
5. Service part price (billing) records
6. Stores location records

When these files are transferred to, and centralized in, a computer system, such duplication would be prohibitive in terms of both cost of storage (perhaps in random-access devices) and cost of maintenance.

In setting up a data base for a computer system, the goal of file efficiency is reflected in the twin objectives of

1. Eliminating or minimizing data duplication, redundancy, different file "versions," and different update levels
2. Optimizing file access and its economy

These are *conflicting objectives*. If the files were stored in their original state, with the duplicated data that made them self-sufficient for the respective application, access would be fast and economical, but cost of storage and maintenance would be excessive. If the duplication is eliminated, it means either that several files must be accessed to retrieve a set of data required for a given application or that files have been consolidated and now contain large records.

In the latter case, sequential processing (e.g., magnetic tape, where every file record, whether needed or not, must be read into and out of memory in each data processing run) will have become quite inefficient, and in random-access processing, multiple accesses for selective data retrieval may be necessary. In either case, larger main-memory capacity will be required to accommodate the large records when they are read in.

It can be seen from this dilemma that the problem is one of determining the best file organization that would balance the advantages and disadvantages. The problem is further compounded, however, by another objective of the data base concept, which is *application independence*. If the number, nature, and frequency of applications were fixed, it would be possible to tailor file organization to these applications in a way that would optimize overall efficiency. But the goal is the opposite—a data base should be organized independently of applications and should serve as a common foundation for all applications and subsystems, both *planned and unplanned*.

In principle, this is a sound objective, because the nature and frequency of applications are subject to change and unknown future applications must not require a reorganization of the data base, which is a major and costly undertaking. Conversely, a change in the organization of a file should not require the modification of all programs which use that file. The best method of accomplishing this is a technical system problem that has not yet been fully resolved. Special software may be interposed between programs and files, so as to minimize this problem.

When we consider what happens (and must happen) to files when they become a part of a computer system data base, another significant characteristic of the data base concept emerges. It is the requirement that files can no longer "belong" to the departments in which they originated. In a modern computer-based system, *information is not "owned" by any one business function*, in the sense that departments which traditionally had autonomous jurisdiction over the contents and format of the respective record files can no longer exercise such authority. This is because records have been stripped of redundant and duplicate data, files have been reorganized and perhaps consolidated, and now serve as a *common* base of *all* applications.

The implications of this development are far-reaching and merit the business manager's particular attention. The establishment of a data base has *organizational and political repercussions*. If the file "owners" lose their former prerogatives and file data now belongs to all, it follows that new, *central organizational machinery* must be established to administer the various functions of file data management, with exclusive authority over file organization, record formats, and system standards (for more on standards, see Chapter 9).

The data base concept provides a classic example of management implications springing from a computer system development effort that, on the surface, may appear purely technical. Computer-aided automation of business functions is characterized by its universality and all-pervasiveness, and the attention and involvement of the business executive is imperative. The data base example shows perhaps most clearly and most forcefully the price of management aloofness and disinterest.

Where the business executive does not understand the organizational and political consequences of data base development and fails to step in to make decisions and give backing to new operating policy, the problem will tend to go unresolved. There will be friction, dissatisfaction, and a serious impairment of the data-base-oriented system. The quality of the data base and the control over this quality are so vital to the proper functioning of a computer-based system that the executive's failure will be reflected in the failure of the system. If system malfunctioning represents a relative failure, the true failure lies in the fact that the computer is not fulfilling its potential for the benefit of the business.

The file management functions mentioned earlier consist of the following:

1. File creation
2. File organization
3. Providing for file access
4. File updating (i.e., transaction processing)
5. File maintenance
6. Establishing inquiry capability
7. Report generation

Some of the above represent largely technical considerations that need not be elaborated on here. Three of these functions, and the problems associated with them, however, merit a review for the benefit of the business management reader. They are file maintenance, already discussed, and the closely related functions of file organization and file access or data retrieval.

A file is made up of a set of like records. Each record, in turn, consists of a number of *fields* containing the various pertinent data or *data elements*. Each record has a *key*, i.e., a field or data element that serves as the main identification of that record. The key is the identifier by which the record is found in the file. Examples are the employee name in a personnel file, the man number in a payroll file, and the part number in an inventory control file. Each file is organized in the sequence of its key.

The file organization and file access problems arise when we wish to retrieve some data other than the key. Such data, although they occupy the same field in each of the records, are not (and cannot be) sequenced in their own right, and therefore it is not possible to find (access and retrieve) them directly, without more or less excessive scanning of the file. In a data base arrangement, this problem is crucial and must be solved through one or more techniques of information retrieval.

If the record (or records) containing the desired data cannot be accessed directly, it must be accessed indirectly, through either of the following:

1. A file *scan* (always possible but most inefficient)
2. A separately maintained *index*
3. A linked record or *chain*

The problem and some of the available solution techniques can best be illustrated using a commonly known file such as a phone directory. A phone book is, in effect, a set of records pertaining to telephone users. Each of these records is made up of three or four fields, i.e.,

1. Name
2. Business or occupation (optional)
3. Street address
4. Telephone number

The name is the key, and the file is, of course, organized in alphabetic sequence. It is not difficult to envision this file residing in computer random-access storage (the application rules out tape) and to pretend that in retrieving information from the phone book we act as a computer program. If we wish to learn the telephone number of someone named Morris, we break the book open somewhere in its third fourth from the beginning, as we are familiar with the key and its sequence and know approximately where to look for the letter M. From the page we have opened, we then conduct a partial file scan, until the desired record is located.

The logic of this technique can be programmed for a computer to follow, by setting up a subsidiary record (which we carry in our head) or *index*, that might indicate, for instance, the range of storage addresses (phone book pages) for each letter of the alphabet. This index would be consulted first, and the subsequent scan would be accordingly limited. But here we are dealing with the name, i.e., the key itself, which in computer systems is not a problem at all, as a number of techniques for minimizing scans or even accessing the record directly are available.

The real problem would arise were we to seek information such as

1. Whose number is 322-7593?
2. Which names represent restaurants?
3. What are all the names with a 48th Street address?

The telephone directory contains all of this information, but how do we locate it short of a total scan? The phone book solves problem No. 2 by means of yellow pages, which represent a duplicate file of the same records organized by a different key, i.e., occupation or business. In a computer system, such record duplication would be unnecessary, as the yellow pages file would only need to contain the names of the restaurants (the key of the primary file) but no street addresses or telephone numbers, which can be extracted by going back to the name records. Such record linkage represents *chaining*, as the contents of one record *point to*, or lead to, the location of another record.

If query No. 1 above were frequent, an index to telephone numbers could be constructed; e.g., all pages on which the prefix 322 appears could be listed in a separate record, along with similar records for all the other prefixes. This would create another small subsidiary file, to be consulted for purposes of limiting file search. Obviously, a more extensive index would limit the search still further, but at the expense of storing a larger subsidiary file. Problem No. 3 could be solved similarly.

It can be seen that if a file is to serve multiple applications, including unspecified future ones, a host of file organization and data retrieval problems arise. The objective of eliminating duplication must be compromised to some extent, and various indices, new chain fields in existing records, and subsidiary record files must be created.

The reader should note that all the data being stored to facilitate retrieval must be *maintained*. As changes are made in the primary records, they must be reflected in the chain structures, indices, etc. The cost of storing and maintaining the subsidiary records represents the tradeoff between the efficiency and economy of file storage on one hand, and the efficiency and economy of data retrieval on the other.

A special case of the file organization and record retrieval problem are two or more files that are interactive but differently organized, which cannot, because of their nature, be made similar in organization or consolidated. An example of this phenomenon is the relationship between a product structure file (Figure 21) containing part numbers arranged by subassembly contents and a file containing a single record for each part number, such as an inventory file or a cost file. For certain applications, such as the calculation of net material requirements or a standard cost buildup, the pair of related files must be processed in conjunction.

PRODUCT STRUCTURE

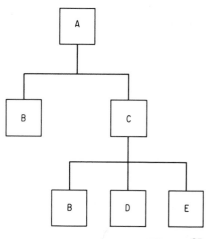

FIGURE 21

The problem is one of record linkage, and it is aggravated by the fact that there is no one-for-one relationship between part number records of the two files. The problem is solved through chaining, i.e., storing in one record the address of a related record which, in turn, may contain the address of another related record. Computer manufacturers have developed, and have made available to their customers, generalized application software packages to handle this problem. These programs are called *Bill of Material Processors*, after their initial application, but they have a much wider applicability. They can be used wherever one of two interactive files represents structure and the other is a master file containing single records for each existing component of the structure.

The bill of material processor programs usually combine the capabilities of file organization, retrieval, and maintenance. The chaining, as represented in Figure 22, is of two kinds, tracing either down (so-called *explosion*) or up (where-used, *implosion*) the product structure.

Thus when calculating material requirements, the chain from assembly record A in the master file leads to the bill of material record of A, which lists as its components B and C. These component records, in turn, chain back to their respective master records in the first file,

CHAINING OF FILES

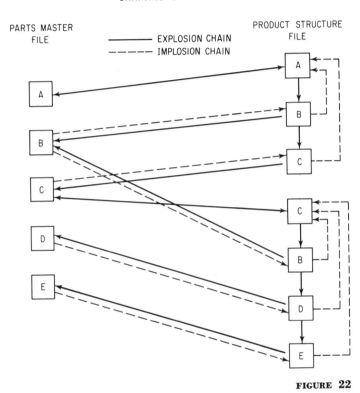

FIGURE 22

so that these can be updated. As C is an assembly in its own right, it has a bill of material record in the product structure file, to which it is also chained. For purposes of tracing *up* the product structure, chains lead from each record of the master file to *all* corresponding records in the other file (see part B). Each component record in the bill of material file is also chained to its parent assembly record in that file.

In a standard cost buildup application, if the cost of part B increased $2, the where-used chaining will assure that the cost increase is carried from master record B to product structure records B and C, from there back to master record C, and again to product structure records C and A, and finally back to master record A, increasing its cost by $4.

A layman might be under the impression that the tremendous speed of a computer enables it to find anything in a file as quick as lightning and that therefore not all the data retrieval aids are necessary. Why are they necessary? Because even microseconds add up. If the Manhattan phone directory, which contains just under 1 million names, were to be scanned from a disk file, assuming that each record were accessed individually (rather than in blocks of records) at 50 milliseconds per access cycle, the total search time would amount to 13 hours.

To conclude the discussion of file and data base considerations, a recap of the main points brought out in the above analysis indicates the following:

1. The scope and costliness of file maintenance in general should not be underestimated.

2. When implementing the data base concept, an organizational solution to the file management problem must be found and authorized by company management.

3. Authority over data base record formats and maintenance standards must be split away from the responsibility for record maintenance —the former to be given to *staff*, the latter to remain with *line*.

4. A compromise, or tradeoff, must be sought between the efficiency of file storage and the efficiency of data retrieval.

5. No effort should be spared and the best available talent should be used for data base architecture, which, at present, is more of an art than a well-defined science.

INPUT DATA INTEGRITY

In Chapter 2 we indicated that a computer, unlike a human being, functions with full success only in a "perfect" environment, which would include error-free, complete, and timely data. When data lack integrity, a computer system tends to fail. The seriousness of the consequences will vary with the application. It may be minor where the computer is used as an analytical tool or rapid-fire calculator. In these cases, resulting outputs are used for evaluation or as an intermediate step within some larger function, but they do not reflect operating decisions.

In computer-based operating support systems, however, many such decisions are programmed for the computer to make. In this type of application, where day-to-day tasks and functions of the business are being handled automatically, system failure may have far-reaching consequences. Low-quality input data heavily contribute to such failure and particularly plague newly developed systems once they go into operation.

The quality of input data varies with their source. Accounting data are, as a rule, the most error-free, followed by engineering, purchasing, production control, and marketing data, in roughly that order. The incidence of error is always the highest, however, in the labor and production data being generated in factory operations, particularly where production workers themselves report (by whatever means) their activities to the system.

In this category of data, which are fed into payroll, cost accounting, and production control functions, the opportunity for committing errors is extensive. Production workers, truckers, stockroom and tool crib employees, expediters, dispatchers, industrial engineers, and foremen contribute data, and all are in position to introduce many different *types* of error. In an average-sized plant with fairly complex payroll, routing, and production control systems, anywhere between 100 and 300 different types of error in factory-generated data may be recognized.

Error rates typically run between 1 (very good) and 3 percent of transactions collected. Thus a job shop with 1,000 employees, which may report, say, 7,000 labor, production, and materials movement transactions per day, can be expected to generate 100 or 200 errors every day. Input data errors cannot be entirely prevented, but it is important that their *effect* be corrected and their impact on the functioning of the system minimized.

The wise system planner *anticipates* the problem of faulty input data and accordingly exploits all avenues open to him for combatting this problem, prior to the operational phase of the system. He knows that *Input data integrity results from education, discipline, system checks, and the capability to investigate and correct.*

Education of the people who will be in a position to generate input data is the most effective error-preventive means available, and its importance cannot be overstressed. Only education will make people realize the importance of proper computer system inputs and their individual responsibility in this respect. Psychologically, if the employee is made to feel that he is a vital cog in the system machinery, he is more likely to cooperate in making the system work rather than trying to "beat" it.

Discipline enforcement, i.e., assuring adherence to procedure, strict observance of cutoff times, and vigilance to ensure the completeness of data that must be supplied for a proper *data flow,* is a management responsibility. Management on all operating levels will have to be educated to this responsibility—and top management will have to demand it.

System checks, both external and internal, will be developed by an experienced system planner as part of the overall system design, and a qualified programmer, who knows that a computer possesses an outstanding ability to check and police its own operation, can incorporate many editing, self-checking, and self-correcting features into a program. The "war" against input errors should be conducted on three separate fronts, i.e.,

1. Erection of a *barrier* to keep errors from entering the system

2. Programmed capability to *detect internally* most of the errors that get through the barrier

3. A procedure for *washing out* of the system the *residue* of undetected errors

The barrier, or filter, against input errors can consist of a number of procedures and techniques. Some form of input audit is recommended, wherever feasible. When new computer-based systems are first launched into operation, many companies establish, at least temporarily, a new job of input data auditor or coding clerk, whose function is to examine transaction entries for correctness of form and content before they are submitted to the computer system for processing. In addition to the value of spotting many errors that otherwise would enter the system, what recommends this approach also is the fact that during the system "shakedown" period, sources of particularly high rates of error are identified. This allows correction *at the source* and also indicates specific deficiencies of education and procedure, which can then also be remedied.

Another part of the barrier against errors is a programmed capability of the computer system to detect and *reject* incorrect transactions at the point of entry, i.e., immediately following the input step and before processing begins. A variety of techniques can be used to test the formal validity of transaction entries, but one merits special mention—the *self-checking digit.*

To provide a dependable basis for the checking of a numerical piece of data, such as part number, order number, account, etc., a so-called self-checking digit can be *computed from* the original number and then appended to it, so as to form its integral part. As such data are entered into the computer, the self-checking digit is immediately recomputed and tested against the digit shown. If it does not match, it is proof of either transposition or some other kind of error.

A convenient example of the use of self-checking digits is the account code on many credit cards (American Express, Carte Blanche, Esso, etc.). This number usually consists of ten digits, the last one of which is computed from the preceding nine. The calculation for account code, say, *193-958-466-8* is performed as follows:

1. Starting with the next-to-last digit, and proceeding from right to left, double every other digit, with a carry to the next value to be doubled.

$$\frac{1\ 9\ 3\ -\ 9\ 5\ 8\ -\ 4\ 6\ 6\ -\ 8}{2\ \ \ 7\ \ \ 0\ \ \ 9\ \ \ 2}$$

2. Insert digits that have not been doubled, except the last.

$$2\ 9\ 7\ \ \ 9\ 0\ 8\ \ \ 9\ 6\ 2$$

3. Add up these digits: *52*
4. Subtract last digit of result from *10* to obtain self-checking digit.

$$\begin{array}{r} 10 \\ -\ 2 \\ \hline 8 \end{array}$$

It can be seen that, if any two digits are transposed, or if the value of any one digit is erroneously recorded manually, or in key punching, the self-checking digit will not add up to eight and the error will be detected. Key punching has not been mentioned as a possible source of errors, but it will, of course, contribute its share, even though very small.

In this connection, it should be noted that data containing self-checking digits can be tested at the point of key punching, thus preventing any errors (whether on the source document or introduced by key punching) from getting past this step. An attachment is available for most key punches which calculates the self-checking digit as the punching progresses, so that the machine "knows" the value of this digit before the last key is struck. If the last digit punched is different from what the machine expects, it will signal the error at once.

The use of self-checking digits is highly recommended, because they provide an extremely effective check that can be routinely carried out by a computer in a matter of microseconds. To the extent that the type of error this technique detects can have serious consequences in a particular application (in inventory control, for instance, an erroneous part number causes the wrong record to be updated, thus rendering *two* records invalid, including the one that *should* have been updated), the expense of incorporating self-checking digits into the system, including perhaps changing the part-numbering scheme, will most likely be a worthwhile investment.

Beyond a formal check such as is possible with self-checking digits, for instance, so-called *diagnostic routines* can be programmed that will conduct other tests prior to the actual processing of input data. For example, the part number, self-checking digit and all, can be correct, but a diagnostic test against an open order file may indicate that no order has been issued against this part number. Or a man reports production against an operation that has previously been deleted from the route sheet.

These diagnostic tests, conducted against files other than those to be updated or against special tables set up for this purpose, cost something in terms of extra processing time, but for computer applications in areas of high input-data error rates they should by all means be programmed. A great variety of this type of check is possible, and when carried out in a computer, it is the swiftest and most efficient way of "catching" errors.

Internal detection, during the actual processing, of errors that get past the barrier discussed above, is also an important system capability that can usually be programmed in. It is distinguished from diagnostic tests mainly by the fact that the checks are made against the file being updated. An example might be a stock withdrawal transaction that passes both input audit and diagnostic tests but is *substantively* incorrect, i.e., reports a withdrawal quantity that exceeds the quantity previously on hand. Or a production worker reports his man number, account code, department worked in, etc., correctly but is signing off an indirect labor activity he never signed in on.

An entirely different kind of test, called *test of reasonableness,* can sometimes also be employed. In an inventory control application, for example, if the usage of a given part averages 100 per month, a computer-generated requirement for month X of 1,000 or 5,000 is almost certainly invalid. A man spots and questions such absurdities immediately—and a computer can be programmed to do the same.

In some cases, a properly programmed computer will be able, if not actually to correct the error, at least to trace it to its source, i.e., to the particular input tape, or disk file record, from which it came. This will facilitate investigation and correction. But as far as a test of reasonableness is concerned, even if the computer program is unable to trace the error in a given case, it can always, by applying this test, *flag* the results that are suspect. The computer can tell the recipient of its output not to use the information without verifying it first.

Washing out residues of errors that escaped detection through other means is a must if the system is to be kept from gradually (perhaps very gradually) deteriorating. It should always be assumed that at least some small proportion of errors in input data will penetrate the system despite all barriers and checks. These errors may be forever undetectable as such, but procedures should be devised to detect their *effect* on system files, and it is this effect that must be removed. This is accomplished by means of various *reconciliation, purging,* and *close-out* procedures. They are analogous to writing off, periodically, miscellaneous small unpaid balances in the accounts receivable file. Examples of this type of procedure are the reconciliation of planned versus actual requirements of a part number, or forecast versus actual demand, the purging of long-unrelieved load from a machine load file, or the closing out of ancient shop or purchase orders that still show some small quantity due.

It is a safe assumption that most systems in the business applications area contain some (small, we hope) percentage of error at all times. This can be tolerated as long as such system-resident errors do not accumulate. Even an accumulation at a minute rate must eventually smother the system. As far as the washing out of error residues is concerned, it is less important how soon after the fact the effect of an error is removed, but all-important that it be removed at some scheduled interval. If a certain level of residual error is inherent to the system, let us keep it constant.

The ability to investigate and correct is a separate and, with newly launched computer-based systems, new function. It is important that it be planned—and budgeted—as part of the new system operation. The capacity and the staffing to do this must be there when the first errors are detected, or else the unresolved errors will snowball and constitute, very quickly, an investigation/correction workload that may prove unmanageable. There have been some instances in industry where this point has been overlooked by system planners, and the oversight led to rather massive fiascos of computer-based systems.

The capacity for investigation and correction pertains to errors detected by all the means enumerated above, plus errors revealed in system *outputs.* There should be the capacity to get at any of these errors quickly, particularly as certain types of error can play hide-and-seek. If left alone, they seem to go away, but they do not really, and will be back. An example of a negative on-hand balance in an inventory record was mentioned above. If not corrected, the next receipt will wipe it out, and the record is to all appearances correct again. In this case, it could be years before the physical stock is once more depleted to the point that would cause the record to turn negative.

We have mentioned the requirement for reconciling data within records. But wherever possible, record data should also be methodically reeonciled with the real physical world. Regular inventory cycle counts, work-in-process checks, and even the less recommended annual physical inventory taking (which often introduces more new errors than it corrects of the old ones) belong in this category. Inventory cycle counts can be coordinated with a computer system for maximum efficiency of this function.

The easiest (and most dependable!) count is at the time the supply of the material drops to a low point. Computer programs can be written to keep track of this, and the system can generate requests for counts automatically. In addition to regular cyclical counts, capability should exist to conduct a count of a specific item at random times, per buyer or inventory analyst request, whenever there is some question about the actual status of such an item.

In conclusion, it can be said that a lack of input data integrity always represents a dangerous situation, because it impairs the usefulness of a computer-based system otherwise well designed and well implemented. A mechanism for a systematic flushing out of errors should be established. Its function is analogous to that of kidneys in an animal organism. If the system poisons are not constantly being eliminated, the system gets sicker and sicker until it dies eventually, i.e., deteriorates to the point of uselessness.

It is not enough to learn how to operate the system without necessarily understanding its internal structure. A pilot merely flies the plane, but the business manager should be able to modify the system in addition to "flying" it.

POST-CONVERSION OPERATION

On a number of occasions during earlier discussions, reference has been made to the operational phase of a computer-based system. Let us now review these references and examine their implications.

Previous discussion generally alluded to the fact that the existence of a new system will affect the mode of operation, and the organization, of user departments. The impact can be expected to be such that these departments will never be the same again, because the installation of a computer-based system will change the operating environment within user departments and may cause profound transformation of the *job contents* of their personnel, including operating managers.

Such changes are the logical consequence of the improvement in the capacity to handle information. The original division of labor had been dictated by the low information-processing capacity of the old system. Hence previous procedures and methods will likely be obsoleted once a new computer-based system goes into operation, and personnel may have to be redeployed to fit in with the new operating pattern.

If difficulties with system operation are to be avoided, these questions must be resolved *prior to* the start of the operational phase. Planning post-conversion organization is one of the tasks of system implementation. For purposes of discussing considerations pertaining to the system operational phase proper, we can distinguish between what we might call the system "shakedown period" and the regular operation following this period.

THE SHAKEDOWN PERIOD

This is the immediate post-conversion period, when the new computer system "goes on the air" and a new mode of operation begins. This is always a rather trying time for everyone concerned, as usually adjustments must abruptly be made to the new situation. The difficulty and confusion of the shakedown period will be in inverse proportion to the care with which conversion has been planned and specific methods of dealing with anticipated trouble have been developed.

We may think of this period as another form of debugging. This time the overall system, including the new operating procedures and the new departmental organization, is being *tested* under operating conditions. Bugs in the *application,* i.e., in the *use* of the computer system (as against bugs in its programming), may be discovered and will require correction. Depending on the nature of such bugs, computer programs may or may not be affected. Sometimes it may only be the (manual) procedure external to the computer system, or the way operating personnel implement the new procedure, that requires correction.

In cases of some obvious malfunction of the computer system during the shakedown period, operating people tend to attribute the difficulty to the poor quality of programming. Before blaming the programmers, one should be careful, however, to distinguish between

1. Errors resulting from faulty instructions executing valid procedure
2. The logic of the procedure behind the instructions

In the latter case of an invalid procedure being correctly executed by the computer program, the system's designers and not the programmers are at fault.

For the duration of the shakedown period, it is a wise course of action not to disband and reassign the whole project task force in anticipation of perfection. The new system, and its computer programs, may require some quick fixes, or *patching*. It is better to have the system development talent standing by temporarily than trying to reassemble it under conditions of emergency.

Backup procedures, discussed earlier in Chapter 7 on System Development Phases, may have to be called into play in the case of system malfunction, and if this becomes necessary, it will prove important to have had operating personnel properly trained in switching to such procedures, so that the operation of the business can go on despite any difficulty with the new system. In areas of critical importance, "fire drills" may be a good idea, to preclude confusion in case of an actual system failure.

Some companies have even organized, and trained, special teams of "firemen" (see also the discussion of conversion, above) to be assigned, during the immediate post-conversion period, to the various operating departments affected by the new computer system. These individuals trouble-shoot, advise operating personnel on the proper use of the system, and in general "hold their hands" during the system shakedown period, so as to smooth the transition.

REGULAR OPERATION

It would be unrealistic not to expect that changes will, sooner or later, affect the operation of a computer-based system. Eventually, there will develop a need to make changes in the application, i.e., in the business function itself, as the environment in which the business must operate changes. There will be new products, new facilities, new competition, new laws. On the other hand, computer program revisions may be desirable for reasons that have nothing to do with the business operation.

Such changes may result from computer system growth, as we discussed in Chapter 4. There may be engineering changes in the computer equipment and changes in the software. There will be changes in the configuration of the computer system. Changes continue, feed upon themselves, and each one can potentially disable the system if proper adjustments are not made.

Regular system operation represents a (continuous) phase of *system maintenance* on several levels. We have already discussed the problem of file maintenance and its importance. But the problem of maintenance is more general. Not only files, but the whole system, including its supporting procedures, its programs, and even the competence of people in using the system, must be maintained.

Psychological factors have also a direct and important bearing on the success of system operation. How effectively a computer-based system actually functions can better be determined by observing the people using it than by a study of the computer and its programming. Symptoms of an unsatisfactorily functioning system will be reflected in the behavior of individuals whose normal duties are in some measure affected by the existence of the computer system.

If employees do not show a sense of understanding of the system and of its purpose—if they do not accept responsibility for its results—system operation can become a serious problem. User personnel action can and does injure the integrity of a system. The following are examples of how operating personnel can impair the performance of a computer-based system otherwise well designed and installed. These examples seem humorous, but they are all taken from life and represent an extremely undesirable situation.

First, there is the oldtimer who cannot bring himself to believe that the right answers could actually come out of the newfangled machine. He diligently checks all the figures in the report that he works with, uses the old time-tested method to arrive at comparative data, and if the results do not match (they rarely do), always gives the old approach the benefit of the doubt and takes action accordingly.

Then there is the man who does not like what the system is recommending (the purchase order quantity is too low, the priority assigned to a factory job is too high), overrides it, but does not bother to have the *logic* of the computer program, which arrived at these unsatisfactory answers, changed. The volume of such overrides should be monitored, as it indicates either that the system's logic is poor, or that people are not using the system properly, or both.

Similar, but not the same, is the case of the man who receives a document prepared by the computer (job instructions, tool requisition, a bill of material) which contains an error, corrects it with a pencil, but fails to report it so that the faulty record in the system's file could be corrected. This ensures that next time the same document is produced, it will contain the same error.

Another example is the party who "keeps his own records." Perhaps the computer-generated output he gets fails to suit his needs, or his mistrust of the new system is total. Either way, a problem is indicated whenever people feel the need for building a protective wall between themselves and the computer system. Clandestine "unofficial" records sometimes found in foremen's and clerk's desks may mean that system files are not properly maintained—a sure cause of system deterioration.

Yet another example of system misuse is the person who "does not tell" the computer or who "lies" to it. Take the case of a buyer whose procedure instructs him that when he receives a shipment of castings that is short of the quantity ordered, and he closes out the order anyhow, he is to fill out a partial order cancellation card and through it inform the system of what has happened. If he attaches little importance to this instruction and forgets to fill out the card, the computer will forever expect the balance of the original order to be shipped. When the computer next time orders this casting in a low quantity (23 are still on open order!), the same buyer makes disparaging remarks about the machine's intelligence and, of course, overrides it once again.

The stockroom clerk who returns a preprinted stores receipt without change even though he received a different quantity of the part, or the production worker who reports completion of more pieces than he, in fact, produced, lie to the computer which takes them at their word and updates its records in an invalid fashion.

Today's computer-based systems are imperfect, and therefore dependent on their users' support. Indifferent or hostile users can defeat a system by a number of means including passive resistance, refusing to exercise judgment in interpreting the computer's output, and following prescribed procedures blindly.

When a new system is not introduced properly, it creates problems of morale. Employees, including professional personnel and operating managers, may undergo an undesirable change in attitude. Those who have to use the outputs being generated by the computer can easily develop feelings of insecurity and frustration, particularly when they regard the computer system as having been designed by "experts" or outsiders who are out of touch with the real world. Just how successfully a computer-based system will function depends a lot on whether its users possess a proprietary feeling toward it. The lack of such a feeling or a measure of pride in the system spells trouble for its operation.

Problems of employee morale, and their adverse effect on the performance of the system, stem from the following factors:

1. Lack of participation in the development of the system
2. Insufficient or improper education, or even a total absence of an education program
3. Lack of concern and positive leadership on the part of operating management
4. Aloofness, lack of commitment, or uncertainty on the part of top management

This last factor, especially, is sensed by the rest of the organization. The leader casts a long shadow, and his indifference will reduce the chances for the system's success.

The process of employee education should be carried on by first-line managers throughout the operational phase of the system. They should motivate people so that they see their role in regard to the computer system as not being to question, verify, and override, but rather to act toward maintaining and improving the system logic.

Operating personnel who communicate with the computer—the buyer, the inventory analyst, the receiving dock foreman, the factory dispatcher, or worker reporting through a terminal—should be made to realize that it is they who actually operate the computer through the data they feed it. They should be made to understand that the computer is their tool and servant, that *they* have effective control over sections of the system files containing records that are their responsibility, and consequently, that they share in the responsibility for the computer system performance.

An important consideration of the regular operation phase of a computer-based system is the training of new employees coming into user departments. This question has previously been brought up in the discussion of education as a system development phase. Procedures and educational aids for the indoctrination of new people on how to work with the computer system should be a routine part of regular operation.

This brings up the interesting question of how a future manager, appointed from the outside to take over a department which operates under a computer-based system, will learn, *if he will be able to* learn, the internal logic and the makeup of the computer system he will perforce have to use as his most important tool. How will he be able to verify the system outputs? We have raised this question previously, as part of the discussion of system complexity. We recommended against complexity of system design, but in the longer run some measure of complexity, resulting from an expansion of scope, an increase in sophistication, and the attainment of higher levels of automation, probably cannot entirely be avoided.

Education, good documentation, and perhaps something on the order of a Link trainer used for aircraft pilot training (to let the man practice under simulated conditions before permitting him to take control of a complex mechanism) are the obvious answers. But with a system sufficiently complex, this may not be enough. Unlike in the airplane example, computer-based systems used for the control of business operations require more than learning how to *operate* the system without necessarily understanding its internal structure. The pilot merely flies the plane, but the business manager should be able to *modify* the system in addition to "flying" it.

The operating manager of the future will, in fact, be less of an *operator* and more of a system custodian, system maintainer, and system improver. Instead of *driving*, he will manage his function by *interpreting* computer system–generated information so as to present alternative courses of action, and their consequences, to top management. But as his information requirements change, he will have to be able to translate them into corresponding system changes. Whether he can make requests for such changes intelligently will depend on how well versed he is in the internal system logic.

Will the business manager of the future be able to learn enough about the internal logic of a complex system? This is an intriguing question to which there is no satisfactory answer known at present. It can serve as food for thought about how to deal with a management problem that now only looms on the horizon and for which special solution techniques may yet have to be invented. This problem, if it persists, may put an end to certain current management practices, such as promoting management personnel from one division of the business to another or hiring operating managers (and executives) from outside the corporation where management replacement talent has not been grown and cultivated on the inside.

If, in the future, computer systems make promotion from the inside a necessity, this will force management to develop competent "home-grown" successor talent. The computer may act to improve the management of business even *that* way.

Chapter Nine
Corporate Systems Considerations

Distinction should be drawn between functional and physical centralization; with respect to the latter, we should distinguish between the location of computer equipment and that of system and programming talent.

CENTRALIZATION AND DECENTRALIZATION

Time and again during previous discussions, we brought out different aspects of how the introduction of computers into business operations affects the enterprise itself. The impact of computers on operating, organizational, and management patterns is undeniable. Because of the tremendous new communications and information handling capacity that computer systems represent, user companies, and the thinking of their management, are changing and in the longer run will change profoundly.

One thing that is already under pressure to change is the management philosophy of decentralization. Industrial corporations today can be labeled as centralized or decentralized according to various criteria, of which the important ones are the degrees of operating autonomy and independent profit responsibility granted to individual divisions, plants, and other local operations of a corporation. The degree of local autonomy is in inverse relationship to the amount of direction and direct control over operations being exercised by corporate management.

By these criteria, we can classify small companies, single-location companies, and companies with homogeneous product lines as tending to have centralized management control, whereas large multidivision and multilocation corporations generally, and conglomerates particularly, are likely to be decentralized.

Does the advent of the computer point to a recentralization of management control over operations in companies that in the past have been organized, and have functioned, under the philosophy of decentralization? At present, this question is tinged with controversy. The tendency of the past has been to represent decentralization as having superior inherent value, as being desirable for its own sake. But in fact, this made a virtue of necessity. Decentralization, which has both advantages and disadvantages, was always *dictated* by the limited span of control that men individually, and corporate managements collectively, possess. The span of control is really a function of time required to be devoted to a job, in view of such communications and information processing capacity as exists.

In the past, when a business exceeded a certain point in its size, and when remote operating facilities had to be established, it became simply *impossible* to manage centrally, primarily because of delay in lines of communication and sluggishness of the flow of information. But now, in companies with installed computer systems which are becoming more and more comprehensive, integrated, and communications-oriented, the opportunity for centralization, or recentralization, is becoming a reality This makes the question of centralization less academic and more a matter of practicality. With extensive and advanced computer systems the formerly compelling reason for decentralization is gone. If corporate management can *have* the information required to control operations, it *can* control them.

The trend in favor of recentralization of management control is already clearly discernible in industry at present. As computers become more universally, and better, utilized, this trend is bound to become more marked. After all, central management control is the natural state for a business. The owner of a small business prefers central control and gives it up reluctantly when the growth of the business forces him to do so. Any business can be expected to tend to revert to this state, if *enabled* to do so.

The increasing ability on the part of computer-aided management to solve increasingly complex problems presages a return to more centralized control. When company top management, exploiting a computer complex capable of instant response acquires—or regains—the capability of centralized planning, communication, and coordination, more decision making will come back into its hands. Thus the corporate executive will no longer make policy exclusively but will become a top operating manager, exercising *control* over the day-by-day conduct of the business. Corporations able to exercise such control effectively should enjoy a considerable advantage over their conventionally decentralized competitors.

This change can be expected to evolve gradually and naturally, as time goes on. Of more immediate concern to business management is the issue of centralization of data processing, i.e., central control over computer system planning, investment, activities, and data processing operations, regardless of the existing pattern of centralization or decentralization of the business.

Centralization of responsibility for corporation-wide data processing means in all cases the existence of a corporate systems staff and likely the establishment of a position of a top data-processing systems executive (see subsequent section on corporate systems management). Beyond that, however, it may mean one or more of the following functions:

1. Control over data processing *expenditures*
2. *Coordination* of systems activities
3. *Direction* of systems planning and activities
4. Control over location of *systems talent*
5. Control over location of computer *equipment*
6. Control over the *selection* (configuration) of equipment

In this regard, there is at present no consistency among corporations that have adopted a policy of data processing centralization. There exists some confusion and controversy about which of the above functions should or should not be assumed by corporate systems staffs. The predominant pattern is for the corporate group to have responsibility for coordination and the right of "sign off" on proposals and expenditures. But in the typical decentralized corporation, the autonomous divisions resist attempts at corporate control over the other functions.

Difficulty and friction in matters of data processing between corporate and local organizations can be expected where the central Systems department has been set up to function strictly in a staff or advisory capacity. In these cases, the corporate systems group lacks a charter giving it responsibility for the *direction* of company-wide systems planning and systems activities and the corresponding authority endorsed by the top executive.

In a number of large multiple-computer-using corporations the corporate systems executive has, however, been given decision-making authority to direct computer system development efforts and to determine the location of computer equipment. In corporations that are currently undertaking to standardize and integrate their computer systems company-wide, the corporate systems office typically has authority also over the selection and configuration of all computers.

Currently, the least well resolved issue is that of control over the staff strength and location of data-processing system talent. In the majority of decentralized companies, such control is still exercised by division and local management. In a few cases, however, powerful central systems groups have concentrated, or are attempting to concentrate, all systems development resources at the corporate level. Such central "empire-building" moves, which strip local operations of all systems talent, are unsound. Let us examine the whole issue of physical centralization.

There exists at present a certain amount of confusion and controversy over what comprises a proper arrangement of system functions and responsibilities in corporations with a policy of centralized control over data processing systems. To aid the concerned corporate executive in sorting out the issues, the following analysis and arguments are offered to serve as a guideline. The two major bones of contention between the corporate systems organization and the divisions are

1. The location of computer equipment
2. The location of system development and programming talent

It is worth noting that, although the first is typically more ardently defended by local management than the second, their relative importance to the success of the local operation is actually the reverse. As a matter of fact, with the computer communications linkages now available, the physical location of the central processor hardware—everything else being the same—is irrelevant. To help in determining how best to allocate the various systems resources and facilities, management should pose the following four questions:

1. *What* are the problems that must be solved; i.e., what should the computer applications be?
2. *When* is information needed (system response required)?
3. *How* are we going to accomplish this?
4. *Where* should (what kind of) computer equipment be located, and where should system talent be resident?

The answer to the first question is twofold, since both local and corporate problems need to be solved. The corporate systems staff should not attempt to answer *both* parts of the question. Definition of local problems, and their priorities, should come from divisional operations and should form the basic material from which a corporate long-range data-processing plan is made up, as we shall discuss in a later section of this chapter.

The determination of the required system response introduces the time dimension to the overall question of what should be done. In the relationship between a corporate systems organization and the divisions, it becomes a matter of who owes what to whom. We have previously examined the relationship between system designers and those who control the computer installation on one hand and the system users on the other. The user owes participation and involvement in system development, and he is entitled to system service, which is essentially a function of response. If this applies on the local level, it must also hold true if we *scale up* the relationship so that the corporate systems group represents the system designer who controls data processing capacity and the division represents the user. Service to the user should in all things be the primary consideration.

The third question of how the goals are to be reached is a matter of implementation, of developing short-range data processing plans and launching system projects. The specific answer to this question will depend on the answers to the preceding two questions, plus the availability of resources that can be applied to system development. The answers to the first three questions are essential to the definition of the total data processing job, and they constitute the substance of the long-range system plan.

Where to place the equipment is the least important consideration. The *location* of the computer need have nothing to do with solving the problems that must be solved and providing the system response necessary to serve the user. But the second part of the fourth question, i.e., where system talent should reside, *is* important. Sufficient system development resources, and systems talent, should exist at the division level to assure effective system development participation and to provide the required user in-house talent which is necessary for valid problem definition and good communications with the corporate systems group.

Reasons for this are analogous to those which have been advanced previously in discussing the working relationship between a Systems and Programming department and the user groups. As far as the issue of data processing centralization versus decentralization is concerned, the foregoing arguments can be summed up as follows: *Distinguish between functional and physical centralization; with respect to the latter, dis-*

tinguish between the location of computer equipment and that of system development and programming talent.

Functional centralization (i.e., coordination and central control over corporate systems activities) is always desirable. *Physical* centralization is a secondary consideration, in which management should distinguish between the location of hardware and the location of systems development resources. The bulk of the latter should remain at the division level even where computing power, for reasons of information processing economy, is concentrated in a central location.

As far as the question of performing the actual data processing work at either a central or division level is concerned, the following list can serve as a general guideline:

At central level

1. Work of the corporate office
2. Company-wide functions (e.g., personnel, payroll, distribution)
3. Divisional work which is not response-sensitive, if it can be done centrally with more economy
4. Work of small divisions that cannot support a computer system of their own
5. Interdivision, interplant functions that are part of a centrally integrated system

At division or plant level

1. Response-sensitive applications that the central computer facility cannot consistently provide (e.g., engineering jobs requiring quick turnaround, production monitoring, local file inquiry, process or test control, etc.)
2. All data processing work that can, for any reason, be performed better at the local level

As a rule, the concentration of computer data-processing power in a central location will afford economies of scale, which will increase information processing efficiency per unit of work performed. In their legitimate search for such economies, however, corporate managements should never lose sight of a basic principle stated earlier: *The efficiency of the divisions' business must take precedence over the efficiency of the corporate computer system.*

In corporations without formal long-range planning the systems staff is often not privy to the business plans of the corporate management group.

CORPORATE SYSTEMS PLANNING

Decentralization and divisional autonomy have certain natural consequences that inevitably concern corporate management. The most serious of such "side effects" of decentralization is poor interdivision coordination. To the extent that the divisions are intended to support a broad corporate marketing mission and are to function so as to enable the corporation to achieve its overall business goals—unless the corporation is a holding company or a corporate shell of a conglomerate—a lack of coordination between divisions breeds waste and excessive costs.

The lesson has been learned from the classic example of the Department of Defense (DOD). When Robert S. McNamara left the presidency of the Ford Motor Company and took over as Secretary of Defense in 1961, his extensive questioning of prevailing practices and of the DOD management system revealed serious cases of poor coordination between the armed services. Famous is the case of the Army, the Air Force, and airlift. It appears that the Army had a number of combat-ready divisions prepared for airlift, but the Air Force had been loath to spend their funds in the proper amount required to support such airlift capability. It preferred to allocate resources under its control to the more glamorous mission of nuclear bombers.

We had troops ready to be airlifted but not enough airplanes to airlift them. This was not necessarily the fault of the generals but rather a fault of the DOD planning and management system then in effect. Because the Army, Navy, and Air Force had been budgeting independently, decision making was too decentralized to achieve a balanced overall program. As can be expected in any situation—government or business—of decentralization without central coordination (but is not *that* a degree of recentralization?), the autonomous operating arm tends to exercise its own priorities and to favor its own unique missions at the expense of joint or common missions.

In the case of the DOD, Mr. McNamara, as is well known, proceeded to correct the situation by overhauling the existing system of management and by instituting new planning and control machinery at the Defense Department, or *central*, level. The results of his reforms were impressive, and "the McNamara approach" became a model that others, both in government (under a presidential directive) and in business, began to adopt for their own. The subject has stirred wide interest. Its various facets have been receiving ample attention in business literature, and its principles are being expounded by speakers and by the new, rapidly growing community of corporate planners.

Because this subject provides a fine framework, or background, against which to discuss corporate systems planning, a succinct review of it is in order at this point. So that the reader may grasp the entire substance of the type of planning and management in question and see its elements in the proper context, the author offers the following comprehensive definition, which represents his subjective view and interpretation of the subject. In this view, planning and management à la McNamara consists of a certain management *philosophy*, certain *methods* used to carry out this philosophy, certain *techniques* to support the methods, and an *implementation and control machinery*, as follows:

Management Philosophy

1. Positive or active (as against reactive), methodical management that *creates* objectives. A forging, influencing, or control over the destiny of the organization.

2. An insistence on a systematic application of *reason* in managing. A posture of consistent objectivity—the opposite of management by intuition or emotion.

3. A striving for control, i.e., quantifiable goals and measurable progress.

Methods

1. Planning *by mission* (as against planning by individual function) as a means of discharging the basic management responsibility of resource allocation.

2. *Needs research*, to maintain initiative in identifying opportunities, challenges, and problems.

3. *Economic choice* as a way of looking at problems, i.e., the principle of cost-effectiveness used for deciding between alternative courses of action and for the setting of priorities.

4. *Formality* of planning, including specific organizational and procedural machinery for review, evaluation, and approval, plus a cyclical time frame to establish the rhythm for a methodical shift in management attention from one planning phase to the next.

Techniques

Scientific, or *quantitative*, techniques for analysis and evaluation (known as systems analysis), including mathematical modeling, simulation, risk assessment, and other Operations Research tools. The main object for the application of these techniques is to provide an objective basis for cost-effectiveness determination.

Implementation and Control Machinery

1. *Planning* process of
   a. Mission selection, via needs research
   b. Creating strategic plans for the accomplishment of missions
2. *Programming* or, more precisely, the program planning process of defining the scope and time dimension of projects, consisting of
   a. Formulation of specific goals, by program
   b. Review and incorporation of programs into an overall long-range (five-year) plan
3. *Budgeting* process, i.e., the setting of a specific final operating and cost plan for a fiscal year

The above summary and classification represents the scope of Mr. McNamara's innovations in the Department of Defense. But many business corporations have analogous internal problems of management system and control. Planning is a business problem, and there are two basic reasons for the desirability of business planning. First, there is the necessity for allocating *limited resources*, which is a prime management obligation. Obviously, if there were no limit on resources, there would be little need for planning. The second reason is the degree of *uncertainty of the future*. If the future were fully predictable, there would be no need for decisions based on studied alternatives.

Formal long-range planning, in the sense that it is being discussed here, is an organized attempt at charting the future, by means of developing programs to reach specific objectives and to influence the future through planning, which then can serve as a guiderail on the way to it. Only through planning is it possible to establish a better awareness, on the part of management, of tomorrow's implications of today's decisions, and to assure that intermediate results are consistent with, and will support, the ones desired for the future.

In commenting on the DOD pattern of planning and management control, as it applies to business corporations, we should first note the management attitude that it embodies. Progress takes place not by inertia but by the organization creating its own momentum. Management does not consist in *ad hoc* reactions to random external stimuli, but in directing and controlling progress toward predetermined goals. Management is scientific in the sense that it insists on facts and proofs, and "hard nosed" in the sense that it will allocate resources as objective analysis dictates, even if that means cutting back, stretching out, or aborting existing projects.

Planning by mission, in a business context, will usually mean identifying, and defining, corporate marketing missions along product lines and the development of competitive strategies and long-range programs by mission, which will cut across divisional and functional boundaries. Needs research, also called environmental analysis, is the tool for maintaining competitive initiative.

As it is necessary to keep a balance between the opportunities and challenges of the market on one hand and the internal corporate resources and capabilities on the other, needs research will effect a subtle but significant shift in emphasis. The process of planning will begin with, and will orient programs toward, the external environment or market. This is opposite to starting with, and fashioning plans based on, an appraisal of internal corporate capabilities.

The principle of cost-effectiveness, or cost-benefit, is self-explanatory and has obvious direct applicability to business decision making. Technically, it is defined as maximizing benefits obtainable for given resources or, conversely, minimizing expenditure of resources to obtain a given benefit. The phrase "most bang for the buck" defines it in a nutshell. The formality of the planning, decision-making, and control procedure assures that plans become structured, explicit documents for guidance. Formality serves as an incentive for members of the organization to analyze and think through their problems and recommendations, as it forces them to document, i.e., to commit themselves "in writing." The formal mechanism also acts to assure the *use* of, and adherence to, plan.

A formal planning process must be supported by an organizational and procedural machinery for its implementation. In the Defense Department, this is the *planning-programming-budgeting* procedure, which serves as the primary tool of management control. A counterpart control system must also be established in a business corporation if its planning is to have vitality and not be a mere exercise in creating documents to be filed away.

Needs research will provide the basis for exercising executive judgment in selecting marketing missions. Formal strategy will serve as an antidote for the usual tendency to continue previous programs without proper recognition, and analysis, of changing needs. The corporate long-range business plan will act as an integrating framework, permitting the individual program plans, or functional plans, to be tied together. In a business environment, planning by function, i.e.,

1. The marketing plan
2. The manufacturing plan
3. The personnel plan
4. The product development plan
5. The capital investment and facilities plan

will normally be more suitable than planning by program such as in the DOD, where the "business" is weapons, logistics systems, etc. Planning by function need not be inconsistent with planning by mission. Missions cut across functions, but functional plans can be derived and *assembled from mission plans.* In a business corporation, the basic difference between planning by program or function on one hand and planning by division on the other is in the *organization* of the plans. The former are organized by object of accomplishment and are therefore *output*-oriented, whereas the latter are, by accounting tradition, organized by object of expenditure and are *input*-oriented.

A most important dimension of program planning, or its business equivalent, is the plan's *time span.* Long-range (i.e., typically 5-year or 7-year) planning provides the full cost-dimension of programs or mission plans and establishes *visibility* of future commitments. This forces some hard choices when it comes to making new commitments and launching new projects, because the long-range plan provides the measure of allocation, or mortgaging, of *future* resources. With conventional one-year planning from one fiscal year's budget to another, attention is directed only to the next year, and this acts as a spur for nominating a lot of new projects, i.e., proposing a large number of new starts for which the full cost-dimension will not become apparent until years later.

This phenomenon is common in the life of corporations where a one-year-at-a-time planning system encourages divisions and various functional groups to make an annual bid for a larger share of corporate resources by submitting sometimes hastily concocted "wish lists." The limitation of available resources acts to defer, stretch out, or terminate projects, but beyond the budget year there always tends to exist a backlog of unrealistic plans, in the hope that "next year" there may be more money.

Management motivation for instituting a better planning process and through it to acquire a more effective corporate management and control system derives from the size and complexity of the business enterprise.

Analogically, as computer systems and data processing activities of a corporation reach a certain scope, complexity, and level of investment, a need arises for more effective systems planning and control. The current growth of formalized, central systems planning in large computer-using corporations represents a reaction to the experiences of the recent past. Even in the best-managed decentralized corporations, divisional computer systems apparently were permitted to develop and grow in different directions, depending on the preferences and ideas of local personnel.

The reason for this, no doubt, was corporate management's view of the computer as being merely another tool, to be used by local managements at their discretion in attaining their operating and profit objectives. The wastefulness and inefficiency of this approach is now, however, becoming very apparent, and many large corporations are currently in the process of overhauling and *unifying* (at a cost of millions of dollars) their computer systems.

Companies that do not see the need at present will very likely be forced to do the same eventually, at a higher cost, because they will not be able to *afford* the continued redundancy and duplication of computer system effort, interdivision system incompatibility, waste of corporate system resources, and inconsistency of management information. This will come about when both the investment in computer systems and the dependency on the performance of these systems reaches a critical point—which is only a question of time.

The corporations that are currently spending a lot of money for a fundamental system overhaul have a powerful incentive for creating a corporate planning and coordinating mechanism that would prevent the need for another such expenditure in the future. These companies are reorganizing and establishing the function of corporate-level system management and control. Such a move not only affects corporate staff organization, but introduces a new philosophy of corporate-divisional relationships by changing the mix of respective responsibilities. It affects divisional systems capability, regulates its use, and usually severely restricts or terminates local autonomy in the sphere of computer system development.

Corporate systems management is a new and significant development. As part of the current discussion, we shall review the most crucial function of corporate systems management, i.e., *corporate systems planning*. Organizational and other functional aspects will be examined separately later.

To establish a meaningful context for corporate systems functions, we need only to transpose, or scale up, many of the principles and relationships expounded in the previous chapters. What applies to the interaction between the user and the computer system on the divisional level, and the arguments on communications, departmental functions, central systems service, coordination, etc., apply to the corporate level also if local operations are viewed in the role of system users.

As far as corporate systems planning is concerned, however, the task is complicated by the fact that systems must be planned and coordinated not only on the level of the division, but also on the level of the various *functions* that are internal to each division but are common to those of other divisions. It is not enough to evaluate and coordinate overall systems activities of divisions A and B. Such coordination must include the purchasing, accounting, and inventory control subsystems of A and B, for instance.

The purpose of corporate systems planning is to

1. Assure efficient utilization of the corporation's systems resources.
2. Permit effective planning, communications, and interaction at the divisional level. This will be particularly important in multidivision corporations with homogeneous product lines and a high degree of interdependence between local operations.
3. Establish a corporate information system about data processing that will yield management information uniformly interpretable by the executive who is attempting to control corporate system activities through the planning and budgeting process.

The task of the corporate systems planning staff is analogous to the DOD planning by mission, i.e., to cut across divisional and functional lines to assure consistency of systems effort relative to common corporate goals. With respect to corporate information flow, divisional boundaries are artificial. The tool of the corporate systems planner is a hierarchy of plans, including corporate and divisional long-range data processing plans.

The specific responsibilities of the corporate systems planning organization include the following:

1. Coordination of divisional systems activities
2. Evaluation, analysis, and recommendations for the assignment of priorities and allocation of resources
3. The watchdog function of monitoring divisional system development progress
4. Making sure that data processing plans are consistent with business plans—that computer systems of the future are adequate to support the business of the future

This requires that the corporate systems planner be able to assess long-range systems plans against long-range business plans. The data processing plan should be a *function* of the business plan. The corporate systems planning group requires a knowledge of the business environment that data processing has to serve. Without such a knowledge, systems planning takes place in a vacuum and cannot be valid.

It is an anomaly that such a self-evident requirement is not universally appreciated by corporate managements. Many companies that do long-range business planning have not given data processing and computer systems the status of a significant business function, so that plans for the latter are not the integral part of the overall formal plan they should be.

In corporations without formal long-range planning, the corporate systems staff is often not privy to the (undocumented) business plans of the corporate management group or those of the individual functional executives. In the absence of some sort of formal scheme of keeping the systems organization informed of future business plans, the systems people are often the last to know. This guarantees waste of the corporation's systems resources which, as some large corporations have now determined in retrospect, can cost millions of dollars.

A well-managed corporation should also manage its data processing systems well. The organizational environment should be deliberately planned to provide for coordination, control, and optimization of the use of vital corporate resources. Computer systems are fast becoming, or have become, such a vital resource. Centrally coordinated planning and not the maximization of operational efficiency of the individual divisions is now the essential ingredient of continued corporate success. Without such planning, the direction of the corporation is merely the sum of the independently set directions of its autonomous divisions.

A corporation will have poor information systems if it does not establish a corporate function of central systems planning and if it fails to relate systems planning to business plans, whether formal or informal. The function of corporation-wide data processing should be elevated to the status of corporate long-range planning. System projects should figure as a separate function in each divisional plan, and the corporate systems planners should have free access to all the corporate business plans, which constitute the only environment against which the data processing plan can validly be evaluated. The data processing plan should be made subject to the same review and coordinating process that governs other business planning.

Central corporate planning for both business and systems functions reclaims the advantage of coordinated pull enjoyed by a small company, as it knocks down the artificial walls between divisions. But what about corporate systems planning if a company does not do, or does not believe in, formal long-range business planning? Even in that case, corporate data processing should be centrally planned. To enable corporate systems planners to assess data processing plans against the future business environment, the flow of formal planning data can be substituted for by means of an advisory group or "business planning committee" appointed for this purpose.

This is the approach currently being taken by a number of national decentralized corporations. The advisory body is intended to meet with corporate systems planners on a regular schedule to apprise them on which way the business is going, and the practice is to be continued until formal corporate long-range planning is established.

> *From the point of view of the manager, sameness is preferable to perfection, and control takes precedence over performance.*

THE MANAGEMENT OF CORPORATE SYSTEMS RESOURCES

In the preceding section we have reviewed problems arising from unplanned and uncoordinated systems activities in large and decentralized computer-using corporations. Many such corporations, in response to these problems, have established a new, central function of corporate systems management. This is a significant, but quite recent, development. To permit the proper exercise of this function, provisions must be made for an adequate organizational accommodation on the corporate level and for its staffing and funding. The corporate systems group should be given a charter of its responsibilities by the chief executive. Otherwise it will tend to be ineffectual acting in a strictly advisory role.

Because of the newness of this corporate function, there is at present a certain amount of groping and a lack of consistency from one corporation to another in how this function is being handled. The organizational pattern, functions and tasks, mode of operation, and the executive status of the head of the corporate systems group vary from case to case. This section is therefore devoted to a review of these considerations in the hope that it can serve as a guideline, to aid corporate managements struggling to implement the concept of centralized systems management and to establish this new function properly. The main considerations related to this subject are

1. *Organization*
2. *Functions* and responsibilities (charter)
3. *Tasks* of a newly created corporate systems staff

CORPORATE SYSTEMS ORGANIZATION

For best results, the corporate systems function should not be organizationally associated with any of the other functional areas of the business. Data processing cuts across all the business functions, and there is no logical reason for assigning responsibility for corporate systems management to Finance (the most common practice), any more than there is for giving it to Marketing or Manufacturing.

The criterion for granting vice-presidential status to a head of an organization, and for direct reporting to a senior executive, is the scope and importance of the function that the manager responsible for it represents. In corporations where the scope and impact of computer data processing is not deemed to warrant executive representation, senior management must by necessity assign responsibility for it to one of the functional executives. But if the scope of computer systems does not warrant separate management representation today, tomorrow it will, as computer use and the associated costs will inevitably grow. Sooner or later, the traditional corporate-level organization pattern must be disrupted, to make room for Data Processing Systems.

In corporations that have acknowledged the increasing importance of computer systems to the conduct of their business and have reflected this recognition in their corporate organization, the functions reporting to the new vice-president vary from case to case. The organization chart in Figure 23 represents a composite of several actual systems organizations.

The executive who heads the corporate systems organization in our composite example (it is interesting to note that a definite trend in industry is to staff this position with a former business manager rather than systems manager) reports directly to the president or the executive vice president. He has *veto power* over system development activities, proposals, projects, and the acquisition of computer hardware. There are no programmers on his staff, with the exception of those cases where the data processing group serving the corporate office has been made to report to him through one of his immediate subordinates, as shown.

The organization is staffed with specialists and people with business management background. Their function is to provide direction, co-

ordinate, plan, and control. In most cases the Corporate Systems department has no *operating* responsibility (with the exception already noted).
But in some cases Systems groups, or even Data Processing Operations
departments located in the divisions or remote computer centers, have
been made to report to the corporate manager of computer techniques
and services (see Figure 23). This the author considers undesirable.

Another aspect of corporate systems organization is advisory bodies.
Some corporations have lately established such groups so as to provide
a corporate-level interface between systems management and business

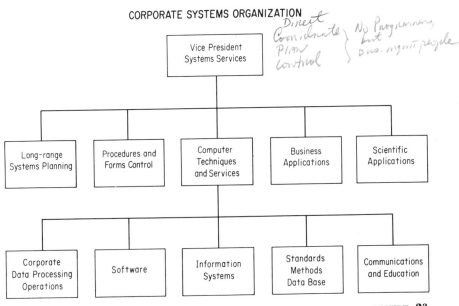

FIGURE 23

management. Such advisory committees play a particularly vital role in
companies without formal long-range planning. There the regular contact between the respective representatives of systems and business
serves to assure that longer-range systems development is kept on the
right track.

The corporate advisory bodies, functioning under many different
labels (system planning advisory committee, business planning council,
systems advisory group, etc.), are composed either of the top executives
representing the various business functions or of their representatives.
The council members are not—or should not be—staff personnel from the

various functional areas. In those cases where the vice-president himself is not a member of the council, he is represented by one of the managers reporting directly to him.

The specific functions, or authorities, of these advisory committees vary. In some cases the committee serves as the final authority on system development project approval, for example, and in other cases their function is strictly to advise the systems organization on business developments and plans. Generally, their decision-making responsibility is in inverse proportion to the strength and status of the corporate systems management group. With the latter properly organized, staffed, and chartered, there is no need for the advisory body to make systems decisions.

In some corporations another type of advisory committee has been established (in addition to the business advisory council) which represents divisional-level functions. Thus manufacturing systems, engineering systems, and quality control systems councils are periodically convened to meet with corporate systems management representatives, for the purpose of exchanging information and views regarding the particular subsystems in question. This arrangement is especially useful in corporations that are engaged in company-wide systems overhaul, integration, or unification efforts.

CORPORATE SYSTEMS MANAGEMENT FUNCTIONS

The mix of these functions and responsibilities is suggested by Figure 23. But the principal functions are three:

1. Long-range systems *planning*
2. Development of a corporate *information system* (this)
3. Coordination and direction of efforts to *unify* or *integrate* division-level systems

Of these functions, corporate systems planning has been thoroughly discussed in the preceding section and requires no further elaboration. The corporate information system function is essentially the goal of assuring, through an analysis of the corporate information flow and of the corporate information requirements, that systems at all levels yield the proper information required to manage the business. A particular objective is to provide top corporate management, and the chief executive, with correct and timely information of the type that they need for managing the affairs of the corporation. Corporate information system development may or may not be oriented toward the creation of a management information system (MIS) in the sense that we have defined it in Chapter 3.

The definition of a company-wide information system is also essential for the proper exercise of the previously discussed long-range systems planning function. An important responsibility of the corporate systems planner is to assess the propriety of data processing plans that come to him for review. The assessment must always be relative to something else. The planned business environment serves as one frame of reference, but a master blueprint of the overall corporate information system (the ideal system) provides another dimension and is a valuable tool of data-processing plan evaluation.

The third principal function, the direction and coordination of company-wide efforts to achieve a unified (integrated, standardized, total, compatible—all these adjectives mean roughly the same thing in their current system-related usage) information processing system, can be broken down into three areas of responsibility, i.e.,

1. Coordination of system development
2. Management of the corporate data base
3. Administration of standards

The coordination of system development proper, and its direction, is achieved in conjunction with long-range systems planning. The planning machinery, as discussed in the previous section, can serve as the means for the exercise of direction and control. Centralized and authoritative management of the data base is all-important in all cases, without exception, of data-base-oriented computer systems. The data base concept, and the related problems—both technical and organizational/political—have already been reviewed in some depth. We have brought out previously that central organizational machinery independent of the data base users, to administer the data base and its maintenance, is a necessity if the related systems are to work satisfactorily.

In corporations that have established a Corporate Systems Management department "with some teeth in it," i.e., the proper charter, status, authority, budget, and competent staffing, the function of managing the data base finds its natural organizational home in this department. In the absence of such a corporate department, it is difficult to see another satisfactory organizational solution. Without such a solution, however, data-base-oriented systems are destined to work poorly, at best.

A function closely related to both system unification and data base management is the administration of data-processing systems standards. Such standards are rules and conventions intended to achieve conformity, alikeness, sameness of as many aspects of computer system development, and operation, as possible. The purpose of establishing, and enforcing adherence to, standards is fourfold:

1. Communication
2. Control
3. Compatibility (exchangeability)
4. Facilitation of data-processing systems work

Standards represent a procedure to follow and a yardstick against which to measure the quality of systems work and system output. The implications of the concept of data-processing systems standards are far-reaching. As computer installations and systems activities grow in scope, they become unmanageable without standards. Unless the same things are done the same way, communication suffers, and the resultant confusion, rework, and malfunction are costly, in more than one way.

Standardization permits uniform interpretation of results, and of information, by the manager who is attempting to control data-processing systems activity and its cost. From the point of view of the manager, sameness is preferable to perfection, and control takes precedence over performance. Without uniformity of interpretation of terms, data, and reports, an executive responsible for multiple operating units cannot exercise control, and therefore cannot truly manage. The divisions may be perfect, but the corporate executive is deprived of the ability to *manage* them.

Without standards, compatibility, i.e., exchangeability of systems and programs, becomes quite impossible. This also means that transfer and exchangeability of computer hardware, products, and even *people* from one division to another becomes more difficult and costly. Without standards, even a transfer of responsibility for system, program, or file maintenance becomes a problem.

Adherence to standards facilitates all facets of systems work and of data processing operations. In addition to improving communications among people, standards assist all classes of data processing and systems personnel in their work, as both interpretation and method selection is made easier; i.e., the number of decisions required to be made becomes less. Standardization is the opposite of reinventing the wheel. Standardization equals efficiency.

Standards can be established for a long list of things in the sphere of computer systems, including system design, user participation (program specs, user's manual, furnishing test data), operating procedure development (a procedure for writing procedure) measurements, testing, program release, machine operation, terminology, etc. The most important standards, however, pertain to

1. Documentation
2. Record format and file design
3. Use of software (including configuration of operating system modules)
4. Hardware configuration

Of these, the last may be of interest to the business managment reader. Some of the large corporations engaged in redesigning and unifying their computer-based systems have established standard computer configurations to maximize corporation-wide system compatibility. This means that a division must order its equipment in the prescribed configuration, with the prescribed mix of special features, regardless of particular local needs. In practice, this probably means that the average division will get, and have to pay for, a computer larger than it would otherwise have ordered.

This may look like a startling innovation, but such a policy will assure that a program written in one location can be used (without modification) at all other locations, that common file formats can be used throughout the corporation, that the manufacture of products can be shifted from one plant to another with less disruption, that personnel can move between divisions without having to relearn new systems, and generally, that the cost of system development, programming, and program and file maintenance can be minimized. In the average computer-using company, this should more than pay for the extra equipment cost.

To administer data-processing systems standards without friction and confusion, there must be central authority held by a single individual. The corporate systems management organization shown in Figure 23 provides the best organizational and systems-authority framework for the exercise of this important function.

CORPORATE SYSTEMS DEPARTMENT TASKS

If a newly created Corporate Systems department is to begin functioning with effectiveness, it must carry out, or at least initiate, a number of startup tasks. As there is little precedent for this, corporate systems personnel often spend a good portion of their first year of tenure trying to define the job that should be done and the methods of doing it. For this purpose, the top management charter that established the new function is typically too vague to be of much help.

To assist newly appointed corporate systems executives in organizing the work of their staffs so as to get off to an effective start, the following "job description" is being provided as a guideline. It is a list of fourteen principal tasks (not necessarily exhaustive) as follows:

1. Define systems management responsibilities and relationships. Identify the specific functions and responsibilities of the corporate systems staff and the corresponding responsibilities (these may have to be assigned) at each level of the company. Identify interrelationships among the various concerned organizations for purposes of communication. This task is intended to establish the overall systems management and communications framework.

2. Design a classification and coding scheme for the unique identification of all systems resources and activities. Establish the procedure for identifying and reportng systems activities that are to be planned and controlled. Provide for a unique data identification to facilitate file management, system design, and programming. Assign identification codes (passwords) to terminal users to implement file security control. Define a coding structure for the control of transaction data.

3. Determine the identifying characteristics of both existing and planned systems. Identify the functions, interrelationships, schedules, outputs, and data sets of these systems. The purpose of this task is to facilitate the function of long-range systems planning in general and the assessment of data processing plans relative to business plans in particular.

4. Determine management information requirements. Assist business executives in defining the information and its characteristics (form, structure, timing) that they need for the effective discharge of their responsibilities. This pertains to information generated by the corporate system, to information generated by divisional systems that serves as input to the corporate system, and to information used by divisional management.

5. Define the long-range objectives for computer systems, and their environment. Determine the requirements of future systems in view of the objectives and requirements of long-range business plans.

6. Analyze management reports, both current and planned for the future. Analyze these reports for their information contents and timing, in relation to management needs as determined in task 4. Make certain that current reports to corporate and divisional management meet their present needs. Identify the best sources and forms that can satisfy these needs, and eliminate unnecessary redundancy and duplication in information reporting.

7. *Identify specific major subsystems at any level which are critical to the support of the corporate information system.* These are the subsystems whose development must be coordinated and controlled. These subsystems must function well, as they are the critical components of the company-wide information system structure.

8. *Develop the technical and procedural machinery for the implementation of the long-range systems planning mission.* Establish a project file, and develop procedures for planning, evaluation, measurement, and control.

9. *Establish principles, standards, and measurements for computer systems and for all systems activities.* These are to be used in the management, development, and operation of computer systems. Formulate standards, particularly in the areas of equipment and software configuration, file data, programming, and documentation. Define principles and other criteria that can form the basis for judging relative excellence of system design.

10. *Develop a master blueprint of the corporate information system structure.* Design (at a macro level) the ideal data and system network for information flow, storage, security, and integrity. The purpose of such a master system blueprint is to serve as one of the criteria for assessing the soundness of both existing and planned computer systems.

11. *Identify the constituent files of the corporate data base.* These are the file data that must be used by several operating divisions. Establish how these files will be created and maintained and how file data will be disseminated. Provide for consolidated acquisition of data and for an acceptable single definition of each data element of the data base.

12. *Establish a well-conceived plan or road map for implementing systems over the long run,* as called for by task 10. This plan will serve to designate the priorities, sequences, and assignments necessary to realize the design and will act as the prime tool for systems resource allocation.

13. Determine hardware and programming requirements. This task is derived from task 12 and those which precede it. It cannot be validly initiated until the results of these tasks are well defined.

14. Identify opportunities for short-range improvements. This pertains principally to existing systems, for the improvement of which the proper action should be initiated.

> *Only* implementation, *i.e., detailing of centrally conceived design, can successfully be subdivided and delegated to multiple local organizations.*

CORPORATE PROJECT ORGANIZATION

Principles and recommendations advanced in all the previous discussions regarding organization applied to a normal or regular mode of operation. But there will be times when a corporation undertakes an extraordinary effort to develop a system of major scope, and at such times the existing organizational machinery will likely prove unequal to the task.

The magnitude of these projects is often such that their funding runs into millions of dollars and systems resources at all levels and locations must be drawn into play. Obviously, how well such major projects are organized will have a direct bearing on both the quality of results and the efficiency of achieving these results.

A major corporate systems project team will have to be composed of personnel with different backgrounds and from different units of the regular company organization. This poses a particular challenge, since corporate as well as divisional people, of both the business and systems variety, will have to serve, even though only for a time, in a common organization. In the absence of good project organization and strong management backing, allegiances and regular reporting relationships may cause friction and unevenness of pull.

Because its components are so heterogeneous and the users of its end product so various, the corporate project organization must primarily be designed for *communication.* This is everyone's project; everyone will be affected, and therefore everyone should be heard.

In the discussion that follows, an imaginary project organization will be used as a vehicle for illustrating the various considerations and relationships. This organization is patterned after certain actual current projects, with some modifications. The company in the example is assumed to be organized and operating, in the computer systems sphere, along the lines recommended in this book. Thus there is assumed to be a corporate central systems organization, but system design and implementation "muscle" resides at divisional locations, etc. For purposes of clarity of example, the corporation in question is assumed to be a manufacturing company with multiple plant locations, and the objective of the project is to develop a unified system of production control for all the plants. The reader may wish to substitute the words "distribution," "sales districts," and "warehouse control" for "manufacturing," "plants" and "production control," etc. The principles and relationships represented by the example are universal.

It must be recalled that a corporate systems project has several major phases, i.e.,

1. Study and proposal
2. System design
3. System development
4. Installation (conversion)
5. Operation

We shall concern ourselves only with organization for phases 2 through 4, as the study will likely be conducted by a small and differently composed group, and operation will be taken over by the regular data processing organization. A special organization will have to be created for phases 2 through 4, but as each phase has its own organizational requirements, the project organization will be composed differently during each of the three phases.

A special project organization on the corporate level will be created for the duration of the program. It can remain virtually unchanged throughout (except probably for staffing strength which may have to vary from phase to phase), but reporting relationships will change with the phases, as shown in Figures 24 through 27.

The corporate project organization chart is largely self-explanatory, except for the function labeled *system support*, which encompasses:

1. Software selection, modification and development, i.e., the writing of any common, nonapplication programs
2. Hardware selection (but see also preceding section regarding hardware responsibilities of the regular corporate systems organization)
3. Simulations and testing programs
4. Central control of project documentation
5. Coordination of project activities related to the data base

The function of project-related activities labeled "education" is actually something on the order of public relations, i.e., selling people throughout the corporation on the desirability of the new system. Education and communications are the tools.

It is important to note that the corporate-level project organization

CORPORATE ORGANIZATION

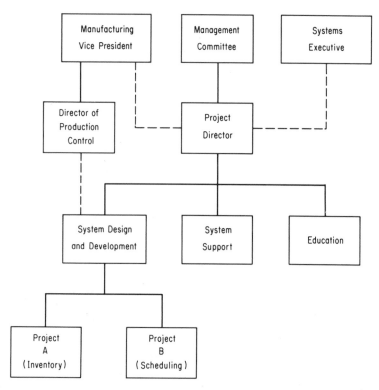

FIGURE 24

does not merely coordinate local project activities but contains system design and development capability of its own. Experience with several major corporate projects has shown that chopping up system design into subsystems and "farming it out" to the various locations proves unsatisfactory. The overall system is then a pasting together of independently conceived subsystems that, even though each might be excellent in its own right, do not really fit together.

Such an approach is analogous to having a house designed by several specialists on kitchens, living rooms, bathrooms, etc., independently of each other. Each may provide optimum dimensions for his room, but together they will not fit into a common floor plan and the house cannot be built that way. The need is for central system architecture, for one system design philosophy. Only *implementation*, i.e., detailing of centrally conceived design, can successfully be subdivided and delegated to multiple local organizations.

COMPOSITE ORGANIZATION — DESIGN PHASE

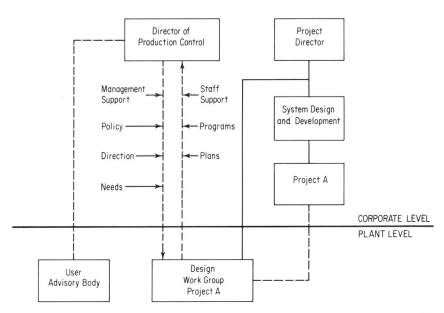

FIGURE 25

The composite organization chart for the system design phase (Figure 25) shows the existence of a so-called design work group which reports, during this phase, directly to the project director. The work group is a specially appointed body that implements system design of one of the subsystems or subprojects. In our example, "Project A" is the inventory control subsystem. The design work group is made up of personnel from all the plants that this subsystem will affect, and it resides at one of the plant locations for the duration of the system design phase. It works closely with Project A representatives of the corporate project organization.

The corporate director of production control is involved and has functional (dotted line) responsibility. Production control managers from all the plants form the user advisory body and participate in the system design phase in this fashion.

The composite organization chart for the system development phase (Figure 26) shows that the design work group has been sup-

COMPOSITE ORGANIZATION–DEVELOPMENT PHASE

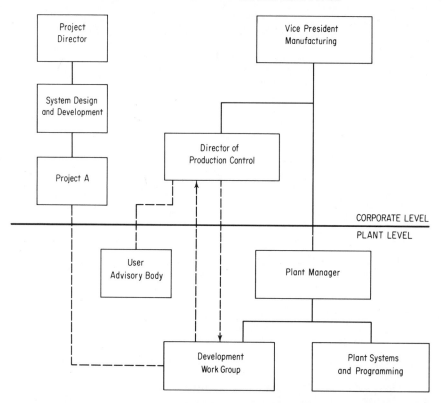

FIGURE 26

planted by the so-called development work group, which now reports to the plant manager at the location of its residence. The switch in the reporting relationship illustrates the philosophy of central corporate system architecture and design coordination coupled with local responsibility for all implementation activities.

The work group has changed not only in name but in composition. Although some original members continue to serve during this phase, others have returned to their home locations, and new personnel with different skills (mostly programmers) have joined the work group. Most of these people come from the local Systems and Programming department, which is now also otherwise connected with the project. User participation continues unchanged.

LOCAL ORGANIZATION (EACH PLANT) — INSTALLATION PHASE

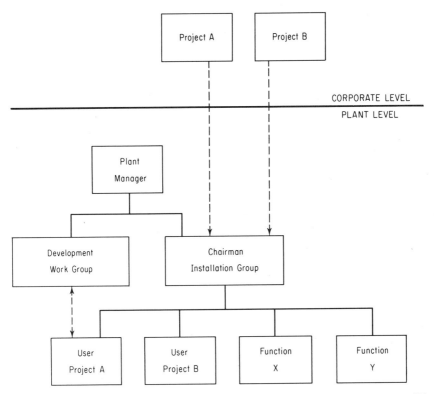

FIGURE 27

A separate organizational machinery is established at each plant location for the installation phase. It should be noted from Figure 27 that not only the subsystem developed locally but all the *other* subsystems will have to be installed. The installation phase organization reports to the plant manager, with dotted lines to the corporate project groups, as well as to the respective development work groups, as indicated. It can be seen that users are organizationally involved in the responsibility for installing the system—a move highly recommended.

In this organization, distinction is made between projects or major subsystems and business functions. Thus Project A or inventory control will affect the functions of production control, purchasing, manufacturing, accounting, etc. These functions cut across projects (or vice versa), and their representatives on the installation team are responsible for seeing to it that their requirements are met, even though they are not the primary users of the respective subsystems.

Good organization is the key to the success of the whole effort. An effective corporate project organization embodies several important principles, all illustrated by the above examples. These principles are:

1. Central direction of system design
2. Local responsibility for implementation (including installation and eventually, responsibility for system operation)
3. Strong user participation
4. Cleanly defined lines of responsibility
5. Flexibility (changeability) of organization
6. Effective communication

Chapter Ten
The Computer
and Management

Obsolete Executives
Firm Fires Controller
for View on Computers
Wall Street Journal
headline (*Jan. 24, 1966*)

The management of the average computer-using company would likely have been incredulous if, seven years ago, someone had accurately predicted that they would be spending as much for data processing as they are, in fact, spending today—about three times as much. It is probably also true that the same company today would refuse to believe that their investment in computers and related efforts is to reach several times its present size in the future, as it almost certainly will.

In 1954, American industry installed its first computer for use in business data processing. In 1968, it passed the 30,000th computer system installation mark. Forecasts, quoted by computer convention keynoters, various news media, and some investment advisory services point up to as high as 160,000 industrial installations by 1975 and 280,000 by 1980.

One facet of the phenomenal past progress in computer technology is reflected in the fact that increasingly more information processing power is being procured per dollar of rental. This takes the form of reduced cost per computer instruction executed, unit of storage used, etc., but it also means that lower-priced machines of relatively high capability have become commercially available. This, coupled with the programming aids offered by computer manufacturers and various systems services obtainable from specialty service firms, has dropped the cost of using a computer to the point where soon practically no company will be able to afford the use of older methods for the processing of its business data.

The overall industry investment in computer systems already is large, but all signs point to a several-fold increase in the future. According to a study released by the American Federation of Information Processing Societies (AFIPS) in 1966, United States investment in computers and related equipment will top $30 billion by 1975, in comparison with previous years as follows:

```
1960–$  1,480,000,000
1966–    7,800,000,000
1970–   18,000,000,000
1975–   35,500,000,000
```

Since the publication of this report, actual performance has been following the forecast well, and there is no reason to doubt that the major part of the investment in computers, before its growth levels off, is yet to be made. This is of special significance to the businessman, because of the need for this investment to be well managed.

At present, computer systems are becoming increasingly important not only for what they *do* but also for what they *cost*. The vast majority of computer-using companies are still in an early stage of the learning process. As they progress from the initial accounting and clerical applications toward the various areas of business operation, and as they make their computer systems more comprehensive, more communications-oriented, and more sophisticated generally, costs go up significantly.

In 1960, outlays for computers represented less than 4 percent of industry's total capital investment budget, but the figure will be closer to 15 percent in 1970. The sales revenue of the entire computer industry amounted to something over $9 billion in 1967; forecasts place the comparable figure for 1975 between $13 and 16 billion. Computer users' costs, it should be noted, are considerably higher than computer industry revenues, however.

A special report by Booz, Allen & Hamilton, Inc., published in the January-February, 1968, issue of the *Harvard Business Review* ("The Computer Comes of Age," by Neal J. Dean), indicates that the total computer system expenditure by the companies surveyed breaks down to

38 percent for computer rental
29 percent for systems planning and programming
33 percent for operating

It is significant that associated costs run almost double what it costs to rent the computer equipment proper. The report, completed in 1967, is based on a survey of 108 leading manufacturing companies. Its findings show that, when expressing total computer system expenditure as a percentage of annual company sales, the median is 0.56 percent, and the range within the group surveyed extends from a small fraction up to 3.4 percent (note the one-to-six spread from median to high).

Another interesting finding is the direct correlation between computer system expenditure and the length of its use. Companies with less than five years of computer experience spend 0.41 percent of their sales dollar for data processing compared to 0.65 percent for companies with ten or more years of computer use. Significantly, the survey indicated that only 4 out of the 108 companies did not anticipate an increase in their computer system costs.

This appears to confirm the premise that the average computer-using business will inevitably increase its expenditure for computer-data processing in the future, probably several times over. The rate of industry expenditure for data processing should be in the *$40 billion per year* range by 1975.

The investment in computer data processing, in terms of not only money expended but also what is at stake for the future of a business, has gotten so big—and is inexorably getting bigger—that it is reaching a point where the business manager will be forced to shift his attention and rearrange his priorities so as to become more directly involved in computer-related efforts and to exert control over them. When the outlay for computer systems approaches $1 out of every $100 of sales, the time surely has come for the executive to take personal charge. But it will not suffice for him to want to provide personal leadership in this new area, with its technical aspects, if he has not also acquired the necessary technical and *managerial* qualifications without which intelligent leadership and effective control are not possible.

Aside from cost, another important reason for active management involvement is the fact that success in making the computer *pay off* tends to depend on such involvement. This was first brought out by the now classic 1963 McKinsey survey (*Getting the Most Out of Your Computer* by John T. Garrity, McKinsey & Company, Inc.). The McKinsey report, based on a survey of more than 300 computer installations in 27 major manufacturing companies, indicated that the most important ingredient of computer payoff success is not the technical skills or the power of the machine but *management direction.*

This survey was the first attempt at an evaluation of how effectively computer systems are used by the companies that installed them, and it revealed that fully two-thirds of the companies surveyed were not being successful in this respect. The McKinsey report also represents the first attempt at an objective determination of the causes of success, or the lack of it, in effective computer use. The McKinsey researchers segregated the surveyed companies into two groups—the successful and the unsuccessful—and looked for common characteristics within each group.

This led to the conclusion that the major problem in obtaining payoff is not technical, but managerial and organizational, and that *computer system success is more heavily dependent on executive leadership than on any other factor.* No company achieved above-average results without active participation by top management. In the successful one-third of the surveyed companies, corporate executives saw to it that operating management take major responsibility for the success of computer applications affecting business operations and that managers play a major role in the development of such applications.

The McKinsey report suggested several questions for the chief executive to ask of himself, including, *"Do I devote to the computer systems effort the time and attention its cost and potential warrant?"* This question, posed in 1963, probably still could not be answered affirmatively by many business executives today. This is, in effect, confirmed by the findings of the follow-up survey by McKinsey (*Unlocking the Computer's Profit Potential,* 1968) of 36 large corporations. This study concludes that, as far as computer utilization is concerned, the economic payoff has not kept pace with technical achievements. When it comes to computers, and their use, executives are uneasy when faced with the requirement for mastering new techniques and making judgments on matters that seem excessively technical. The fact is that to acquire reasonable qualifications in the field of computer data processing requires certain effort, but too often we see a reluctance to make the effort.

Top business executives seem willing to commit money and men, but not their *own time,* to computer systems efforts being undertaken in their companies. Unfortunately, it is still quite common to see senior management abdicating their responsibility in this respect and letting junior managers and technical specialists make too many decisions that are of vital importance to their business.

In his own defense, the executive who is in default takes the position that "he does not know anything about computers" (a commonly heard expression) because the subject is too complex and esoteric. Too technical, anyhow, and that is why he assigns responsibility for all systems decisions to the "third echelon," below the vice-presidential level. Such an executive is delegating not only responsibility for execution of information system policy, but the very making of this policy, which entails basic decisions that bear on both the makeup and the functioning of the whole business organization.

Today, what is required of business executives in computer-using companies is effective leadership in computer system activities and "homework" on their part that is necessary to equip them to provide such leadership. Instead, some executives who are unable to overcome their distaste for acquiring the required knowledge and for direct involvement in matters of data processing attempt to delegate something that really *cannot be delegated* or to buy on the outside what *cannot be bought*. The responsibility for the health of the business they head is theirs.

No responsible executive of a computer-using company can avoid the need to educate himself about computer systems, avoid active involvement, or avoid responsibility much longer. A senior business executive was recently quoted as saying, *"Before we can really use these new techniques, we'll need a new generation of management. The older group just wasn't educated for it."* But the point is that the computer phenomenon is moving too fast, and we cannot wait.

So far in this discussion, we have tried to prove the necessity of management involvement on the basis that the increasing investment in computer systems deserves to be well managed and on the basis that computer system payoff is dependent on management. But there is still another reason which overshadows the other two in its importance to the future of a business. And that is the all-pervasive nature of computers introduced into business operations.

The universal applicability of the computer causes computer systems inexorably to expand. The computer system, in time, becomes inextricably one with the organizational and procedural machinery that drives the business. In the longer run, no company can be better than its computer system. The business executive should therefore exert the type and the degree of influence on computer system development that is commensurate with the importance and impact the system will have on the future conduct of the business. A main tool is in the making, and the executive should participate in its forging.

Some of the specific elements of top management's involvement are as follows:

Decisions

1. Grand Scheme
2. Data processing plan
3. Application priorities
4. Computer selection

Direction

1. Goal setting
2. Policy
3. Organization
4. Authority/responsibility assignments
5. Staffing of study and project teams
6. Monitoring of system development progress
7. Lower-level management attitude and participation

The concern and active interest of the top executive solves nothing if it exists in a managerial vacuum. It merely creates the atmosphere, the environment, in which imaginative system development efforts of men working under such an executive can bear fruit. Lower-level executives and operating management must actively participate in, and assume responsibility for, the systems work and its *results*. They also need to educate themselves and to acquire competence in this new responsibility.

Willingness on the part of management to step in and assume direction of computer system efforts is, of itself, not enough. The business manager must become *qualified,* through education and the acquisition of the required new management skills, to provide the intelligent leadership in this sphere that is expected of him.

We have begun the current discussion with a quotation of a newspaper headline proclaiming the obsolescence of executives. Executive obsolescence means loss of qualification to manage. In these times, business executives and operating managers can become obsolete, as their old skills become obsolete. Probably many business managers today *are* obsolete and serve on borrowed time.

The author hopes that the business management reader has found this book of value for keeping his own skills up-to-date.

Appendix
Fundamentals of Computer Design and Technology

In the following fifteen pages, divided into sections on

1. Computer System Characteristics
2. Computer Technology

the most frequently used technical terms are concisely defined, and the fundamentals of both computer function and technology are explained with maximum admissible brevity. The first part deals with *functional* aspects of computers irrespective of size, make, or technology. Preceding discussions of a number of management-level subjects have assumed the reader's familiarity with these functions and the related terms.

The second part attempts to explain what goes on under the cover of the machine and what enables it to do what it does. This is described in terms of how characters of data are represented and manipulated internally, and what the technological aspects of devices employed to accomplish it are. This material is included for the benefit of the business management reader with intellectual curiosity about "what makes a computer tick," but it has less relevance to the body of this book.

COMPUTER SYSTEM CHARACTERISTICS

1. STORED PROGRAM

A computer is an automatic information handling machine that can execute instructions in a predetermined and *self-directed* manner. This self-direction is its outstanding characteristic. The fact that a computer is designed not to depend on instructions being supplied from some external source during the execution process, but instead to have the ability to read its instructions in advance, and to remember them (by storing them in an internal memory unit), means that it need not be reinstructed as the job progresses. It can thus perform tasks of considerable complexity from start to finish without operator intervention.

The instructions for the execution of a data manipulation process are linked together into a logical arrangement called a *program*. This internally stored program represents the series of steps that must be taken to produce a desired result. The computer has the ability to proceed automatically from one instruction to another; because its internal circuitry is so fast, it is important that it be able to *access* its instructions equally fast. The earliest computers had to read-in their instructions from punched paper tape or a similar medium, with the result that the overall speed depended almost entirely on the time required to read these instructions, which, in turn, was dictated by the speed at which the medium could be moved physically. In modern computers, only a stored program can be made available to the instruction execution circuitry on the same speed level at which the latter is able to function.

It is this speed of access to the instruction, plus the capability for program self-modification and conditional branching (see below), that makes the computer so versatile and prodigious as far as information processing work is concerned. The program can execute a given set of instructions over and over again, using different data each time. Program *self-modification* consists, in essence, of executing an instruction that changes another (previously executed) stored instruction. Thus the program, in successive iterations or *loops*, need not necessarily be repetitive.

The so-called *conditional branching* is the capability of certain instructions to cause the machine to determine, at that point of program execution, whether a given condition exists and, depending on the outcome, to follow alternative instruction sequences or program paths. For example, in a payroll application, when calculating net pay, the computer program will, in effect, ask itself "Has the Social Security withholding limit been reached previously—yes or no?" (Does the total withheld year-to-date equal sum X, the withholding ceiling currently in effect?) If no, the program will next execute instructions that will calculate and deduct the prescribed amount. If yes, it will proceed directly with the calculation (different instructions) of net pay. It is the ability to execute conditional branch instructions that enables the computer to perform *logical operations,* or to make decisions.

2. CENTRAL PROCESSOR FUNCTIONS

The central processing unit (referred to as the CPU in data processing jargon) is the heart of a computer system, and it controls and coordinates the operations of all the interconnected devices that comprise this system (see Figure 28). It regulates the movement of data in and out of the system, activates the appropriate programs, and executes the individual instructions. Functionally, the central processor is made up of five subunits, as follows:

1. Input control unit
2. Output control unit
3. Main memory
4. Central control unit
5. Arithmetic and logic unit

FUNCTIONAL MAKEUP OF THE CENTRAL PROCESSOR

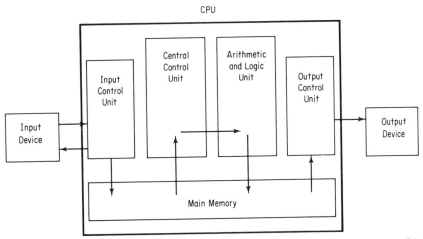

FIGURE 28

Input and Output Control Units

In a computer system, all input-output devices are under program control; i.e., none functions automatically. Each step of an input or output operation is taken in response to an instruction of the program that is in control, either directly or indirectly, through an attached input-output control device, which is interposed between the central processor and the individual input-output devices. In the latter case it is said that the program *transfers control* of input-output operations to the intermediate device by instructing it to execute an operation and *returning control* upon completion. Thus, the central processor, in effect, delegates this type of work to the intermediate device, which then, in turn, executes a series of *commands* that control individual input-output steps.

Within the central processing unit, the circuitry and related internal devices that *interface* (provide the connection) with external input-output machinery, including intermediate control devices, comprise the input and output control units.

Main Memory

The memory is the focal point of all data movement. It is the part of the central processor that stores information in a unit of hardware whose technology (see section on computer technology below) affords rapid access. The speed of access to memory is one of the prime determinants of the overall power of the system, and it is expressed in terms of *cycles* per second, i.e., rate of consecutive accesses. Scientific terminology designates a thousandth of a second as a *millisecond,* a millionth as a *microsecond,* a billionth as a *nanosecond,* and a trillionth as a *picosecond.* Depending on make and model, computer memories cycle upward of a million times per second. In the memory are stored:

1. All the (active) instructions
2. Tables of reference data, as required
3. Blocks of data being processed

Because of the relatively high cost of its hardware, computer main memory is always of rather limited size compared to other storage devices, and the information in the three above categories resides in it only temporarily. It is transferred in and out, as required, between memory and either secondary-storage (see below) or input-output devices.

Main memory is organized into small subunits called *words,* each of which is uniquely and permanently identified by a so-called *address,* i.e., a number or other code preassigned by the computer manufacturer. The addressing scheme for any given model and make of the machine is always part of its design specifications. The size of the word will vary with individual computer design, from 1 decimal digit or character up to about 12 such characters. Instructions in a program refer to the contents of each word by specifying its address. The instructions, at the time of program execution, also reside at specific address locations in memory, from which the central control unit automatically and successively retrieves them for purposes of execution.

The technical data-processing jargon employs terms taken from Latin and Greek to express magnitude, size, and rate. The convention is to use Latin terms for fractions (small values), such as the millisecond, etc., mentioned above, and Greek for multiples (large values). Thus memory size is expressed in terms of how many thousands, or K (for *kilo*), of addressable positions it contains. Because the current core memory technology (see below) makes it convenient to manufacture memories, i.e., to string cores on wires, in square arrays or grids, the basic unit is 64 × 64, or 4,096 positions. This is usually labeled as 4K, and memory capacity of any given computer is always a multiple of 4,096. For example, 16,384 or 16K, 32,768 or 32K, etc. Another Greek term is *mega* (for 1 million), used in data processing literature in terms such as megacycle (1 million cycles per second) or even megabuck ($1 million).

Central Control Unit
The principal functions of this unit are to:

1. Receive and interpret instructions
2. Send appropriate signals to the executing hardware

An instruction is moved from memory into a *register* of the control unit, where the latter is said to "look at it" to determine what it is and how it must be executed. The signals generated that will cause the instruction to be executed send addresses to the memory unit to read-out or to store data, directing the arithmetic and logic unit to operate on the data, and initiating the flow of data between memory and input-output devices.

As instructions move into the control unit, so-called address registers are activated that keep track of the addresses of the last instruction and of the one to be retrieved next. Other registers monitor the substeps of both retrieval and execution operations, to assure coordinated function and the proper alternating between the *instruction state* (retrieve and interpret) and *execution state* (execute).

The central control unit also receives signals indicating special conditions. Internal error-checking circuitry will generate special signals. Attached devices will send special signals at the termination of data transfers. External mechanisms, such as clocks or sensors, can be wired in to provide special signals. Internal mechanisms of various sorts will send signals to the control unit to alert it to the occurrence of some condition. On receiving a special signal, the control unit may cause the central processor to stop, or it may *interrupt* the active program and transfer control to special sets of stored instructions designed to deal with the condition being signalled.

Arithmetic and Logic Unit

This unit of the central processor performs the *mathematical operations* as well as the so-called *logical operations*, i.e., branching and decision operations (choices between alternate sets of instructions). This is the unit that actually operates on and modifies data. Its circuitry will perform all the basic arithmetic functions, but may, in less expensive models, use limited methods for accomplishing this. For instance, addition circuitry cannot only add but, through *complements,* does subtraction as well. Furthermore, with the additional capability to *shift* numbers (left or right from the decimal-point position), it can also be used to do multiplication and division. To achieve higher speed of arithmetic operations, other models will have special circuitry to perform multiplication, etc.

Logical operations are basically of two kinds:

1. Branch on condition
2. Compare

In the first instance, branching (as defined above) takes place if a condition exists; this is being *tested* at that point in the program. For example, a sign of a number may be tested, or the existence of a card in the reader, or the position of a switch that can be set externally. In the second instance, two numbers are *compared* for magnitude or two non-numeric data for alikeness, and depending on the outcome, alternative instruction sequences are executed. The testing, comparing, and branching capabilities of a computer system permit the construction of highly sophisticated programs to handle the most complex of jobs.

3. INPUT-OUTPUT DEVICES

This family of devices, also known as *peripheral equipment,* provide the means of entry of data into, and egress of data out of, the system. Some of these machines have only one function, e.g., input only, such as in the case of a card reader, or output only in the case of a printer. Others combine both functions, e.g., a console typewriter. Others still are, strictly speaking, *secondary storage* units, such as magnetic drums or disk files.

Input devices receive data from an outside source and *encode* them, or else receive them already encoded, in *machine-readable* form, so that they can be manipulated by the computer. The group of these devices includes:

1. Punched-card readers
2. Paper tape readers
3. Attached typewriters
4. Plastic badge readers
5. Key-driven terminals
6. Optical scanning devices
7. Magnetic-ink sensing devices
8. Various sensor devices
9. Voice recognition devices

Output devices display data or record them on one of several media, either encoded (for subsequent use as input) or *decoded,* i.e., presented in *man-readable/recognizable form.* The group of these devices is varied and includes:

1. Card punches
2. Paper tape punches
3. High-speed printers
4. Attached typewriters
5. Visual display (cathode-ray-tube) units
6. Graphic plotters
7. Audio response (voice answer) devices including telephone
8. Other signal-transmitting (lights, sound) devices

4. SECONDARY STORAGE

Devices in this category provide a means of storing large quantities of data, and they have four common characteristics:

1. Data is stored in machine-readable form.
2. Relatively rapid access to this data is provided.
3. Relatively inexpensive form of storage.
4. Data in secondary storage must always first be transferred to main memory (primary storage) before processing can begin.

The common technology of the current family of secondary storage devices is the *magnetic surface* on which encoded data can be *written* and *read* from by so-called *read-write heads*. These heads utilize the principle of the electromagnet to magnetize, or sense the polarization of, tiny areas of the surface passing under them at high speed. The magnetic tape unit, the magnetic strip or data-cell unit, the disk file, and drum storage belong to this group of devices.

Magnetic Tape Units

This type of device provides the capability of reading and writing, as a reel of magnetic tape is unwound and rewound onto another reel. Data are written onto the tape in *blocks* separated by blank *gaps*. One block at a time is read into main memory. The gap signals the end of block to the system, which stops the reel. After the program has dealt with the block of data, another instruction will cause the reel to start unwinding, and the next block will be read into memory.

Tape speed, or *data transfer rate* between the head and memory, is measured in terms of tens or even hundreds of thousands of characters per second. As many millions of characters can be stored on a single reel of tape, this method of secondary storage is both low-cost and of unlimited capacity, because tape is reusable and the reels removable. Both programs and data files can be stored on reels kept in a *tape library*, from which the operator retrieves them for mounting on tape units or *tape drives*, as required.

Until mounted, the tape-reel data are said to be *off-line*, i.e., not immediately accessible by the computer. Another limitation of magnetic tape is the necessity of *sequential processing*, because every data block must successively be read into memory, whether or not it is needed for the data processing job in question. Thus, a record that may physically be located in the middle of the tape can only be read after the reel has been unwound, in successive starts and stops, to that point. The delay inherent in accessing any specific record on tape makes this method of secondary storage unsuitable for applications requiring direct, or *random access,* to file records.

Magnetic Strip Storage Units

To overcome the limitations of *sequential access* inherent in magnetic tape storage, devices in this category utilize what is in effect tape cut up into small strips. A *cartridge* containing a number of these strips (or magnetic cards of larger width which function as several strips of tape mounted side by side) is inserted into the storage unit, which can then select individual strips directly and mechanically transfer each under the read-write heads.

Random access is thus provided, while retaining the read-write speed and low storage cost of magnetic tape. The delay between records, however, is much longer because of the mechanical operations of strip retrieval and return to cartridge. Machines in this category are considered *low-speed access* devices.

Disk File Storage Units

These secondary storage units utilize rapidly rotating disks, on which data are recorded magnetically in a series of concentric *tracks.* A disk file module may consist of one or several disks mounted on a common shaft. Each disk has two surfaces that can be accessed. An *access mechanism* or *arm* equipped with read-write heads provides the motion between the rim and the center of the disk. Data records stored on the various surfaces and tracks can thus be accessed directly, and either a whole track or a portion of it can be read into memory (or, conversely, written).

The obvious limitation here is the time it takes for the physical movement of the access arm from track to track. Faster units are equipped with more than one arm per disk module, permitting simultaneous access to multiple tracks and overlapping of access so that while one arm reads or writes, another is in motion to the next position.

Modern disk storage units can operate at very high speed, the data transfer rates being on the order of several hundreds of thousands of characters per second. The number of disk units that can operate *on-line* to a single computer system is limited, but maximum capacities are counted in billions of characters. Another feature is the removable disk module or *disk pack,* which, like tape reels, can be stored off-line in unlimited quantities.

Disk storage units afford fairly high-speed random access to file records. Aside from access mechanism motion delay, there is also the inherent *rotational delay* determined by rpm of the disk module. These delays, which make up the record *access time,* are measured in thousandths of a second.

Magnetic Drum Storage Units

A cylinder rotating along its axis at very high speed represents the fastest method of secondary storage. Data are stored in tracks on the circumference of the cylinder, each track continuously passing under a stationary read-write head. As there are as many heads as tracks, there is no access motion delay but only rotational delay. The multiple heads, of course, raise the cost of the unit. The capacity of magnetic drums is limited, but the data transfer rates are upwards of a million characters per second.

These drums are used primarily to store programs rather than data files. In many computer applications, it is important to be able to bring a new program into main memory fast. To the extent that such programs can be stored on high-speed access drums, the main memory need not be as large.

It is the main memory (primary storage, directly accessible by the central processor) that is the fastest of all storage devices, because it has no moving parts causing mechanical motion delays—but it is also the most expensive.

COMPUTER TECHNOLOGY

In concept, computer design logic is independent of the technology utilized in implementing it. The technology of the hardware varies and changes in time. The "state of the art" determines the specific technology selected by the computer manufacturer based on performance characteristics, reliability, cost, and size of components.

1. CHARACTER REPRESENTATION

Although technology may vary, all digital computers have one central characteristic in common, i.e., the capability to represent *characters,* numerical, alphabetic, and special, internally within the machine componentry. The requirement of internal representation of characters and the ease of their manipulation is basic, and the universally employed method is that of *binary,* binary-based, or binary-coded characters.

This is because the simplicity of the binary method—as explained below—permits the utilization of a wide range of mechanical, electromechanical, electronic, and magnetic devices that can be brought into *one of two different states*, such as positive and negative, on and off, etc. There are many different schemes (codes) for character representation, but all define the various characters by means of strings of subcharacters or positions, each of which can have one of two values. These values are commonly represented as 0 and 1, but can also be thought of as *yes* and *no, positive* and *negative, on* and *off*, etc. Under each code, the meaning of each combination of the two values is assigned by convention.

For instance, the letter *K* in the 5-position Teletype code is represented as in Figure 29. In the 7-position U.S.A. Standard Code for In-

Position				
1	2	3	4	5
•	•	•	•	
1	1	1	1	0
Yes	Yes	Yes	Yes	No
On	On	On	On	Off

(or, or, or)

FIGURE 29

Position						
1	2	3	4	5	6	7
1	1	0	1	0	0	1

FIGURE 30

formation Interchange (USASCII) the same letter is represented as in Figure 30.

This general method of representing characters by way of groups of two-value or *bistate* symbols permits both internal storage and manipulation using electricity-related technologies, especially magnetics (bipolar devices) and electronics (pulse-switching devices), which lend themselves to character handling and character manipulation at very high speed rates. As much of such manipulation is arithmetic, computers use the binary method of representing numerical values to take advantage of the simplicity and speed of *binary arithmetic*.

2. BINARY NUMBER SYSTEM

The decimal system of numbers that we normally use has 10 symbols (0 through 9). In this system, 10 is the base, or *radix*, because the positional value of a number is assigned in increments of the power of 10. Thus, the number 438 represents 8×10^0 plus 3×10^1 plus 4×10^2, or 8 plus 30 plus 400.

The binary (or base two) system of numbers uses only 2 symbols, 0 and 1; the radix is 2 and the positional value varies with the power of 2. Thus, the number 111, expressed in *binary digits* or *bits*, represents 1×2^0 plus 1×2^1 plus 1×2^2 or 1 plus 2 plus 4, for a total value of 7.

	Positional Value of Bit						
	64	32	16	8	4	2	1
Binary Representation	1	1	0	1	1	0	1

FIGURE 31

ADDITION

	0	1
0	0	1
1	1	0*

*Carry 1

Decimal	Binary
5	101
6	110
11	1011

FIGURE 32

MULTIPLICATION

	0	1
0	0	0
1	0	1

Decimal	Binary
5 × 6	101 × 110
30	000
	101
	101
	11110

FIGURE 33

The number 1101101 in Figure 31 represents the value of 109, or the sum of 64 plus 32 plus 8 plus 4 plus 1. With only two symbols available, it took seven positions to express a value which in decimal requires merely three positions. Binary is less compact than decimal, but its advantage lies in the extreme simplicity of its arithmetic. The logic of binary addition and multiplication, for example, is summarized in Figures 32 and 33. Relatively simple circuitry can be devised to automate binary arithmetic, but that presupposes that data are expressed in straight or *pure binary*, such as the value of 30, or 11110, in Figue 33. With computers used for commercial applications, it would not be practical to convert decimal input data to binary and in turn reconvert to decimal for output purposes. Internal representation is, therefore, *binary-coded decimal.*

Since a group of four bits can represent sixteen states or combinations of ones and zeros, such a group can be arranged to represent any of the ten states (numbers) in the decimal system. In the binary-coded decimal representation, each decimal position (and its value) is represented by a separate group of four bits. Thus, 30 would be written as 0011 and 0000 (3 and 0, respectively). Such a system has a *mixed base,* and it is necessary, in doing arithmetic, to convert from one base to another. For instance, when adding 5 and 6, the addition is:

$$
\begin{array}{r}
0101 \\
0110 \\
\hline
1011
\end{array}
$$

The sum of 1011, which has the value of 11, must be *decimal-converted* to 0001, which represents the value of 1 to be retained in that position of the sum. There must also be a decimal carry of the value of 1 to represent the 1010 (10) carried to the next most significant position. Obviously, such a carry is not inherent in the binary-coded decimal system, but it can and must be provided by special circuitry.

3. CIRCUITS AND THEIR "GENERATIONS"

Computer circuitry is the complex of paths that the signals generated by the computer-driving mechanism (pulse generator or *clock*) must travel. These signals, depending on the technology employed, can be electrical pulses in electronic computers, light in optical computers, fluid in hydraulic computers, etc.

The makeup of individual circuits varies with their function, but generally consists of an assemblage of components that *conduct* (wire), *regulate* (diodes, resistors), *switch* (transistors), *delay, amplify,* and *terminate* signals.

It is the switching devices that permit the variety of internal signal manipulation (and, therefore, character and data manipulation). The basic function of a switching device is to open or close a *gate*, or switch, in the circuit, thus permitting a signal either to travel through, to block it or to direct it onto an alternative path. It is fundamentally the switching devices (relays, vacuum tubes, transistors) that represent the technology being employed and determine the "generation" of a particular computer.

The relay, the vacuum tube, and the transistor serve the same function in, respectively, the electromechanical, electronic, and *solid-state* electronic technologies. With technological advancement, the device becomes smaller, faster, cheaper, and more reliable.

The transistor deserves special mention because, although it serves the same function as the vacuum tube, it does the job so much better. It can work faster and perhaps 1,000 times more reliably, at 100 times less cost. The transistor itself is a layered piece (called *chip*) of semiconductor material (such as germanium), with each layer having different electrical properties. The current that flows across, or through, the different layers can be controlled (i.e., stopped or let go through) by an electrical pulse applied to one of the layers.

Integrated circuits, which represent an advanced generation of solid-state technology, are fashioned into a single piece of material (that is why they are also known as *monolithic circuits*), the various circuit elements not being assembled but rather *deposited* onto this material by chemical, photographic, and similar processes. The microscopic dimensions attainable through these processes permit the *miniaturization* of circuits. This in itself enhances the speed of such circuits, since the electrical signals that travel at a finite speed—the speed of light—have shorter distances to traverse.

A still more advanced technology is the so-called *large-scale integration,* or LSI, which fashions multiple connected circuits on one chip of material. In the ultimate stage of LSI, a single chip could conceivably contain all of the circuitry of one of the functional units of the central processor. In commercially available computers it is the cost, rather than the latest advancement in the state of the art, which dictates the choice of technology to be utilized.

4. STORAGE DEVICES

Retention, or storage, of digital data is a characteristic capability of a computer. Technologies employed to store the data vary and change with time, but functional distinction lies in whether storage is *primary* (so-called "memory," directly accessible to the control and arithmetic units of the central processor, with very high read-write speed) or *secondary* (lower access and read-write speed rates and can only be read into memory rather than directly into the control unit), as described above.

The main memory acts as the working area of the computer where data and instructions are temporarily stored for instantaneous access by the central processor and where the results of arithmetic and logical operations can be stored at the same high rate of speed that the central processor works at. As jobs are completed, the memory-resident programs and data are typically transferred to secondary storage to make room for new programs and data.

In modern computers, the individual memory positions (generally, one-character storage areas) are directly accessible-addressable. This contrasts with secondary storage, where typically only a whole record, or block of records, can be accessed either directly (random-access storage devices) or sequentially.

After the initial variety of experimental technologies used in the first computers (magnetic slugs, drums, etc.), manufacturers universally settled on magnetic *cores* (small ferrite toroids or "doughnuts" strung on wires) for main memories. Although core memories proved highly reliable, as well as susceptible to considerable miniaturization, the methods of their manufacture are rather clumsy, and their cost, therefore, quite high. For this reason, they are bound to be superseded by technologies that will minimize or eliminate the need for mechanical assembly and that will lend themselves to further miniaturization.

5. COMPUTER DESIGN LOGIC

The "power" of a computer is thought of in terms of so-called *through-put*, i.e., capacity to perform an amount of work per unit of time. This capacity derives, aside from technology, quality, and speed of components, also from the approaches and methods of function (known as *design logic*) incorporated in a particular model design.

For instance, characters of data can be transferred between memory and the central processor control unit circuitry in either *serial* (one at a time) or *parallel* (several at a time) fashion, arithmetic can be performed in either binary or decimal mode (the latter requiring more complex circuitry), utilizing either *fixed-point* or *floating-point* registers. Main-memory design can utilize the *fixed word* (or field) *length* versus the *variable field length* principle, the former assigning a separate address only to relatively large strings, or blocks, of bit or character positions (typical word length: 32 bits), the latter partitioning the memory into individually addressable characters or *bytes* (1 byte = 8 bits).

Another design problem is devising an *addressing scheme* that would permit addressing the largest number of individual memory locations while using the most compact address format—a conflict in objectives. Because memory addresses are part of each instruction, the larger the memory size and the more unique addresses the instruction format must accommodate, the bulkier the programs tend to get and the more storage space they require.

Because the central processor is so much faster than the input-output devices, it tends to waste too much time waiting for a given read-write operation to be completed. This problem can be solved by interposing a so-called *channel* between the central processor and the input-output units. The channel, actually a small limited-capability special-purpose computer, will accept and store *commands* from the central processor and will execute them by initiating, monitoring, and signaling the completion of input-output operations. The independent control over the latter by the channel enables the central processor to do other work (i.e., execute other instructions, perhaps of another program) simultaneously with these operations.

Another example of alternate design logic is the so-called "scientific" versus "commercial" computer. Scientific computation typically calls for limited input-output capability but high speed of arithmetic (enhanced if done in binary mode) using floating-point registers and fixed field length, whereas commercial work usually requires high input-output and data handling capability but only limited fixed-point arithmetic in decimal mode, plus variable field length. The best of modern, general-purpose computers combine all these capabilities, alternately called out, through special instructions, depending on the type of job being run.

Index

227